# CONFESSIONS OF A GOOD GIRL

Andrea McLean's warm and sparkling personality has endeared her to millions of *Loose Women* viewers. But in *Confessions of a Good Girl*, she describes her years of bullying at school and the panic attacks she suffered as an adult. She relates how, at GMTV, she got her first big break as a weathergirl, the hilarious disasters she experienced as a showbiz reporter and how television can be a treacherous place for a nice girl. She opens up about the destruction of her first marriage, the guilt that drove her to the edge of a breakdown and her struggles as a single parent. Looking for happiness in her second marriage, it took almost dying to give her the impetus she needed to change her life.

ANDREA McLEAN

# CONFESSIONS OF A GOOD GIRL

*Complete and Unabridged*

# CHARNWOOD
*Leicester*

First published in Great Britain in 2012 by
Sidgwick & Jackson, an imprint of
Pan Macmillan
London

First Charnwood Edition
published 2013
by arrangement with
Pan Macmillan, a division of
Macmillan Publishers Limited
London

The picture acknowledgements on page 333
constitute an extension of this copyright page.

A catalogue record for this book is available
from the British Library.

ISBN 978–1–4448–1592–4

Published by
F. A. Thorpe (Publishing)
Anstey, Leicestershire

Set by Words & Graphics Ltd.
Anstey, Leicestershire
Printed and bound in Great Britain by
T. J. International Ltd., Padstow, Cornwall

This book is printed on acid-free paper

*For good girls everywhere*

# Contents

# Prologue

The first thing I felt was the shock of cold liquid pouring into the veins in my arm. Someone was shouting, and a mask was roughly pushed onto my face, forcing life-giving oxygen into my gasping lungs.

Voices, from far away. Someone was telling me to *breathe, breathe* . . .

A million questions exploded in my head. What had happened? Why had I stopped breathing? I knew I was in hospital, I'd had an operation, and I'd been recovering, but something had obviously gone terribly wrong.

As the drugs snaked their way through my veins, awakening my senses and stabilizing the medication that had caused such a terrifying reaction, a shiver of cold fear ran over me. What if they hadn't been able to make me breathe? I could feel my heart starting to race again and I forced myself to inhale slowly and fully, calming myself down. The question remained, poking me until I acknowledged its presence. What if that had been it? If my life had ended there and then on a bed in a quiet hospital in Surrey, my husband by my side and my children blissfully unaware back at home; who would have died? A good wife? A good mother? A good daughter, sister, friend? A pushed-about TV star, a bullied schoolgirl, a woman who smiled and said everything was fine, just fine.

1

Only an hour before, the nurse had popped into my room and checked that I was feeling OK. I wasn't; I had been feeling a little strange, but I didn't want to mention it because she looked busy and it was probably nothing. If I had spoken out then, if I had been honest with myself and with her, and said, 'Actually, I don't feel too good . . . ' all of this could have been avoided.

That one moment summed up my whole life: always saying I was happy when I wasn't, making do and smiling, not wanting to make a fuss. I had spent my life trying to be perfect, to be good and make life easier for everyone around me, and where had it got me? Almost dead on a hospital bed, aged forty-one.

I had a feeling my life would never be the same again. And I didn't want it to be.

# 1

## The Sweet Smell of Childhood

You know when you fly away on holiday, and they open the doors of the plane and the heat hits you in the face, and the air smells strange — of heady flowers, heat and dust? Well, that's the smell of my childhood, mixed with the sweet smell of sugar carried on a hot tropical breeze.

Just as evocative are the sounds of the Caribbean: frogs *krricking*, bugs humming and unnamed things shuffling and scuffling under a wooden floor; the whirr of an electric fan that soothes you to sleep. I still love it when the night is so hot you have to use a fan. Sometimes, if I have trouble sleeping, even in the depths of winter, I'll put a fan in the corner of the room, face it to the wall and turn it on. In minutes I'm asleep, dreaming of the Caribbean.

In the mornings, as it was getting light, I would lie in bed and watch my thin cotton curtains bulge and flop with the fan's light breeze. It was always noisy around our house at this time of day, with birds chirping, flies buzzing and the rumble of tractors and trailers in the distance. The trailers usually sounded empty — the cane cutters would be on their way out to the fields by then, sharpening their cutlasses and preparing for another long day of chop, chop, chop.

The dawn would turn the air suddenly cold in those first few moments as the sun came up. The smell would get stronger as the wind changed direction, and I would lie in my narrow wooden bed inhaling the sweet scent of molasses. A huge sticky mountain of factory-chewed and spewed sugar cane sat in the nearby yard, waiting to be burned in the factory furnaces, making steam to drive the machinery that produced beautiful Caribbean sugar.

And then it would start: softly, and low, so low I could feel it in my tummy; then louder, higher, the noise would get into its stride . . . the bellow of the old air-raid siren that called workers to site in the morning, then sent them home again at the end of the day. Quiet at first, a rumble that grew in volume and urgency, drowning out any thoughts of further sleep, its roar would hang in the still morning air, even after it had wound down and been put away until the afternoon. That was my morning wake-up call, and soon after, my mum would appear at the door to say, 'Wake up, girls!' and my sister Linda and I would heave ourselves from our beds and begin our day.

From the age of five I went to the company school with all the other children whose fathers worked in the factory. We were a mixed bunch, some of us expat kids of British parents, others born and bred islanders of mixed heritage — African, Indian, Chinese, Spanish and French. The classes were small, up to ten children at the most, and we started each day with the Lord's Prayer and the national anthem.

We were also taught the British national anthem as the island was a former colony, and alongside a picture of the President in the head teacher's office was a portrait of the Queen.

Sometimes, after coming home from school, I would creep in to see Alison, a local woman who helped look after us. She would be lying on her bed in her room, having her afternoon rest. Not sleeping; just lying still with the thin curtains closed and the fan on, reading her Bible. I would crawl onto the bed next to her, snuggling into her, comforted by her smell: warm skin, Vaseline and Johnson's baby powder. It was cosy in her room. Alison never seemed to mind that I crept in to join her, as long as I kept quiet and didn't fidget too much. We rarely spoke during these little afternoon visits; I would just lie next to her, trying to make sense of the tiny words in the worn book. Ten minutes was usually enough, before the twitches started and I crept back out again into the afternoon sunshine to ride my bike.

I grew up on the Caribbean island of Trinidad, which is quite an unusual thing for a girl from Glasgow to do. My parents had met while they were teenagers, married a few years later and then my dad was given the chance to travel to Trinidad to work as an engineer in a sugar factory. This was quite a feat for a couple who had barely been any further than Loch Lomond, and my mum apparently sobbed every night for six months, she was so homesick. They got used to it, though, and ended up living there for eighteen years, gradually making lots of friends with whom they are still in touch today.

Two years after arriving in Trinidad, Mum became pregnant with me, and they decided it was a good time to travel back to Scotland. I arrived one month early during one of my granny's get-togethers. The neighbours had popped in to see Jack and Betty and 'bump', McEwan's Export was poured, whiskey flowed and it didn't take long for the singing to start; my granny loved a good sing-song. It was a fine old night, apparently, but Mum started to feel a bit peaky, then a bit damp, and thought in her excitement she'd wet herself. She took herself off for a lie down. When my Auntie Norah found her she was lying on the bed saying she wasn't feeling very well, and could Dad please stop singing long enough to come and see her. Everyone rushed in, and in their wobbly state deduced that she was in fact having a baby.

Dad helped her into the passenger seat of his mum's little red van (she worked for a bakery in Glasgow), and, with cheers ringing in his ears, raced off into the night to deliver his own little bun. The party resumed without them. An hour later I was born in Glasgow Southern General Hospital, weighing four pounds eleven ounces. I was rushed straight into an incubator, where I stayed for a week, red and small with arms like spaghetti. Once I was allowed out, their mission was to feed me up enough so I could make the journey out to Trinidad, and so a round-the-clock feeding routine began, the main problem being keeping me awake long enough to drink. I still have that problem today, much to Denise

Welch's annoyance.

At the time, my parents were living on a sugar estate in Brechin Castle in the middle of the island. It was one of the original estates built in the early 1950s, and housed expat and local workers from the factory. Any medical problems were seen by the company clinic and everyone went to the company club to swim, and play tennis and golf. It was kind of like being in the army, with regulation houses and furniture.

I don't remember much about the early years there; my first memories are of my younger sister Linda being born. This time there wasn't any singing involved, but there was a midnight dash. Mum had woken in the night feeling a bit odd, and Dad found her a while later waddling round the garden. After dropping me off at a friend's house, Dad was once again bundling her into the car, this time to race into Port of Spain, a good forty-five-minute drive away, with my Auntie Mary (not a real auntie; everyone is called 'auntie' and 'uncle' in Trinidad) squatting in the back footwell as Mum lay on the back seat with her feet pressed against the window. Dad was shouting at her not to dare have the baby on the back seat, and Auntie Mary, who used to be a nurse, was shouting at him to shut up, that she'd have the baby wherever she wanted and he wasn't being helpful. My mum just bit her lip. Always very dignified, my mum, even when she ended up having the baby in the first room the nurses could find as Dad was signing her in and paying their deposit at reception . . . Apparently they got a rebate, as she hadn't used the delivery

7

room — or a doctor, for that matter.

I can remember the day Dad and I went to hospital to pick up Mum and my new little sister. It was very exciting to be coming home with a real live doll that was now going to be living with us. It took a few weeks for the novelty to wear off, and the reality that the red-faced, screaming bundle that was my little sister was actually going to STAY didn't live up to my four-year-old expectations. After repeated requests to 'take her back please', and 'why does she have to stay in my room?' I resigned myself to having to share the limelight. And I've liked having a sister ever since, now that I've grown out of standing on tables, lifting my dress to show my knickers and screaming, 'Look at ME! Look at ME!'

That's not to say we've not had our ups and downs . . . She may be small, with her trademark 'cute hands and feet', but Linda is terrifying when she loses her temper.

At the age of five, she nearly threw my mum out of a rocking chair when she got upset that I had laughed at her drawing of a horse.

'It's all right, it doesn't matter,' Mum said, glancing up from her book at the commotion.

An innocent enough response, you'd think, but not to a very cheesed-off little girl. There was silence, stillness and somewhere a dog may have barked. And then, from nowhere, came a piercing cry of, 'IT DOES MATTER!' and Mum was flung backwards in her rocking chair, book flying and arms flailing. It's become our family battle cry ever since. I might even see if I can get it made into a family crest; the picture would be brilliant.

* * *

Apart from molasses, there's another smell that takes me straight back to my childhood: Opium perfume. And with it comes the image of my mum, glamorous and beautiful in a long evening dress, bending over to kiss me goodnight. Her scent would hang in the air after she'd gone, and sometimes settle on the pillow. (It wasn't until years later that I realized the glamorous dresses had all been handmade from patterns, run up in a day or two, with leftover material used to make clothes for my Barbie.) I wanted to smell like that when I was a grown-up, but I have tried to wear Opium and it didn't seem right. It was as if I was wearing my mum. Even now that she wears lighter scents, with the occasional bit of Chanel No. 5 splashed on for a special occasion, Opium remains forever Mum's smell, not mine.

I sometimes wonder what smell will remind my children of me. I hope it's a nice one. It will probably be a dab of Jo Malone or a splash of Clarins, possibly with a dash of spaghetti bolognese or fish fingers.

* * *

Every Sunday our family would make the hour-long drive to Maracas in the north of Trinidad, one of the nicest beaches on the island. The trip took a lot of preparation, mainly by my mum, who would make tuna-fish rice to be eaten cold with a salad, sandwiches and biscuits. Dad would pack the cooler, with Carib beer for him, Cokes for Mum and juice for me and Linda. Then there were the towels, the bikinis, the baby oil (this was before the days of sunscreen!) and the goggles.

We would set off at about nine-ish (timings in our house were always 'ish' when Dad was involved). Mum would have had us up and ready by seven o'clock to miss the beach traffic, but Dad always seemed to start a hundred things and never finish them, before deciding to check if he had enough ice for the cooler. Then, when he was ready, he'd sit in the car and start the engine, shouting, 'Come on, girls! Hurry up!' while we all raced downstairs. The car was parked under the house, which was on stilts. Like most of the homes in the Caribbean it was like a bungalow perched high in the air to allow the tropical breeze to flow through. It was an L-shape, with three bedrooms down one limb, and the living room and kitchen on the other. When the water came out of the tap, sometimes it was brown. I would test it by pouring a glass of water and letting it sit for a while, until it was water on the top and silt on the bottom. We rarely drank water from the tap — Mum usually boiled it — but after a lifetime, it didn't kill our tummies like it did the tourists'; it just smelled and tasted funny.

When we finally arrived, me feeling slightly sick in the back seat because of the mountainous road and my dad's driving (he still makes me feel sick whenever I'm in the car with him, even now; I always have to sit in the front), the dark green sea and creamy yellow sands of the bay at Maracas would stretch out in front of us. As we parked the car and opened the doors to the heat, the smell of freshly frying 'shark and bake' would jump up our noses, and my poor mum's efforts at making tuna-fish rice and sandwiches would be wasted. We would hold off as long as we could, but after a couple of hours swimming in the sea, even our parents could appreciate that there was nothing better than standing in line in front of the concrete-walled, thatched-roofed stall of the beach vendor, listening to soca music booming from a rasta blasta, salivating over the smell of deep fried shark.

'Shark an' bake! Shark an' bake!' came the rallying cry, and resistance was futile. There was something hugely exciting about eating this beast of the sea, smothered in batter and enveloped in a soft white bun, hot and tangy on your tongue, all the while knowing that more of these creatures lurked just beyond the breakers, dead-eyed and waiting for a lone swimmer. Tit for tat, I guess, in the cut-throat world of tucker. I never saw a shark, but that didn't stop the fear. As children, we all ran into the sea clutching boogie boards if we had them, ready to bodysurf the rolling waves back to the shore. We would fight our way past the waves to tread the deep water behind, chatting and giggling and keeping one eye peeled for the next big swell. A kick of feet, a push with the arms, and whoosh! Either we would rush triumphantly towards the beach, seeing just how far we could get before the wave ran out of steam; or it would go horribly wrong, and we would tumble head first into the surf, banging foreheads and elbows and knees into the grating yellow sand. Sometimes it was funny, but sometimes it went on and on and on and I didn't know which way was up and ran out of breath so that I'd swallow a bellyful of bitter sea water. Somehow I always made it to the surface, choking and gasping and seeing spots in front of my eyes. For a little while after that I'd sit it out on the beach, running up to my chatting parents and their friends and quietly helping myself to some rice and a drink, wrapping my shivering body in a towel and trying not to look like I was frightened.

Other times, when my friends and I were bobbing on our boards in the deeper water, I would feel the current suddenly change and a rush of cold would push through my legs. I always thought of sharks then, and would swim slightly further in, drawing my legs up under me, hoping that someone else was further out and looked tastier.

One Sunday, when we hadn't gone to the beach for some reason, two sharks were spotted. Lifeguards shouted and blew whistles, and everyone was called out of the water and stood on the shore watching as two fins slowly made their way up and down Maracas Bay. I was never sure if I wished I'd seen them or was glad I hadn't. Either way, it proved they were real, and boogie-boarding was never quite as carefree after that.

The trip home from the beach was normally quite eventful, as car after car full of damp, sandy children and pink adults headed through the winding mountain roads towards the outskirts of Port of Spain. The roads were narrow and sometimes a bit scary, as cars would stop to allow passing traffic through on blind bends with lush wet vegetation to our left, and a sheer drop down to the Caribbean Sea on our right. If we were quiet, we could hear the chatter of unseen monkeys high up in the trees, and occasionally spot the bright green and red plumage of a watchful parrot. Then we would head on to the highway south for the rest of our journey home. Sometimes we'd stop off for a Kentucky Fried Chicken (as it was called then) and that would keep us busy in the back seat as we munched away, wrapped in towels and trying to keep the gritty sand off our drumsticks and fries, oblivious to the dangers of not wearing a seat belt. If it was very late, we would lie on the back seat and nod off to sleep, listening to my dad singing John Denver's 'Take Me Home, Country Roads' all the way home.

When most people think back to their childhood, they remember every day as being sunny; well, with me, it really was. It was even hot when it rained, so I spent every day of my young life in shorts, a T-shirt and bare feet. In Trinidad, I swam almost every day. I was good at swimming, and I liked it. The pool area on the estate where we lived had the air of a 1950s holiday camp about it. The pool itself was enormous and very deep, and had three different levels of diving board: normal; bit scary and bouncy; and ridiculously high. When I was a teenager I used to do handstands on the very top diving platform, holding myself still and strong, before pushing away with my arms into a perfect arrow-straight dive. My dad taught me to do it, and spent hours coaxing me away from the edge of the ladder; first getting me to jump off into the pool, then to do a normal dive, then finally the handstand.

I was very proud that I could do it, and I once tried to show my cousins at some swimming baths in Scotland during a family trip back home. It all went horribly wrong. There was a big queue of people behind me, someone shouted, 'Wid ye get a bloody move on!' and I wobbled . . . and landed with the loudest belly flop ever heard in Kilmarnock. I sank, mortified, to the bottom of the pool, wishing I would drown, or at least lose consciousness, rather than face the laughter at the water's edge. But I didn't; I just ran out of breath and slowly bobbed back up, pulling my costume out of my bottom as I rose, red-faced, to the surface. That was one of my first lessons in life: no one likes a show-off, and the forces that be will see to it that you look an arse if you do.

As well as swimming, another favourite pastime was (and is) going to the cinema and losing myself in an unfolding story in the dark, sometimes even on my own. People moan now about the noise in a cinema, but I don't mind the munching or even the mutterings of people confused by a plot. No; it's rude disinterest,

14

which manifests itself in texting or outright chatting, that gets on my nerves. There has always been noise in cinemas — it's bound to happen if you stick a bunch of people in a dark room and expect them to sit still for two hours. In the UK, I can remember struggling to see the screen watching *The Rescuers* through the thick haze of cigarette smoke that hung in the air — it seems crazy now!

Going to the cinema in Trinidad as a child was a totally different experience to the UK, as it was OUTSIDE. You know the bit in *Grease* where Sandy and Danny are at the drive-in listening to the movie through speakers on posts either side of the car? Well, that's how we used to see all the latest releases. It was brilliant. If the film was a little dull, or got to a boring bit, us kids would get out and go to the playground behind all the cars, arching high on the swings in the dark while watching films like *The Pink Panther Returns* on a huge wall. The air would be filled with the sounds of the movie and kids' shrieks as we spun on the roundabout. There was always a parent we knew standing by to look after us, and somehow you always found your way back to your parent's car in the darkness, and there was never any fear. It was just what we did; we played with other kids and looked out for each other, and only went back to the car to pester our parents for hot dogs when we got peckish. There is something truly magical about watching a film outside while on a swing in the dark; it's something that all the 3-D cinematic experiences in soft comfy chairs will never replace.

I also liked riding my bike and, because we were allowed to tear around the estate without a grown-up constantly keeping a nervous eye on us, I was quite good at it, too. Before I'd learned about the rules regarding the forces of nature versus the show-off, however, I saw my arse in a fairly spectacular manner. Some of you, if you have nothing better to do and have studied my face with any vague intensity, may have noticed that I have a wonky nose. There is a reason for this, which comes from an incident involving a chopper bike, an eight-year-old girl (me), a very steep hill and my inability to tell my left from right.

My bike was shiny and went very fast, which was all I asked of it. Our little gang of girls used to ride around the estate after school, keeping out of the way of the boys. We had our tree house and they had theirs; we had our water balloons, they had their water pistols made from old Fairy liquid bottles. Half the fun was just screaming and cycling away from each other, as fast as our legs would take us.

One day, our legs were going like the clappers and we tore down the road, heading for my friend Laura's house. Laura happened to live at the bottom of a very steep hill. We were screaming and pedalling and laughing and I was in front, thrilled that I was leading, and going really rather fast, when I thought I'd better slow down a bit, as the bike was starting to wobble. As it did, I remembered that my dad had told me always to squeeze the left brake when going down a hill, as that was for the wheel at the back.

I squeezed with all the strength my fingers could muster.

Nothing happened, so I squeezed a little bit harder. Too late — as the front wheel gripped the road, my back wheel left it. Even in my little eight-year-old mind I knew that the consequences of getting my left hand and my right muddled up would be bad.

The whole back end of the bike rose and propelled me forwards, in an arc, sailing over the handlebars and into the bright Caribbean air. I flew for a while, and then landed on the tarmac, nose first. This was closely followed by my lips, chin, arms, stomach, knees and feet. I cruised along the road on my face, in the style of Wile E. Coyote when he has failed yet again to catch the elusive Road Runner. By the time I eventually ran out of momentum, I had left most of my skin behind. My friends were scared to look when I slowly peeled myself off the tarmac, but judging by the scream that Laura's mum let out when she saw me stagger, bloodied and battered, to her door, I gather it wasn't a pretty sight.

Somewhere, in the heart of Trinidad, is an imprint of an eight-year-old girl's face, and I'm sure if you look hard enough you can still see the dent in the road where my nose used to be.

# 2

## Down the Islands

By the time I was fifteen years old, I had lived in eight houses, moved country five times and been to nine schools. I used to tell people that my dad was a bank robber and that was why we were always on the run.

Our first big move away from Trinidad happened in 1977 when I was eight, and we returned to the UK as Dad's contract had ended. We lived for a while with Granny and Granda in their council flat in Cardonald in Glasgow, before my dad took up a position at the Tate & Lyle head office in Bromley and we decamped to Beckenham in Kent. Dad went to work every day in a suit and tie, and got fatter and fatter on business lunches. We moved into a small flat, and for two girls used to running free in the Caribbean it was like trying to cage two wild birds. We were noisy and messy, much to the annoyance of the elderly lady who lived below, who kept her fitness levels up by storming up the stairs to bang on our door and shout at my mum.

I went to the local primary school, and can't remember much about it except that there were thirty children in my class instead of five like I was used to, and the teacher told me no one wanted to hear what I had been up to at the weekend as they didn't have time to listen to everyone. So I learned to be quiet, and the first little spark of life was snuffed out. How often do we do this to our own kids, I wonder? It's because of this that I do what my parents did to me and my sister: I let my children talk at me until my ears feel like they're bleeding and I'm wishing for bedtime. At eight it's a hard lesson to learn that people aren't always interested in what you have to say, and I hope my two don't learn that lesson for a little while yet.

We spent the summer holidays playing in the local park, making dens under bushes and splashing about in a little stream; all things that health and safety would probably put an end to now. At the weekend my sister and I were taken to the Saturday morning kids' film club to watch Tarzan and cowboy films. It was before the days of endless kids' TV at home (unthinkable!) and it gave our parents a few hours to themselves to do whatever they wanted. We were a little scared at being left alone in the dark with all the other children, but quite excited by it, too.

I didn't really make any friends while we were there, because I think I knew we wouldn't be staying long. And, sure enough, along came the next big move — this time to the Philippines. Linda and I were dressed in matching red jumpsuits and joined Mum and Dad on another flight around the world. It seemed to take days to get there — and, as it was 1977, it probably did. We helped the stewardesses collect the trays and tidy up, just for something to do, and I remember being very proud when they gave us a badge with wings on it, telling us that we were such good girls we were now honorary air stewardesses. That was in the days when stewardesses were nice to children, rather than seeing them as pint-sized peace-and-quiet terrorists, only there to get on your nerves.

We flew to Manila, and then on to the island of Mindanao, and the scruffy, haphazard town of Cagayan. After that was a five-hour drive up and down muddy, slippery and very bumpy dirt roads until we came to our estate in Bukidnon. I use the term 'estate' loosely, as it only involved four bungalows stood next to a sugar factory in the middle of nowhere surrounded by sugarcane. It was so new that it still smelled of sawdust and mud, and Linda and I played in the unfinished building site as there was nothing else to do. There was no school, so for the next year my mum used one of the rooms in the guest house (used for employees who would fly out to work and weren't bringing their wives or family with them) as a classroom. My mum was a qualified hairdresser, by the way, she wasn't a teacher — but suddenly she was OUR teacher. You can't moan to your mum that you've got too much homework when it's your mum who has given it to you. You can't lie to the teacher and say you didn't have time to revise, when it's your mum standing in front of you with a raised eyebrow. My mum was a novice teacher, but she was a damn fine shot. She could throw things from one end of the classroom to the other and still get you on the head when she'd finally had enough of you.

'Owww-wahh! You can't do that to me! You're my TEACHER!' I'd splutter, outraged.

'No, I'm your mother when I do that, so sit down and finish your work.'

Power cuts, spiders the size of a man's hand, the occasional rat and a late-night intruder featured during our year in the Philippines. At night, the power was switched off to save the generator, so we would sit in the glow of hissing gaslights, listening to the *krrick* of frogs and the hum of beetles. There was no TV, so we played cards or back gammon, or even our own version of mahjong. It was and is hugely popular in the Far East, and I loved the sound it made, pushing all the smooth, cool ivory rectangles into the middle of the table before making our selection. But we had to play by candlelight as it was completely dark, the kind of dark you don't really see in this country, as there is normally some kind of light pollution close by giving its distinctive glow; the kind of dark where you couldn't see your hand in front of your face, but your ears could pick out the tiniest of sounds. In the hills in the distance we could just make out a scattering of glowing orange lights that my dad told me were fires lit by guerrillas in their camps. It was years before I realized he didn't mean *gorillas*, and I was kind of disappointed. It was 1978 and opposition to President Marcos was rumbling.

It was here that my fear of the dark was formed, cemented one night by a would-be intruder creeping around the outside of our bungalow, looking for a way in. It was pitch black

21

as usual, as our generator had been switched off. I don't know what stirred me, but I woke and heard the noise of slow, stealthy footsteps at my window. I lay rigid in my single bed and held my breath, straining to hear above the blood rushing in my ears. Was it a rat? Something bigger? Silence. My lungs were close to bursting. There it was again: a quiet footstep and, more terrifyingly, whispered voices. The hair prickled on my head with shock and fear. I wanted my mum and dad — NOW.

I slid silently out from under my sheets and tiptoed into my sister's bedroom. I shook her gently.

'Linda, wake up,' I whispered. She groaned in her sleep and I prickled with fear. I didn't want the men outside to hear us through the mosquito screened window. I shook her again, and then sat her up and managed to guide her, half-asleep, to Mum and Dad's bedroom.

My dad was already up — I could see his outline sitting on the bed. Linda crawled in beside him and had fallen back to sleep in seconds. As I got into bed and clung on to Mum, Dad got up and walked quickly towards the bedroom door.

'Jack, no!' Mum whispered, and she sounded scared. I hung on to her. 'Stay here!'

Dad ignored her and disappeared into the dark. We heard him padding down the wooden floor of the corridor, the rattle of the front door being opened, then more footsteps. Mum was sitting up now, straining to hear as I gripped her side. The silence was as terrifying as the darkness. Then, BANG BANG! Gunshots, so loud and close we saw the bright flash from the gun and our ears rang.

'Jack!' my mum screamed, and I burst into tears of pure terror. 'Oh my God! Jack! What's happening?'

There was confusion. We heard footsteps running, some shouting, more voices, all male . . . Was it our guard coming to help? Then a gaslight was bobbing and hissing its way towards us. Someone was coming down the corridor towards me and my mum as we lay in her bed. Who? Who? A dim white light swung into the room and Dad was swearing and shaking as he sat on the bed and gathered us to him. We all screamed at him for going outside. I say 'we all', all except my sister Linda, who slept soundly through the whole thing. It was a guard who had fired the shots at our would-be intruders, frightening them off into the sugar cane.

Since that night I've always been afraid of the dark. Even today I need some kind of light in my room, and still sleep with either the hall or bathroom light on if there are no street lights outside to shine through the window. I can't breathe if I can't see in front of me and fear of the unknown threatens to swamp me. I *never* make fun of my kids if they say they are afraid of the dark; I comfort them and make sure their night lights are on, taking them with us wherever we go. I know what it's like to have the bogeyman tiptoe outside your window, unseen but heard, and I will never forget it.

The next day Linda, Mum and I were put in a

four-wheel drive and sent to catch a plane to Manila, where we would wait for Dad to come and get us. He had decided that enough was enough; there had been a kidnapping a short distance away, and stories about a teenage girl being snatched and murdered some years before, and he didn't want to run the risk that our night-time visitor had been hoping to snatch the valuable assets of a nine-year-old and a six-year-old girl. He handed in his notice with instant effect, thinking only of our safety and getting us as far away from there as he could — we would worry about making ends meet later. He stayed behind for a few days, packing our few belongings, and then he met us in Manila and took us all back to Blighty.

We found ourselves back in Scotland after that. Mum and Dad bought a little two-bedroom bungalow in the village of Tarbolton in Ayrshire, and tried to settle into Scottish life. It was very odd for us all though; I think my parents were probably still reeling from our Philippines experience, and my sister and I were over-whelmed by the fact that we were in a school with other children again. As ever, Linda adapted really well, and within weeks had made new friends and settled into a group. Despite the fact that I am older and have the more public job, Linda has always been more confident than me, sliding into new situations with enviable ease.

I didn't find the transition from wilderness to civilization quite as easy, and hung on to the first person who was nice to me. Luckily, she turned out to be a really lovely girl called Marie, who lived next door but one. Marie walked with me to school and introduced me to her friends at Tarbolton Primary School. I was an alien creature compared to the other children there; I felt like Mowgli from *The Jungle Book*. I didn't understand anything about living in a village that wasn't an estate where everyone worked at the same place and all knew each other. I had never bought anything from a shop in Britain before, because I had never been in a shop without my parents — at the age of ten I had no concept of British money, and would just hold my hands out and let the shopkeeper pick out what they needed. It never occurred to me that they would be anything other than honest.

Luckily, the people of Tarbolton were polite and friendly to the two strange little creatures who wandered round the village in bare feet speaking in West Indian drawl, and whatever they may have thought of us, they made us feel very welcome.

Our bungalow was heated by a coal-fired burner that we called Sparky, because that's exactly what it wasn't. It was always going out. Linda and I would lie in our beds refusing to get up until the fire was lit, watching the steam leave our mouths and scraping the frost off the inside of the windows. Dad decided he would like to start a DIY business and be self-employed, and he and Mum spent long hours planning the details. I don't remember it being a stressful time; it was just nice to have him around. He looked a bit different — he was scratchy a lot of the time, as he'd decided to grow a beard — but it was good to hear him pottering around in the workshop he had made for himself in the loft upstairs, turning wood on his lathe, making lamp bases and other things to sell through the DIY business. He put an offer in on a shop in Irvine town centre and was disappointed when it fell through, but fate had other plans. Out of nowhere came the call I think he had been quietly hoping for: it was Tate & Lyle. How did he fancy returning to Trinidad?

'I'll think about it,' he said . . .

Weeks later, we were boarding the plane to Port of Spain, all of us excited and me pale, sweating and covered in chicken-pox spots.

'If anyone asks, tell them it's acne,' said my dad, as we weren't sure whether I was really supposed to fly.

When the hot sweet smell of Piarco International Airport hit me I keeled over, and had to wait for our bags with my head between my knees. Not the best homecoming, but that was what it felt like; we were coming home.

★   ★   ★

Being ten and moving back to Trinidad was great. The sun had been waiting for us! Even though old friends had moved on and it was a bit strange slotting back in again after two years away, I was still happy. Tennis lessons started again, and swimming lessons. I had swum for a team in Kilmarnock while I was in Scotland, so I had kept up with my training, but this was so much better! No cold changing rooms, trying to pull tights up over damp legs; this pool was in the sunshine and I swam and swam and swam.

My parents were happy, too; they seemed to feel more at home out in the Caribbean than they did in our little village in Scotland. My dad worked hard and thrived on a renewed sense of purpose, and my mum, like me, quietly took her time finding her feet and making friends. It was easier for Dad, I think; he was thrown back into a work environment where colleagues became golf partners and then pals. My mum had to cope with finding a circle of women who were happy to let her 'back in'. Mum is quieter than Dad, and, like with me, this is sometimes taken for aloofness when it's actually shyness. But, like me, once Mum makes a friend it tends to be for life, and it didn't take her long to find her feet again.

My parents at this time were thirty-four; it seems so young to me now! I thought they were a very glamorous couple: Dad with his jet-black hair and ready laugh, and Mum with a cigarette held aloft while she read a book in the sun. My mum has always been a smoker, with only occasional breaks over the years, and apart from when we were trapped on transatlantic flights next to her as she nervously chain-smoked her way to and from the UK, I grew up thinking it was a very glamorous thing to do. My mum has always been the strong, silent type, and over the years I have become more and more like her. We set certain ground rules and we expect them to be listened to, and in the case of my mum

. . . well, it was do as I say *or else* . . .

I'm glad I was in Trinidad for my between-age and teenage years; I think I avoided a lot of the stresses that come with growing up in the UK. Mum made some of our clothes, and it didn't occur to me to care; I spent most of my time either in school uniform or shorts anyway, riding my bike, roller skating and climbing trees until I was fourteen. I was a VERY late starter, and I think my parents liked it that way. I was very gullible and straight, as Mum and Dad were much stricter than the other parents, but I didn't really mind. I didn't think of rebelling, as I liked how things were; watching Doris Day films with my mum, *The Love Boat* and *Little House on the Prairie* with my sister, and all of us going to the beach on Sundays with my dad. What more could a girl want? I had an idyllic childhood and early teen years, and all I wanted was to be like my idol, Doris Day. Mum and I would inhale these movies, me watching Doris and loving the fact that she was bright, perky and always got her man by being her lovely self. Mum was probably keeping more of an eye on Rock Hudson and James Garner, but I didn't notice them until much later.

By fourteen I was pulling at the leash a tiny bit, although not so much that anyone else would have noticed. I was friends with Ingrid and Rachael, two girls whose dads also worked on the estate, and who were a year older than me. A year at that age counts for a lot. They had 'taken off' with (snogged) boys, and slow danced to Barry Manilow's *Mandy*, while I was left

28

sitting at the side, pretending it was all fine and terrified that someone would ask me to dance, only to be embarrassed and relieved at the same time when they didn't.

I would sit, skinny, awkward and listening bug-eyed while Rachael told me the gory details of 'taking off' with some boy the night before. It sounded disgusting, all that business of tongues and teeth and breath, but I was jealous that at least someone wanted to 'take off' with Rachael, with her curvy legs and short shorts and proper breasts that needed a bra.

During the holidays I would walk round to Rachael's to see if she was about and wanted to climb trees and make mango chow (she made the hottest and *best*). I have no idea how she made it, I just know it involved not-quite-ripe mangoes, water, vinegar, chilli, Tabasco and probably a load of other things that I would find disgusting now, but back then we devoured it! Or we would lie on her bed and look at her posters of Andy Gibb, David Cassidy and Scott Baio. I had posters of Tracy Austin and Sue Barker, and a big one of a Holly Hobbie rag doll. Rachael's room seemed so grownup in comparison.

Sometimes her big brother John would come in, all long-limbed and brown, and he never seemed that pleased to see me. Maybe it was the way I gazed moon-faced at him whenever he was around. 'Oh, *she's here*,' he'd snarl, ignoring my feeble smile. He'd then jump hard on Rachael's bed, punch her arm, push her off and walk out of the room. Sometimes Rachael would laugh and ignore him, other times she flew at him, pulling his hair so his head jerked back, punching him as hard as she could, screaming. They would really fight. Not play-fighting or pillow-throwing like my sister and I did; it was all-out war. They threw punches, they rolled on the floor, banging into Rachael's single bed and thrashing about until their mum came in and pulled them apart. I would stand as far into the corner as I could get while they forgot about me.

Sometimes we would carry on where we had left off, with Rachael rubbing her bruised arm where John had given her a Chinese burn. Other times I just crept away, a little bit scared of the noise and banging, but a little bit excited by it, too. It was so different to our house. In Rachael's house, she had big brothers who shouted and slammed doors. John drove his mum's car, and it had an eight-track stereo that played really loud music. He liked Adam Ant, and sometimes he would shout 'Dog eat dog eat dog eat dog!!' right in my face, while I stared back, just happy that he was looking at me.

One day, John and his older brother Ralph got a copy of The Texas Chainsaw Massacre on video. I was so pleased to be allowed to stay and watch with them and their older, bigger friends, who had wispy moustaches and smelled of their dad's aftershave, that I squashed down the little voice that whispered in my ear, 'Dad says you have to ask first. Mum and Dad have to watch all your videos first to make sure they're OK.' I sat quietly on my chair, staring at one little fixed point in the corner of the screen and trying not to watch as bodies flailed and blood poured. I gritted my teeth and bit my lip so I wouldn't scream out when the chainsaw roared. I ran, ran, ran all the way home when it was over, shaking and wet with sweat, and couldn't tell anyone what I'd seen because I wasn't supposed to be there anyway. The nightmares stayed for months.

The club house where our family spent most of our time was also a golf club (a grand title for a not very grand building) and sat close to the edge of a large pond. I heard stories of golfers who had gone to get their balls from the rough, only to run screaming from the shrubbery with an angry crocodile lumbering after them. In fact, I was told that crocs could really shift once they got going, especially angry females who thought their eggs had been interfered with, and the only way to outwit them was to run in a zigzag line as they couldn't bend very well. I have no idea if that is true or not, and, despite going paddling in the pond when Mum and Dad weren't looking (who says I wasn't a rebel?), I never had to find out.

My fear of crocs was just as potent as my fear of sharks. Even Linda joined me on this one, and she never seemed to be scared of anything. We were both convinced that there were crocodiles under our beds at night, and had to sleep with the hall light on. This was so that a shaft of light shone on the floor, and we decided between us that that was a safe place to walk. If I needed the loo in the middle of the night, I would stand up on my bed and jump over to Linda's, then jump onto the pool of light shining in from the hall. I did the same on the way back, and Linda never woke. Linda could sleep through a hurricane, and when she was five, she actually did. She used to talk in her sleep, sometimes loudly, sometimes just snuffling, and I spent many nights chatting to her while she slept, stifling giggles behind my hand as I tried to get my little sister to say something I could embarrass her with the next day. If I wasn't so tired now and likely to fall asleep well before her (I'm the older one; I'm more knackered), I would still do it — it's hilarious.

★ ★ ★

Most summers, my parents and little sis and I joined forces with two or three other families, and we all headed off for a week 'Down the Islands'. Men, women and children were packed into tiny motor boats called pirogues, which chugged out of Port of Spain and along the coastline until they came to one of the series of little islands dotted around the north coast of Trinidad. They were pretty much uninhabited, but a few had holiday homes on them, some better than others. The sugar company owned a two-storey wooden house, with a few basic bedrooms and bathrooms. Us children slept in a huge room lined with bunk beds, while the adults had their own rooms. I loved being Down the Islands, but best of all was staying at Mayaro, another beach in Trinidad. It wasn't as pretty as Maracas or even Down the Islands, but lots of families had second homes there and would decamp for the weekend. Houses there were far enough from the sea that creepy crawlies didn't get in.

Down the Islands, the house seemed to creak like an old boat, and quite often crabs wandered in, and silverfish wriggled on the damp wooden floors at night. There was always sand underfoot and freshly caught fish in ice-boxes waiting to be gutted and barbecued. There was no TV, no Nintendo DS or Wii, only a stereo on which the adults played their country music, soca and Sixties medleys loudly until the wee hours.

The only things to do Down the Islands were fish, sail and swim. I got bored hanging a line over the jetty waiting for fish to bite, as it never happened like in the cartoons — it took AGES. I was also secretly frightened of the deep, dark water and only went in to swim if there was someone else there with me. A barracuda had been seen nearby on one of our trips, and that was enough to scare me out of the water. I liked sailing in the little boat, but only if someone else took me out in it; I wasn't skilled or confident enough to try it on my own. I could probably have sailed off all right; it was finding my way back that would have been the problem. And again, I was frightened of falling in; this was the very thing that made me a good sailor, as I could contort myself into any position while the boat bucked and rolled and the sail whipped around my head, just to avoid the bottomless green water.

So I would babysit the others. To stay busy I'd keep an eye on my little sister, who didn't seem to have half the fears I did, jumping off the jetty

33

into the unknown at a moment's notice. She'd done it once on an earlier stay, while Mum was having a quiet afternoon swim. She'd jumped straight in, armbands on, and doggy-paddled up to Mum. Then she'd flung her arms around her neck and clung on, while Mum's head went under. It was a great game to a four-year-old, and soon she was squeezing her arms around Mum's neck and giggling, while Mum went down into the deep green sea. Whenever Mum's head came up, and her mouth opened to gasp for breath, little sis squeezed harder and pushed her down. Eventually, one of the other grown-ups noticed that mum wasn't playing, she was drowning, and he dived in fully clothed to rescue her.

It had all happened in full view of about fifteen people, and for a long time Mum was quietly pissed off that she'd nearly come a cropper courtesy of a four-year-old girl, while her friends got merrily drunk on rum punch. I've had a few near misses myself with my children Finlay and Amy's clinging arms — but the difference is I'm not afraid to yell, while my mum was lady-like to what was very nearly the end.

On one trip Down the Islands, when I was about twelve, we hadn't even arrived at the house when calamity struck. Our boat had been chugging along, laden with provisions for the week: food, drink, snacks . . . and cigarettes. There were a load of children, a few mums and a couple of dads; everyone had got muddled up as we'd piled into the different pirogues. There were a couple of planks nailed from side to side for us to sit on, and some of them had little awnings to shelter you from the sun. Life jackets weren't compulsory in those days, so we were all in shorts and flip-flops when suddenly there was an almighty crunch, and the boat slammed to a halt and flipped sideways. Everyone fell into the sea and onto the rocks that the driver of the boat had obviously failed to notice. There was pandemonium, screams and cries and shouts as the grown-ups panicked about righting the boat and keeping the children out of harm.

'Get to shore. Get to shore!' someone shouted, and we made our way through the shallows and onto the outlying rocks. We all sat shivering with fear and excitement as we watched the adults right the boat, and swim around frantically trying to capture the provisions that were floating in the surf. The boat was half full of water, and didn't look capable of taking anyone anywhere. Images of being ship-wrecked and rescued and staying overnight while waving at passing boats flashed through our minds. An adventure! How exciting!

It was an adventure of the best kind; it actually only lasted an hour, until one of the other boats passed by, saw what had happened, laughed at us for a bit, dropped off their load, then came back to get us. And in that hour, my strongest memory is of my mother, calmly but deter-minedly laying out packs of sea-soaked cigarettes on the hot rocks, willing them to dry.

★　★　★

35

It was Down the Islands that I had the experience every girl dreams about: her first kiss. Fuelled by romantic novels and hormones, I just *knew* that when it happened the world would stop spinning in its orbit, fireworks would explode and Disney-type music would swell from somewhere in the background.

By all accounts, my first kiss should have been a show-stopper. I was thirteen and away for the first time without my mum and dad, on a weekend Down the Islands with some friends and their parents. We had spent the day on a speedboat, driving much too fast and squealing as we skimmed over the sea. We were all walking back through the holiday complex where we were staying, the moon was out and, when I looked around, I was alone with one of the boys. His name was Alfred, and I had felt him looking at me all weekend. I'd liked it — he was friendly and tall, and at eighteen seemed very grown-up compared to the other boys. We had chatted and laughed together a lot, but this was my first time alone with him.

I felt hot and prickly and a little sick as he stopped, turned me round to him and bent down to kiss me. My heart was going to explode with excitement. This was it! This was what everyone talked about. From every Mills & Boon book I'd ever read, I knew that I would want to melt, that I would feel blood rush to my head and I would hold him tightly . . . He kissed me, and I waited. I felt his soft lips, with tufts of downy hair on his chin, and I could smell his father's aftershave. I closed my eyes and relished the moment — I,

Andrea, was one of the gang; I was taking off with someone!

Then he opened his mouth a little wider, and there it was — he slipped his tongue inside my mouth, just like I'd heard girls talk about. I panicked a little; I'd never really cleared up what I was supposed to do with mine, so I tentatively stuck it out. It seemed to work; he made a noise and pulled me tighter. I could feel how hot he was and, scarily, I also felt something move in his shorts. Then he opened his mouth a little more . . . and a little more . . . and his tongue began to swirl. I was a little alarmed; what was I supposed to do now? I kept my eyes tight shut and swirled my tongue back. After a few minutes, I waited for my knees to feel weak, and for him to pull away, hold my face in his hands and tell me tenderly that he loved me; although that would have made things a little tricky, as I definitely didn't love him.

My knees didn't feel weak, but my neck started to hurt; he was a lot taller than me. I opened my eyes and looked up at the moon. It was huge, and seemed to be peering over his shoulder to have a peek at us kissing. The stars were twinkling, palm trees swayed in the breeze . . . and I waited. By now his mouth was open as wide as it would go, and his tongue was swirling and thrashing around in my mouth like a sock in a washing machine. With my eyes open, my body slack and my arms lightly resting around his neck, it began to dawn on me. *This was it.* There wasn't going to be any trembling of knees and declarations of love and face-holding tenderness.

This was what it was all about: standing with a sore neck while a boy sucked your face and slobbered on it and ground his front with the rock thing in his shorts into your tummy. The disappointment was heavy. This couldn't be what everyone got all excited about; this was *horrible*.

After about fifteen minutes, my neck couldn't take any more and my face was starting to feel raw. I let my arms fall to my side, glad to feel the blood return to my fingers. He didn't seem to notice, and carried on sucking and swirling and grinding. I wanted to stop, but wasn't sure how. If I pulled away suddenly, he'd be left with a wide-open mouth and sticking-out tongue, and that would just be embarrassing. So I gently tried to ease myself away, and to close my mouth so that he would do the same. It was a long, slow process, and by the time I had managed to extract myself, my face was sore and wet. He looked down at me, smiling and seeming pleased with himself.

'I've got to get back,' I stammered. 'The others are waiting for me. I'll see you tomorrow.'

And I ran, wishing I could just go home to Mum and Dad.

# 3

## A Good Convent Girl Gone Bad

St Joseph's Convent in San Fernando in the south of Trinidad was my favourite of all the schools I went to, and I had a lot to choose from. It was in the heart of the bustling town of San Fernando, a few miles away from St Madeleine sugar factory where my dad worked. The school was on the side of a big hill with a promenade outside it, shaded by trees. It was pretty but careworn, a mixture of sun bleached wooden buildings and a three-storey modern concrete block which housed the fourth, fifth and sixth formers and a two-storey block for the first, second and third years, who all together made up a few hundred girls. The odd stray dog would wander around outside, plonking themselves on the side of the road to furiously scratch their mange-riddled skin. The young me wanted to bring them all home and love them back to health; I was regularly hauled out from under the club house on the estate, covered in fleas and scratching, trying to cuddle the stray dogs and cats that made their homes there.

Outside the school there was an underlying whiff of drains. Car fumes hung in the air, and the smell of fried food would drift over the walls into our classroom. It was noisy; cars beeping, people laughing, vendors shouting, 'Snow cone!

39

Who want snow cone?' I used to buy one every lunchtime from the vendor who pitched up on the promenade outside the convent, until one day I saw him unzip his trousers and pee right next to the huge block of ice lying on a cloth on the ground. The same ice that was chopped up and ground through his machine, then covered with red syrup. It never had the same appeal after that . . .

From passing my eleven plus to get into the first form, until I left at the end of the third year, I count this as my happiest school time. This time I had joined the school at the same time as everyone else; we had all been frightened little first years in our brand new blue pleated skirts, crisp white shirts and sparkling clean Bata pumps. I was the only white girl in my class, and it was something I hardly noticed. It didn't matter; here, I was just me, a laughing girl who was good at art but terrible at maths. The most rebellious thing I ever did was sliding down the banister, only to be greeted at the bottom by a frosty Miss Earl. She was a large black woman who dressed in bright, tight dresses, and always wore gloves, like a lady from the 1950s. She looked down her nose at me, pursed her full lips and squeaked in her strange, strangled voice: 'Young ladies don't *do* that. Don't let me catch you at it again.'

Actually, that wasn't the most rebellious thing I ever did; it was just the one my parents knew about. I was regularly told off for reading Mills & Boon books in class when I was supposed to be revising Spanish. I was often sent to the chemistry lab to have nail polish removed. I was separated from my group of friends on a weekly basis for giggling too much and driving the teachers crazy. And at least once a month I would stand with the rest of the class when a teacher entered the room, hoping they wouldn't notice one of my shoes hanging precariously on the top of the door. The whole class would spend the rest of the lesson squirming in their seats, waiting to see if it would land on someone's head as they walked in and out of the room.

I was liked. I worked hard enough that the teachers let me get away with things, and I was fun enough that no one thought I was a square. So when I was thirteen and 'the incident' happened, it seemed fair enough that I got away with it.

It started as a simple enough idea. A group of us had been sitting around moaning about the end-of-term exams that were coming up, and the fact that none of us was good at everything, and at least one topic always brought our average percentage down. Then someone hit on an idea. We were all good at different things, so why didn't we just help each other? Whoever was good at maths would pass the answers around. Whoever was good at English would do the same; and Spanish, and French, and History . . . and that way *everyone* would do well.

'I is good at math, nah?' volunteered Nicole, a tall, curly-haired girl.

'An' I can help with de chemistry?' chipped in Afrose; she was good at that.

'I can do de French an' ting, eh?' grinned Janine.

It seemed like the perfect plan. Our parents would be happy, the teachers would be happy; everyone would benefit. We never really saw it as cheating; it was just, well, *helping* . . .

And so when exam time came, notes were zooming around the classroom like flies, and not a single teacher noticed. It was such an unthinkable thing that I guess it had never occurred to them that we would do it. And we would have got away with it. However, with every ointment there is a fly, and in every class there is a person who really *has* swotted for every subject, and she objected strongly to the 'help' offered by her classmates. She was the *only one* who hadn't taken part and, as such, was not at all happy when her grade average was pretty much on a par with everyone else's. So, the truth was told and the whole class was ordered into the principal's office.

We were terrified. We were all good girls who had never even stolen a sweet, so to be hauled in front of Sister Theresa on charges of cheating was pretty scary. We stood in a line as Sister Theresa paced slowly in front of us, and we all stared at the polished wooden floor as she told us how disappointed she was. As an older West Indian woman it was impossible to guess her age, but she seemed at least seventy. In truth, with her beautiful caramel skin and white hair she could have been in her fifties; either way, to us she seemed *ancient*. I liked her, she was softly spoken, but firm and fair, and I was devastated by her disappointment.

Sister Theresa sighed, and then spoke softly: 'Your parents will be very disappointed in you girls.' The weight of those few words sent a few of our line-up into instant sobs of remorse. 'You have let the whole school down. But, more importantly, you have let yourselves down in the eyes of God.'

She looked at us, a sorry lot, lined up in front of her in the cool of her office. It was a sunny day, and carefree traffic beeped outside, unaware of the misery occurring just a few feet away.

Sister spoke to us again, firmly this time: 'I am going to ask you now, before the eyes of God, to answer a question that only you know the answer to. Depending on what answer you give me, God, and myself, will deal with you accordingly.'

One by one, she stood in front of each shaking girl and asked her straight: 'My child, did you cheat in your end-of-term exams?' And, one by one, each girl answered.

The answers varied according to the courage or — depending on which way you looked at it — the duplicity of the girl. Those who answered, 'Yes, Sister!' and collapsed into tears were told to walk to the front of the room. Those who stared at the floor with burning cheeks and answered, 'No, Sister,' were sent back to their classroom to wait for their form teacher to return.

I was near the end of the row. The room was almost empty; only around four girls had crumpled under the pressure. Sister Theresa stood in front of me. I could feel the warmth from the nun's body, and noticed a tiny blue ink stain on the front of her crisp white dress.

'My child, did you cheat in your end-of-term exams?' It was a straightforward question, and needed a yes or no answer. I kept my head bent to hide the betraying blush on my face.

'No, Sister,' I said quietly.

'Return to your class, please,' said Sister Theresa, and I turned and walked out, keeping my head down, not looking at my weeping classmates. Back in the classroom, it was quiet . . . and three-quarters full of fearful, guilty-as-hell young girls.

When my report card came through and I handed it to my parents to sign, my mum looked at the note on the bottom.

'So there were no percentages given out this year because of an incident in class? What happened?'

'Oh, some girls got caught cheating.' I kept my head turned away from Mum and looked out the window.

'Cheating? At the convent! What a shame some people have to spoil it for others. You normally do so well; it's a shame you can't see how you did this year . . . '

Mum signed the card and handed it back to me, smiling. It was never mentioned again and I never did it again. The adult disappointment in my behaviour weighed heavily, and it would be many years before I felt that level of shame again.

I kind of did my penance (if you want to call it that) for cheating by volunteering to sit with the elderly in San Fernando General Hospital. It was a short walk from the school, and once a month Sister Mary, a tiny little Irish nun with sparkling blue eyes and pale freckled skin, would escort a group of girls down the road. We were supposed to go along and talk to them, read the Bible to them and listen to them. In truth, I went because I felt it was a good thing to do, but I always kept a quiet eye on my watch. Just walking into the place made me feel sick, and I would have to hold my breath and try to breathe through my ears for the hour I was there, so I wouldn't reel from the smell of urine, sweat and death.

Most times, the old men and women didn't remember who we were, and had no idea why they were being visited by strange girls in uniform. Some thought we were grandchildren, and talked long and earnestly about family members I had never heard of. I always found this strange; I was white and they were black, so the chances of me being a granddaughter were remote. Still, I went, and I held my breath, and I listened, and stroked hands and joked and laughed, and was relieved when Mum arrived to take me home. Sometimes I would go back and a particular favourite was gone, replaced by another equally frail-looking patient. I hated that part the most; it made it real. We weren't just visiting sick people in hospital; we were talking to real people who didn't know where they were, and who were slowly, patiently dying. I was always quiet on the way home, and would have a shower when I got in to get rid of the smell that was a constant reminder of the frailty of life.

Every Monday and Friday afternoon I would

go to tennis lessons after school with my friend Ingrid's mum, Auntie Cheridah, and on a Monday I would get changed from my tennis gear straight into my swimming costume, ready to dive into the nearby pool and pound up and down for another hour of training, this time in front crawl, breast stroke and butterfly. I was super fit and really loved sport. But I was never going to be an Olympic swimmer or a Wimbledon star as I've always lacked that competitive streak, and quite often I would let the other person win if it looked like they were getting upset or angry with themselves. I can still hear Auntie Cheridah shouting, 'For God's sake, Andrea! RUN FOR DE BALL!', but as soon as sport got serious, the fun went straight out of it for me.

On Saturdays we would often go to Gulf City, a shopping centre on the edge of town, which had been the pinnacle of excitement when it had first been built. It was 1982, and this, the first proper shopping centre in southern Trinidad, was somewhere to go and 'lime'. Liming was basically just hanging around with your friends, but it was much, much more than that. Best clothes were worn, often tight drain-pipe jeans, with lashings of lip gloss. Our style was influenced as much by what was going on in America — which was closer and was seen more on the local TV — as by the UK, where most of us came from and to where we returned every summer, bringing back outfits from Chelsea Girl. The shops themselves were almost irrelevant as we couldn't afford any of the expensive

American clothes, but we cruised the mall anyway.

There was a lot of giggling involved, and stomach-churning excitement, and heart-stopping moments when the boy you fancied looked up at you from the ground floor to the first and your eyes met . . . I was desperate to lime, and only managed to do it once. Going to the mall with your parents didn't count — you had to be dropped off and left to your own devices for at least two hours, so that you could giggle and look pathetic without being embarrassed by them asking, *What the hell did you think you looked like?*

On one particular Saturday I was dropped off by Mum, who told me she would be back in a couple of hours. I hung around on the fringes of the group, so thrilled to be there I could hardly speak, just following the pack wherever they went, and whatever they did. They were friends of some of the coolest girls in school, and I didn't know them very well, but I really wanted to. Then someone suggested going to see a movie. Not a bad suggestion, but it meant that I had to pipe up that my mum was picking me up in half an hour, so I wouldn't be able to go. This was well before mobile phones had ever been thought of, so there was no way of asking Mum before she had set off in the car through the busy traffic to come and get me. Not a problem, everyone agreed; they'd just ask her to come back again in a few hours' time. Obviously not a problem to a bunch of teenagers who had nothing better to do, but for a busy mum forced to drive back and forth into San Fernando twice

47

in one day when driving wasn't something that came naturally, it was a bit of a no-no. I saw the look in Mum's eyes change as soon as I started to ask, but it was too late; the words were out.

'I don't think so,' said Mum.

'Oh, come on, Mrs Mack-Leen,' said one of the (in my eyes) gorgeous boys. 'It will only be for a few hours, nah? We will look after huh!'

Mum's eyes narrowed and my heart sank. Rule number one with Mum was *Never, ever ask for something in front of people when you know the answer will be no . . .*

'All right, Andrea,' said Mum, her eyes cold. 'I will pick you up in two hours. Enjoy the film.'

I didn't. I had no idea what the film was and spent the next two hours feeling physically sick. I had shown Mum up in front of my friends. Mum was *not happy.* That was not a good thing. I was in trouble; big trouble.

Two hours later, in the car on the way home, Mum had hissed through clenched teeth: 'Don't you *ever* do that to me again! Don't you *ever* make me look bad in front of your friends like that! You know you aren't allowed to see a film unless we see it with you or watch it first! And when I say a time to pick you up, I mean *that time*, not when you feel like it!'

I felt hideous and was grounded for a month.

It's strange; when we got back to the UK two years later, liming in shopping centres was the last thing that I wanted to do; it seemed like such a waste of time. It must have been an age thing, because Linda got straight into it and seemed to spend every waking moment she wasn't at school doing just that.

'I don't know what we're going to do with her,' my parents said, as they watched her walk to the bus stop. That had been the drawback of Trinidad. You couldn't just walk to a bus stop to go and hang out with your mates; parents had to be called upon day and night to drop off and pick up, and generally be at your beck and call. Maybe an island paradise had its drawbacks after all, lack of public transport being one of them . . .

# 4

## Back to Blighty

Daydreams are funny things. What are they? Ambitions? Hopes? They keep us going, get us out of bed in the morning, whisper in our ear *What if?* They make us hot, and numb, and spaced out in our head. They put a bounce in our stride, they make us smile in shops and hum in supermarkets.

And they crush us. Why did we think they would work? When will our turn come? No smiles when we're out and about now, just scowls and muttering and shouting at people who cut us up at traffic lights.

And then, after a time, a dream arrives again; a little one, small and apologetic, taps on our window and we let it in. Because without it, where would we be? We would all be traffic wardens.

My dreams weren't unusual for a girl. They started small; when I was five, I wanted to dress up as the Queen of Hearts at the school carnival, a tiny version of the infamous annual celebration from Trinidad that is now enjoyed in Notting Hill in London.

Then at seven, I wanted to be Cinderella in the school play. Instead, I was one of her two mice and I got to wear a black leotard with red and yellow shiny flamenco ruffles and shake a maracas and sing 'La Cucaracha'. I loved it when everyone clapped, and was happy to be a mouse, but deep down, I wished I'd got to wear Cinderella's ballgown and have everyone say, 'Ahhhh,' when I danced at the ball.

When I was ten, I desperately wanted to have real furniture. Not company stuff that everybody had, with little numbers written on the bottom. I wanted a white, curly bed, not a plain dark wooden one. I wanted wallpaper, and matching curtains and bed covers, like I saw on the TV. I desperately wanted a carpet. My dad really tried to help, and during one trip to the UK we bought wallpaper and curtains and a cover for the bed. My dad wallpapered one of my bedroom walls, and for a while it looked almost like a girl's bedroom in the UK. Then the humidity got to work, and the paper started to peel, and before long it was bubbly and strange and didn't look quite right. And it was blue, when really I'd wanted pink.

When I was fourteen, I didn't want to move around any more. I didn't want to be the new girl; to stand alone on the first day at school, hoping that someone would notice and speak to me. I hated not knowing where to go, or where to sit, or who was nice and who to avoid. I just wanted to be the same as everyone else. I wanted to be in a place long enough for people to really know me, to include me; to be part of a gang. For people to notice I was there and to want my opinion; to be invited along. Apart from during my time at St Joseph's, that never really seemed to come — no matter what school I was at, or what part of the world, I was never quite *in*. And the older I got, the more difficult it became, as groups had formed, and friendships had been knitted tightly shut, too tight for someone new to wriggle in. So, usually I just waited, and soon enough 'my' group would form, made up mostly of whoever else wasn't in a little clique. That suited me fine — I had never, and still have never been, 'in with the in crowd'; I just like who I like, and that's it. But, just as I would find my little group, we'd up sticks again and I'd be back to square one, clueless and friendless.

At forty-two I know that I will never be 'cool' and that doesn't bother me in the least — I am very happy with who I am and have made some wonderful friends along the way. A mistake that many people make about me is that I am aloof or distant, or that I think I am better than anyone else. That's not the case at all; it's just that if I don't know what to say, I don't say very much. And I don't presume that everyone wants to hear my take on things, my personal opinion. When I am with my family there is no shutting me up, but outside of that I prefer to listen and blend in. But, like most people, at fourteen I didn't have the self-confidence or self-knowledge I now have.

'You can start again,' my dad said, when he announced that we were moving back to the UK so that Linda and I could finish our education there. 'You can be whoever you want to be, because nobody knows you. Isn't that exciting?'

As a teenager, it wasn't; all I wanted to be was myself. I was so jealous of my cousins in Scotland, who had lived in the same town since they were born, who had had the same friends, and went to the same school. In 1984, when I was almost fifteen, we moved back to the UK for the final time and settled in Leicestershire, as that's where my dad had found work. I didn't even know how to catch a bus. I was British, but I didn't feel welcome here. Even going to the shops was an ordeal, trying to understand the notes and coins, and hoping no one would laugh at my Caribbean accent.

Sometimes it seemed as if there was only one place I had felt at home; it was on the top branch of the wonderfully named Flamboyant tree in our garden in Trinidad. It was a beautiful tree, with flaming red flowers, and my dad nailed a plank of wood up there so I could sit and read, and feel at peace as I watched the sugar cane flutter in the breeze. It was cool up there, and the tree swayed and made a whishing noise, and it felt like a big hug.

I would write my diary, or munch on tamarind picked from the garden and peeled and rolled in sugar, salt, pepper and chilli. They were hot and sweet at the same time and I could eat a bucketful. I devoured books up there, anything I could get my hands on. Jane Austen's *Pride and Prejudice* was inhaled at eleven, along with *What Katy Did*, and *What Katy Did Next*, and all the Malory Towers and Famous Five books. Plus, of course, my mum's Mills & Boons, where I formed my ideas on romance. Those novels became my guidebooks to later years. Fact: men would always be tall, dark and brooding. Men didn't like brash, loud women who wore lots of make-up and smoked. A handsome man would eventually notice the hidden beauty of the girl in the corner, and she would blossom under his gaze, and they would live happily ever after.

But instead of being safe in my tree, daydreaming, I was in England and about to face some of the toughest times of my life.

Bullying. It doesn't matter how old you are, it doesn't go away, and it doesn't hurt any less. All that changes when you become an adult is that the children get older and taller and the playground becomes the rest of the world. I don't believe that children 'don't know any better', in the same way that no adult is 'driven to it'. Bullying is cowardly, sneaky, dangerous and absolutely inexcusable. It takes many forms, but just because it may not involve physical pain, that doesn't make it any less potent. In the same way that verbal and psychological abuse is just as painful as physical violence, the old adage that 'sticks and stones may break my bones but words will never hurt me' is NOT TRUE. I was bullied. In fact, sometimes I still am; the difference is I know now how to deal with it and can see it for what it is. It is weak.

I was six years old the first time I was bullied, by a boy in my class in Trinidad who used to whack me in the face every chance he could get. I didn't say anything for a while as I just hoped he would stop it, but one day I broke down in tears at home and told my dad. He did what any father should: he told me the next time it happened to hit him back as hard as I could, and then run. The next day at the dinner table Dad looked over at my bruised eye.

'What happened?' he asked, appalled.

'I forgot to run,' I admitted.

The funny thing was, once I whacked him back, that little boy and I became friends. The bullying continued for a while, just not to me; he would grab the smaller children's hands and force them to hold on to nettles, laughing as they cried. That stopped soon after as well, as I stepped in and told him to cut it out. By the time I left primary school I was five foot six inches tall, and stood a good head and shoulders above the rest of the school, so anyone who felt threatened would run to me and all I had to do was walk over and 'look tall' at whoever was causing the trouble. I liked helping the smaller ones out, it made me feel good to stop them being picked on. I didn't care about being called 'beanpole' or anything else by the boys, as I knew they were desperate to be as tall as I was!

When we moved back to the UK for the final time, I had left a convent school where you stood up every time a teacher entered a room, or whenever you were asked a question, so life in a Midlands secondary school was a bit of a shock to the system. Robert Smyth School was an ex-grammar school, and by all accounts had a good reputation, which is why we moved to Market Harborough so I could go there. It also helped that it was the same village that my godfather lived in, and he had told my dad that there was a job going in the animal feed factory where he worked. Dad applied and luckily got the job working alongside someone he knew, which made the adjustment to UK life easier. My godfather, 'Uncle' Mike, and his wife, 'Auntie' Frances, helped Mum and Dad settle into their new life, and their daughter Jane, who was the same age as me, would be going to the same school, which would help. Jane and I had been christened together back in Trinidad as children, but she had returned to the UK with her mum and dad when she was two, so we didn't really know each other that well.

Jane was to become my very best friend, but this didn't happen while we were at school together. She already had her group of friends and I didn't want to push myself in and cramp her style, so we mainly saw each other after school and when our parents were together. We shared the same ridiculous sense of humour and can still make each other cry laughing, even now.

From my first day at school I stood out like a sore thumb. Dark eyes, dark skin and a broad Caribbean accent were the first things that set me apart.

'Did you live in a tree?' asked a boy at my new school one day, his spotty face tinged with curiosity.

'No. Why?'

'You speak like a monkey and you lived with all the black people, and they all live in trees!'

'No, dey don't!'

'Yes, they do! And they eat bananas!'

'What's bananas got to do wit it?'

'All black people eat bananas, and you talk like them so must be like them! You live in a tree! Ha ha, ha ha!'

A white girl who spoke like a black one — you didn't get many of those in Leicestershire. The rest was just my generally strange behaviour. I stood up every time a teacher spoke to me, which was hugely embarrassing until I weaned myself off that particular habit. I was polite, well mannered and tried hard, so I was instantly annoying. I didn't understand the dialect — how was I supposed to know a cob was a bread roll? But after a few weeks I began to feel that I was being cautiously accepted; like a new breed of pigeon joining a coop. I made a small group of friends and settled into my new life, learning about the wonders of *Top of the Pops* and the intense joy of taping the weekly Top 40 countdown on Radio One, trying not to get Bruno Brooks' voice mixed in with Frankie Goes to Hollywood. A month or so later, however, everything changed.

We were in the girls' changing room; the setting for many an unhappy teenager's memories. I was OK at sport, so I usually looked forward to it; I had yet to experience a British winter, and the torture of hockey and cross-country in the half-dark of February. We were getting changed, everyone busy doing their own thing and chatting while they dressed. I heard a low laugh coming from the other side of the changing room and glanced over. A group had crowded round Anne Marie, a plain, large girl with few friends. Egged on by the rest of the group, one of them pulled out a can of deodorant while the others sniggered.

'Go on, do it, she stinks!' said a small,

dark-haired girl, as the leader held her arm out towards a blushing Anne Marie. I buttoned up my school shirt and watched quietly.

'You STINK!' shouted a red-haired girl, and she pressed the nozzle down and sprayed. Soon the air was thick with the choking fumes of aerosol deodorant, and the rest of the girls in the room just carried on getting ready and made their way outside. No one did anything. Anne Marie was now soaked through with spray, choking for breath and crying weakly. The girls surrounded her, sneering and laughing. 'You still stink, you bitch!'

'Stinking cow!'

'I can still smell her breath! Get her mouth!'

By now I was fully dressed, and the changing room was almost empty. I picked up my bag and walked over to them. 'I think that's enough now, don't you?'

One of them turned and looked at me incredulously. 'What?'

'I think that's enough. Leave her alone.'

The spraying stopped but the air was thick with it. Anne Marie grabbed her things and ran out of the room, her shirt wet and stuck to her chest. The red-haired girl turned round and looked at me, as if seeing me for the first time. If I had known better I would have been afraid, but I was naive enough to think we could reason this out.

'What's it to you?' she said, looking me up and down. The others were quiet, but gathered round us.

'It doesn't mean anything to me,' I replied. 'I

58

just think you should leave her alone.'

'Why? You her friend? You her *girl* friend?'

There was laughter, and more girls picked up their things and walked out of the changing room. There was now just me and the very scary group of girls left. With blinding clarity I saw what I had done. I had got involved in something that didn't concern me, and now they were all looking at ME. Anne Marie was long gone, and now I was the one standing in her place. From that moment on, my life at secondary school would change forever.

My tormentors must have thanked their lucky stars the day I came into their lives. I was perfect fodder; new and completely lacking in street smarts. I didn't have a clue. I thought you stood up to a bully, they backed down and life carried on, but sadly that only happens in American movies. It didn't happen in the Midlands. Instead, it became open season on Andrea McLean — for two years.

It started small: whispering in corridors that erupted into laughter when I walked past. Kicking the toilet door when I went in during lunch break, and throwing things over the top so they rained down on me as I tried to relax enough to urinate. A foot stuck out as I walked from one lesson to another, sending me and my books sprawling. Screwed-up balls of paper bounced off my head whenever the teacher turned his back in class. A drawing pin, point up on my seat. I had to be on my guard at all times, without looking like I noticed or cared. It was petty, so I said nothing. They were subtly destructive and clever, and always seemed to catch me on my own.

When it first started I thought that if I just ignored them they would get bored of me and move on, but that never happened as I was far too good a target. I could usually manage to put them out of my head when I was safely at home, but even popping into the village to buy a record from Woolworths was a nerve-wracking experience in case I bumped into them. I worked as a Saturday girl in Freeman Hardy Willis with Jane, which thankfully sold shoes too hideous for any teenage girl so they never came in, but I would see them sidle past, looking in at me and laughing at my rubbish job. I played down how horrible it was to Jane and didn't talk to her about it as I knew she would end up getting involved. Her school life was jogging along quite happily; she didn't need anything like this to happen to her. She has told me off for that since then, and maybe things would have been different if she had known, but at the time I felt it was best that she didn't know the full extent of it.

My daily walk to school was usually OK as they arrived later than me, so it was only when the bell went for the first lesson of the day that the knot would really twist in my stomach. Walking down the corridor among the throng of black-and-white uniforms, in a fug of cheap aftershave, *Impulse* body spray and teenage angst, I'd hoist my bag onto my shoulder, put my head down and brace myself for the first insult of the day.

By now my tan had faded and my skin, used to daily doses of sunshine, reacted by breaking out into spots that took until my twenties to clear. My shoulder-length brown hair went lank, so my mum decided that the best thing for it was a 'wee perm'. One afternoon I came home from school to see a Toni & Guy home perm kit sitting on the pine kitchen table. An innocuous-looking thing, it came to represent the worst moments of my teenage life.

Settling me down on a kitchen chair, Mum set to work with scissors, chopping the ends off my hair and trying to even out my stubborn fringe. I had (and still have) a cowlick, which means my fringe never, ever lies straight, so sometimes it would take a few goes to get the angle right. By then, the hair may have been straight, but it was also only an inch from my hair line. 'Don't worry, it'll grow,' Mum chirped as I whimpered to myself.

Using tiny rollers, my mum pulled my hair into tight curls and smothered it in sharp-smelling solution. Rinsed and washed at the kitchen sink, I retreated upstairs to my bedroom, to blow-dry my hair and stare at my hideous reflection. Unknowingly, my mum had just given my enemies a new shipment of ammunition; I was now tightly permed cannon fodder. I didn't really consider that my new look also put off the boys, which it did — I had already figured out that they weren't interested in me anyway.

There weren't many school discos during those years, but there were enough to sort the winners from the losers when it came to love. If

61

it had been invented then, I would have had the 'L' shape of 'loser' waved at me every time. I would spend hours with my girlfriends getting ready, carefully smearing on electric-blue mascara and frosted pink lipstick, backcombing my hair and slipping into something pastel, while bopping to Madonna's *True Blue* album in my bedroom. In a frenzy of nerves we would arrive, worrying about who would be there, who would notice us, and who would ask us to dance in those terrifying last few minutes when Dead or Alive was switched off and we stopped spinning round like a record, and George Michael's 'Careless Whisper' was switched on.

One by one my friends would be plucked from their positions holding up the wall and be led falteringly onto the dance floor by a boy who was either shorter, skinnier or at the very least spottier than them. And as I watched the girls who made my life hell during daylight hours getting their faces snogged off by boys I fancied, and my friends nervously shuffling in the arms of sweaty hopefuls, I realized it wasn't going to happen for me. So I pretended to be busy getting my coat, or that I needed the loo, or I tidied away plastic cups full of secret stashes of cider; anything other than look at people doing what I so desperately wanted to do — dance with someone. And every time, my dad would be waiting outside to take me home, and he would smile at me as I got into the car.

'So, did you get a dance tonight?' he would ask, and I would smile back.

'No.'

He'd reach over and squeeze my knee and say, 'That's because you're too beautiful,' and look like he meant it. And I would look through the windscreen at the wet orange-lit road and silently thank him.

I never said a word about being bullied to either of my parents the whole time it went on, for two reasons. First, I knew it would upset them, as I had so enjoyed my school life in Trinidad and had never experienced anything like it before. Second, I knew they would want to get involved, and that it would only make things worse. So, like many teenagers who are bullied, I kept quiet.

By now, I was used to having things thrown at me and whispered about me and I was able to block it out. We had settled into that age-old dance of tormentor and victim, whereby I took what they gave me and moved on and they just kept coming back with more. I had hoped that they would have moved on by the time I reached the fifth year, but no. Now that we had been put into classes according to our 'O' level options, I had some moments of peace and could relax, but I seemed to be rubbish at the same subjects as them, so was forced to sit with them in the lowest sets for Maths and French, and in Art, which was a mixed class. That meant anyone who was doing it as a dosser's subject was put in with the same group as those who wanted to take it to another level — either A level or beyond. Of course, I was one of those, and the subject went from being my favourite to my most dreaded.

The teacher seemed like a nice enough woman, but I couldn't understand why she would put us all on to tables together, like we were at primary school, and make us do 'group work'. Which meant I had to sit facing the very people who were threatening to set me alight during chemistry class or murder me during RE. And I had to 'help' them as I was 'so good at art'! It was horrendous for me and playtime for them. Paint would be 'accidentally' poured over my work, pieces would go missing and end up in their folders, and finally, my O level exhibition was found ripped in half and hanging off the wall the morning it was to be judged.

'Oh, what a shame,' exclaimed the teacher. 'Who would do something like that?'

I decided she was obviously dumb as well as blind and deaf, and grimly Sellotaped it back together again as best I could.

★ ★ ★

There were two teachers who seemed to notice what was happening to me, and who actually *cared*. One was my English teacher, Mr Gallas. He was a lovely man, with auburn hair and a cheerful moustache, who was as passionate about English as I was. I LOVED it, and I loved his lessons. I saw him fight every day to keep his class under control, when stupid boys smoked at the back of the room with their feet up on the desk, daring him to throw them out so they could rampage out the door, kicking over tables on the way. Most of the time he managed it with good humour and grace, and admirable wit, which even the dumbest of pupils had to raise a smile at. If he was ever to be played in a film, it would be by a twinkly-eyed Kevin Kline.

He saw and heard, and occasionally narrowed his eyes and said 'enough' when things were said behind my back, just loud enough for everyone to hear. He didn't kick up a scene, which I am glad of as it would only have made things worse, but it was good to know that he was aware of what was going on.

One day I showed him a short story I had written about a girl who was being bullied at school. I had changed the details to be about sport, but it was obviously about me and how I felt. The next day he handed it back to me and quietly said, 'I think you should send this off somewhere. It's good enough.' And inside I skipped.

My favourite magazine at the time was *Just Seventeen*, and I was always sending things off to them and other girls' and women's weekly magazines. I was fifteen and I already had a folder stuffed full of rejection letters, but I kept going because I really, *really* wanted to see my name above something I had written. So I sent my story off, called 'Will to Win', about a girl who was good at running but was bullied by another girl who was jealous of her. And one day, what felt like a decade later, I got a reply. I quickly scanned the letter, looking for the word 'unfortunately'. It wasn't there. Nor were the words 'sorry' or 'next time' . . . They wanted to print my story, AND pay me £150 for it!

I spent the next month in a state of anxiety, excited beyond belief that not only was I going to get something printed at last, but in my favourite magazine! However, I was also terrified about what would happen when the girls read it and realized it was by me. Would this just make everything worse? Every week I checked the magazine stand in Woolworths, and one day there it was. My name. I bought it and shoved it into my bag, tripping over myself to get to school. I knew who I wanted to show it to. I hadn't told anyone else as I hadn't wanted it to get out, but I knew one person who would be pleased for me. Mr Gallas was in his Portakabin classroom setting up for a lesson when I knocked on the door.

'Hello, Andrea,' he said, surprised.

'I have something for you,' I said and fumbled in my school bag. He looked at me, confused, then his eyes widened when I held out my brightly illustrated double-page story, with the words at the top: 'By Andrea McLean'.

'Aaaarrr!!!' he yelled, and he picked me up under my arms and swung me around the classroom. 'You did it!' He looked like he was going to cry, or burst, and I just grinned back at him.

'Don't tell anyone,' I said. 'It could make things a bit awkward.'

He looked at me and frowned. 'It shouldn't be like this, you know. It's not fair.'

'I know, but this is how it is. So please don't say anything.' And he didn't. But we knew what I had done, and it was lovely.

There was one other teacher who kept an eye out for me during my time at Robert Smyth School, and who in her own way could see that I was a bit different to everyone else, and would probably never really fit in. Like Mr Gallas, she didn't get involved, or make things worse by saying anything; she just quietly kept an eye on me. Mrs Johnson was our PE teacher, and she was fabulous. She was funny and bright with greying curly auburn hair, jolly blue eyes and the windswept face of a woman who spent most of her time outdoors. She could put anyone in their place with her wisecracks and lovely smile. She made sure no one cheated or illegally whacked an ankle during hockey and she shouted at us to keep going as we limped through muddy fields during cross-country. She also sometimes let me sit with her at lunchtimes and eat my sandwiches in her little office, just the two of us, chatting and munching. It helped on days when I knew they were on the prowl for me; on days when they stood too close behind me in the queue for the tuck shop, whispering hotly in my ear, 'Can't believe you're buying chocolate, you spotty bitch. That's the LAST thing you need . . . '

Sometimes, she invited me to hers for tea, so I popped over to her house across the road from the school and watched as she fed her chickens and stroked her smelly, toothless old dog, and made tea for her strapping son, who was also in my year at school. Soon, the door would slam and Martin would stomp into the house, take one look at me sitting at the kitchen table and roll his eyes.

'Oh,' he'd say when he saw me. 'I'll be in my room.' And he'd stomp upstairs to wait until I had gone. Mrs Johnson and I would smile at each other, and she would roll her eyes as if to say, 'Boys . . . ' and I would roll mine back as if I understood.

Martin Johnson went on to captain the England rugby team and become the pride of Leicester and the nation. His wonderful mum died a few years ago, and apparently was as warm and supportive to the team as she was to me, a gawky, unworldly girl who didn't really fit in. I hope she knew how much of a difference she made to me during those years, and I'm sorry I never got the chance to meet her again and say thank you.

On the last day of the fifth year, before we broke up for the summer, I was sixteen and, like everyone, was in high spirits. We had finished our exams, and for some it would be the last time they would ever walk through the school gates in their life: an exciting day, as it meant that they were no longer bound by the rules or expectations of the head teacher, who, to be fair, seemed to have pretty few where his pupils were concerned. If he didn't see it, it didn't happen, appeared to be his motto. As we walked out of our last lesson I felt a shove from behind and my arm was gripped hard.

'Know what day it is today, Spotty?' snarled a voice in my ear. 'It's the last day of school. That means once we get through these gates no one can stop us, understand?' There was pack laughter from the five behind me.

'Start running, Spotty, because this time we are going to get you.' My school bag was ripped off my shoulder and thrown into a bush, to much laughter.

'Stupid bitch!'

'Ugly cow!'

I did what any self-respecting coward would do and legged it. I never saw them again.

As I said, bullying doesn't stop just because you leave school; it just changes form. I have had bullying bosses and bullying colleagues, and have met bullying drivers, shop assistants and neighbours. I strongly believe that if you have it in you to be cruel and hurtful to another human being then you will carry on doing so throughout your life — you will just find different ways to do it. I have worked in the television industry for fifteen years, and of course I have experienced bullying during that time. IT HAPPENS. And like my teenage self, I deal with it in my own way, and that mainly involves quietly getting on with it and letting things go until it becomes clear that they won't just pass and need to be dealt with. I'm not afraid of confronting someone who is behaving badly towards me, but only if I think it has gone far enough. I don't want to make a fuss, or get anyone on 'my side' or against anyone else. I just want things to be pleasant, and if someone takes pleasure in making other people feel uncomfortable or bad about themselves, then to me that makes them a bully.

I have had quiet words in corridors with people who have shouted their mouth off about me to my peers, but have blustered and flushed when cornered on their own. Before I worked in TV, or indeed journalism, my first job after graduating was in sales and marketing. I didn't last long, about six months, as I spoke out to bosses who paid me less than younger, less qualified boys, purely because I was female, and then when that didn't work I went to their boss, and then their boss and then, once a precedent of fairness had been set, I quit, as I didn't want to work somewhere that thought bullying female employees was fair. In work I keep my head down and my nose clean, but it doesn't mean that I don't care — it's just that in television the rules of combat aren't as clear-cut as they are in other industries: either your face fits or it doesn't, and there is nothing you can do to change that.

I have heard whispers about myself that I am not 'as nice as I seem', which years ago would have cut me to the quick, and now just make me laugh. I have realized that you can't win: if you are too nice you will be walked all over, and if you do well you will be bitched about. Of course I'm not as 'nice as I seem'. That would make me sickly and saccharine — and bloody dull! What I am is straightforward. I don't always need to be the centre of attention, but I do want to be recognized fairly for what I have done. I am not pushy, but I am not a pushover. I am not a bitch, but I am not Snow White either (the name Coleen Nolan once gave to me on *Loose Women*); I'm just a girl trying to be good in a crazy fairytale world where the normal rules of play don't apply.

★ ★ ★

A few months before my eighteenth birthday, I moved for the last time with my parents, this time from Market Harborough in Leicestershire, where I had spent the past four years, to Chester as my dad had been promoted. We moved halfway through my A levels, and by now my heart was mutinous. I was tired of having another move sprung on me just when things seemed to be settling down. The bullies had left school and I had been free to relax and enjoy friends, a social life and even my classes without fear of retribution. But now I was having to start all over again — moving to another new school, but this time in the final year, where everyone was already settled into their groups of friends and the syllabus was completely different.

I had to ditch everything I had spent the past year working on and start again from scratch with my A levels. The school wasn't impressed with me at all. They had wanted me to go down a year and start again, but for the first time in my life I stood firm. I would rather have extra tuition every night than go back to the lower sixth; it would make me nearly *nineteen* when I left school. What idiot would want that?

I spent most of that year at Christleton High School trying to learn two years' work in two terms. I had a lot to get through — extra lessons every night with sympathetic teachers, and battles to be fought in classrooms with the ones who thought I was insane to try and do what I was doing. One in particular never let me forget just how far behind everyone I was. The worst part of it was that it was my favourite subject, English, in which I had always got straight As, since primary school and through my O levels, and now I was behind. She would make me so nervous I couldn't read aloud in class, and I could see her rolling her eyes at her favourite pupils — two boys who took great pleasure in mocking every stammer and stutter as I struggled to read the words in front of me. Eventually, the teacher would snap, 'Oh, just sit down, Andrea!' and get one of her little pets to read instead.

I still think of her, and of them, when I read the autocue at *Loose Women* every day, gliding through the words as they scroll up the screen, keeping the timing and intonation just right. And I allow myself a little 'Ha!' as inside I blow a raspberry to them all, thinking, *See? I can read out loud, you horrible lot.* Or words to that effect! It wasn't all bad during that time, as I made friends with girls I still keep in touch with today. And, most importantly, it was here that I was to meet the boy who would steer the course of my life for the next seventeen years. It was here that I fell in love for the very first time.

# 5

## My First Love

I can remember the exact moment it happened. It was my first day at Christleton, and I was a few weeks away from turning eighteen. I walked into the sixth-form common room, and it seemed dated and immature compared to my last school. There, we'd had a whole block to ourselves, separate from the rest of the school, and we were treated like adults. Here, we just had a room and had to wear the same uniform as the first years, and to me, it seemed that because they were treated like children these sixth-formers still behaved like them. The boys giggled and sniggered at the girls rather than seeing them as equals, and the main talk seemed to be about how much they'd puked at the weekend. Surely they'd grown out of that by now?

I stood alone, waiting to see what the score was here. Everyone was excited to see each other again after the summer holidays; they had all known each other if not right through their school lives, then at least since the lower sixth, so I stuck out like a sore thumb. A couple of girls looked at me curiously, and then came over to introduce themselves; they were called Claire and Vicky, and they were to become two of my closest friends during that time. I'm lucky still to be in touch with them today.

Vicky was half Finnish, all blonde curly hair and bright blue eyes, and she thought the boys were as ridiculous as I did. She strode like an Amazon among them, and I loved that they were scared of her. Fiercely bright, nothing fazed her, and I felt like she watched over me protectively in the years before family, life and air miles got in the way. Claire was different; softer, and trusting, with big puppy eyes and a heart aching to be romanced. She saw the good in everyone, which balanced out Vicky's worldly cynicism and my inexperience, and the three of us made an unusual but loyal little gang.

A group of boys larked about in the corner, laughing at something one of them was saying. I wasn't close enough to hear, but I could see he was the centre of the group; the lads were hanging on his every word. He was about 5ft 8, with thick, wavy brown hair that hung to his collar — the only boy not wearing his hair in short 1980s spikes. He had a school shirt on with the sleeves rolled up to his elbows, flecked trousers and black slip-on shoes. His dress sense was clearly awful, but then so was everyone's back then. Vicky and Claire saw me looking over at the laughing group of boys.

'Oh, don't bother with them,' scoffed Vicky. 'And especially *him*. He thinks *everyone* fancies him.'

Clare sighed and looked across the room. 'I think he's *gorgeous*.'

One of the boys saw us looking at them and glanced over, and soon they all turned round, including the one who was holding court; the one with the longer hair. He turned round, wondering why everyone wasn't listening to him any more, and then he looked at me.

BOOM. It was just like that. As straightforward, old-fashioned and clichéd as that — I looked at him and a bolt of lightning shot through me, time stood still, everyone else disappeared and I fell in love with Nick Green.

Well, for me it may have been that simple, but of course life isn't like the movies. He seemed to snog most of the school before finding his way round to me, including a best friend I had invited up from Market Harborough to meet the boy I was head over heels in love with. That was an awkward Sunday morning at the breakfast table, when Mum cheerily asked whether she had met Nick, and what did she think!

I sat behind him in Geography and marvelled every time he ran his fingers through his dark wavy hair. Then we were put together on a project and were forced to sit together at lunchtimes to work on it. I discovered he had moved around a lot as well; his dad worked for a bank and he had spent most of his life down south, which was why he had a different accent to everyone else. We bonded over that, and a shared love of terrible American soft rock music. I was the only girl he knew who had heard of Bon Jovi *before* the *Slippery When Wet* album, who thought that Van Halen rocked and Def Leppard ruled. He began to *notice* me, not just as the new girl with the strange accent but as someone he could have a laugh with. We started meeting up on Saturdays during our lunch breaks from our weekend jobs, and he seemed much friendlier away from the rest of the boys. He would practically ignore me at school in front of them, but during our lunches he let himself go and I felt like I was seeing the real 'him'.

He was the coolest boy in school, and he knew it, which made him even more amazing. And for some strange reason, he wanted to go out with *me*. Despite my perm, spots, extra tuition and Doris Day attitude to life, he chose *me*, and I was beside myself. He asked me out in the Davies Chippie on Lower Bridge Street in Chester, while I was on my lunch break from my Saturday job at Barratts shoe shop, and he was on his break from Habitat.

We were standing waiting for our fish and chips when he turned to me awkwardly and said, 'Er, if I asked you out, what would you say?'

I blushed red hot with joy. 'I would say yes.'

He looked at the floor. 'Good. Well, I'll bear that in mind.'

I felt prickly with embarrassment. What did that mean? Were we going out or not? We paid for our food and walked outside to eat. I decided to take the plunge and ask him straight out.

'So . . . does that mean we're going out then?'

'I guess so.' Silence, as we munched our chips and blushed.

'So, can I pick you up tonight then? About seven?' he eventually asked.

'OK.'

'Alright. See ya.'

And that was it.

That day two of his friends also asked out two

girls from school; they had agreed they would all do it that Saturday, so on the Monday morning, suddenly I was in a gang for the first time in my life. I didn't know them that well, but before we left school we went out together, went to pubs and parties, danced to Erasure and later the Happy Mondays, and just hung out when I had the time in between my studies. Those two other couples are still happily married, which proves it can last if you get together young, and I'm thrilled for them.

Meanwhile, Nick and I were starting a journey that was to last seventeen years, and back then, who knew where it would lead? My A level results, when they came, weren't fantastic. I had gone from being predicted As and Bs in Leicestershire to getting two Cs and an E. I didn't get my Warwick University place to study English and Theatre Studies, and had to go through clearing to get on the first course that would take me: Modern Studies (History, Politics and International Relations) at Coventry Polytechnic. It is a university now, but back when I went there it was known as Coventry Poly. It wasn't a coincidence that it was only a few miles away from Warwick University, where Nick had been offered his first choice . . .

I had no history qualifications, and had never studied European history of any kind, but I was keen to learn, and more importantly keen to start off on my own. Don't get me wrong; I've always adored my parents and knew I would miss them, but I was ready to do something for myself, to move somewhere that *I* wanted to be, to make my own decisions. I was tired of being accommodating and considerate, and I wanted to be selfish for a while, to not answer to anyone about where I was and what I was doing and how late I would be out doing it! It was normal healthy rebellion, I suppose, and I was lucky that I was able to do it.

For the first time since sitting my eleven plus, I started something at the same time as everyone else. During freshers' week I was so excited that I joined every club and society going and was completely carried along by the buzz of doing something for myself. They eventually got whittled down to just the one: the Musical Society.

I had enjoyed being in plays at school, and I thought it would be fun to try something like it again. It wasn't exactly Footlights but we put on some very cheery shows, and I even managed to say a couple of lines — in total, that is, over the three years I was there. I was a very keen and consistent chorus member — bright of smile, heavy of step and very out of time. But I didn't care. I was having a whale of a time, and for the first time ever I felt like I was getting to know the real me.

I made a lovely group of friends from my course, some of whom I am still very close to today, and we laugh about my terrible hair and love of awful music, and how I quietly fumed while fellow students spoke a lot of political shit during seminars. They were so angry, and I couldn't understand why. They had never experienced real poverty — they were middle class and had been given a grant to spout politics and thrust the *Socialist Worker* in people's faces on their way to the Mandela Bar. They'd never been to a Third World country, never mind lived in one, and they couldn't see how bloody lucky they were.

My favourite lectures and seminars weren't the heated political ones, though they were interesting. No; it was the ones about colonial history, because I understood them. I had seen it, I had lived through the aftermath of it, and those lectures came to life for me. I may have nodded off during a couple on Thursday mornings after the usual Wednesday night at the Biko Bar, but I hope my lecturers didn't think it was them — it was all me. They were wonderful, and in my final year I majored in Indian, East African and South African History, and wrote my dissertation on the Jewish diaspora and the creation of Israel. It wasn't a thesis that would ever set the world alight, but I enjoyed it, knowing that my family on my dad's side had fled Russia and Poland as persecuted Jews to seek a new life in Scotland. Our family are not Jewish any more, but I have always known of my heritage, and I liked studying it in more detail.

I was perfectly happy with the Dezzy I was awarded after my three years. I got a 2:2 (a Desmond Tutu, or Dezzy as it was called then), which was an average grade for an average student, but I was the first in my family to get a degree and my parents almost burst with pride.

Nick meanwhile struggled for the first year, moving from being a big fish in a small pond in

Chester to, well, being just one of lots of fish at Warwick. But we saw each other every weekend, and sometimes on a midweek night too. Our lives were separate enough that we did our own thing without interfering with each other, but close and regular enough that our relationship matured. We spent Friday nights drinking in student haunts, Saturday mornings hungover in either my or his single bed, and Sundays stressing over notes that hadn't been made and revision that hadn't been done. We were normal students, and those three years were among the happiest of my life.

He was my first in every way — my first real boyfriend, my first love and, later, my first husband . . .

# 6

## Bullets in Bangkok

After we finished our degrees, we decided to go travelling, and spent a year living with our parents and working every hour in offices, shops and pubs to save up enough money to go. Finally, in April 1992, when I was twenty-two, Nick's parents drove us down from Chester to Heathrow to catch our Aeroflot flight to Delhi. It was my first time going so far away without my parents, and our first time away together, but I was so excited, I couldn't wait for our adventure to begin! As the plane bumped down the runway I looked out at the drizzly skyline and grinned — we were really doing this! I turned to Nick in excitement, and my smile faded. He was pale and sweating, gripping the seat in front of him like his life depended on it, flinching with every jolt of the old airplane.

'What's wrong?' I asked, horrified, thinking he was ill.

'I fucking hate flying . . . ' he muttered.

Our year travelling the world was full of ups and downs, and the downs weren't just due to the time spent in aircraft. India was a shock to the system in every way, and as two naive first-time travellers we didn't cope with the country as well as we could have done. We arrived by local bus from the airport to the heart of New Delhi, where we must have looked like wide-eyed lambs being led to the slaughter. We trudged our way to the hostel we had booked into from the UK for our first few nights, had a wash, looked at each other and cried. Both of us.

We survived on peanuts taken from the plane for the first two days, we were so scared of eating local food. The initial experience was such an assault on the senses it was like someone had turned up the volume, on EVERYTHING. The sun was hotter, the cars were noisier, people didn't talk — they shouted, there were more of them in one place than I had ever seen in my life before and they all seemed to be pushing to go in different directions. Men hawked and spat huge great red globs of betel nut juice onto the street, splashing your feet if you were unlucky enough to be wearing flip-flops. Children tugged at our clothes and women tugged at our bags, and everyone wanted the same thing from us: money, money, money. It was exhausting and, at first, I hated it.

We left New Delhi by train and made our way down to Agra to see the famous Taj Mahal, and it was here that I finally understood what travelling was meant to feel like. It was calmer here, and we stayed in a hostel filled with seasoned travellers who were able to give us tips on where to go next, how to get there and where to stay. It was invaluable advice; even with a well-thumbed copy of the *Lonely Planet* you couldn't beat first-hand information. I was getting used to the thumb-sized cockroaches on the bed and in the sink, and just flicked them to one side and carried on. The Taj was everything I had hoped it would be and more, and we ended up going three times, just to see it glow a dusky pink in the sunset. It was beautiful.

After three weeks of travelling round India we were returning by train from Himachal Pradesh in the far north back down to New Delhi, ready for our next flight to Bangkok in Thailand. We had spent a wonderful few days there, walking in the mountains, listening to stories about the Dalai Lama, watching orange-clad Buddhist monks file their way through the streets to prayer. On the train I started to feel a little queasy, which wasn't unusual as we were in India and I'd already felt a bit rough earlier on in the trip. It was a long, slow train journey, and by the following morning I was hunched over the hole in the floor that passed for the toilet, trying not to get my leggings covered in other people's poo and wee. I was ill, really ill, and we only just made it to our hostel in Delhi before I collapsed on to the bed, shaking. I spent the next twenty-four hours in bed or on the toilet, shaking and sweating, and convinced that the walls were moving, that the covers were writhing and that the building itself was wobbling from side to side. I managed to take enough Imodium to get me through the flight to Bangkok without embarrassing myself, but once we were there, I spent another two weeks lying on a mattress on a floor, in a room filled with other backpackers, weak and shaking and never far from the loo.

I tried to go to hospital one day but couldn't walk the length of the street to make it to a taxi.

I had been told I needed to take a 'sample' with me, so I managed to get some into a film case and sealed the lid. Or so I thought. Nick honourably took the sample with him to the hospital as I staggered back to my mattress, but as he hitched a ride on the back of a moped from a friendly local, the lid popped open and, well, he ended up with a nasty brown stain running down his leg that didn't even belong to him . . . He wasn't best pleased when he got back, and I didn't blame him. Yuk. In the two weeks that I was very poorly, Nick had to keep himself entertained, which wasn't much fun for him, and he ended up doing most of the sightseeing around Bangkok on his own. I felt bad about it, but I could barely walk to the bathroom myself, so there wasn't much I could do.

Eventually I was strong enough to make it to a doctor in the street nearby, who didn't speak or understand any English but gave me a bottle of pills to take. They took the edge off things, but by then the damage had been done to my stomach, and years later I would be told that was the cause of my dairy intolerance.

After a fantastic few weeks touring round the north of the country we decided to return to Bangkok before venturing south. The day we arrived, we were sitting eating noodles in our hostel on the Khao San Road when we heard what sounded like a car backfire. We didn't pay much attention, as Bangkok is a noisy city filled with bangs and pops, so this wasn't anything too unusual. Then there was another, then another, and we looked at each other questioningly.

Suddenly there was a roar and a thundering sound, and we all stood up to see what was going on.

People were running down the road like their lives depended on it, shouting and waving their arms. None of us understood what they were saying, but the owner of our hostel charged through us all, and began pulling down the shutters to the front of the building. People outside threw themselves under the metal slats before they touched the ground, then once they were in place and locked solid, the unfortunates left on the street began hammering on them, leaving dents and shaking the aluminium. What was going on?

Then the popping started again, but it was louder this time, and closer. *Pop! Pop!* We heard screams from outside, and the thundering of more feet.

*Crack!*

We heard shouting now, and I could taste the fear in my mouth; what was happening?

Gradually the story unfurled through backpackers who had been caught up in it all. For the past few days while Nick and I had been visiting Kanchanburi to see the infamous bridge over the River Kwai, protesters had been gathering in the streets of Bangkok in support of the opposition to the ruling government. We hadn't read a newspaper for two months and had no idea what was happening in the world, so this was news to us. The protesters had been peacefully gathering around the Democracy Monument in the centre of Bangkok, which happened to be in the next street along from the Khao San Road where we were staying. When the police and then the army had tried, unsuccessfully, to break up the protesters, things had turned ugly. The pops and cracks we heard were gunfire, and the people thundering down our street were the fleeing protesters.

We absorbed this information in shocked silence. What should we do? My first instinct was to get the hell out of there, so as soon as the shutters were tentatively opened we crept out into the street. It was eerily quiet. The street traders were gone, the food stalls had all been abandoned, and now the street was filling up with anxious backpackers and Thai men and women, making their way to the end of the road towards the Democracy Monument to see what was happening. As we got closer, a bottleneck was forming, and the crowd of people grew thicker and more packed in. We soon discovered why; the army had stretched huge coils of barbed wire across the road, and a line of soldiers stood with guns stopping people from entering and leaving our street. It was the same at the other end. I mustered up the courage to approach one of the fierce Thai soldiers, who stood looking angry in his uniform marked with 'US Army' on his shoulder. He told me abruptly and in broken English that the road was blocked 'for our protection' and moved me along.

Nick and I headed back to the room in our hostel. I started to pack up my rucksack; we may not have been able to leave now, but I wanted to be ready for when we could — I wanted OUT.

As it became dark, the mood in the hostel grew tense; what would happen tonight? Luckily our hostel was one with a food area, so we ate our chicken and rice and waited in groups of young, worried travellers, wondering what was in store.

This time when the pops and cracks rang out, we all knew what it meant: gunfire. I moved us to the back of the room as it filled with people running in off the street, reasoning that if they were being chased then we wouldn't be first in the line of fire. It was chaos; people were screaming and crying, some angry, some frightened and some, strangely, loving every minute of it. One backpacker ran into the throng, a tall blond English boy we had met a few times. His T-shirt was streaked with dirt and sweat and his eyes blazed with excitement and possibly something illegal as he whooped into the room.

'Fucking HELL, that was AMAZING!'

People gathered round him, desperate to find out what he'd seen. He had been with the protesters to 'show his support' when the gunfire had started, and all hell had broken loose. There had been a surge forward towards the police and soldiers, who had fired over their heads, then things were thrown, smashed and trampled and he'd been swept along by it all. He didn't look afraid; he looked like he'd just got off the Nemesis ride at Alton Towers.

'You gotta come with me, man!' he was shouting at Nick. 'We gotta help these fuckers!'

Nick's eyes shone; drama! A story for back home!

'No,' I said. 'This is not our fight.'

The blond backpacker looked at me scornfully. 'If everyone said that, the world would be run by fascists! We gotta fight!'

I looked at him levelly. 'No, we don't *gotta fight*. We don't even understand what's happening, never mind jumping in and getting involved.'

He saw he wasn't getting anywhere and turned to the others huddled round him. 'Come *on!*' he roared, and ran back out into the melee.

*What an arsehole*, I thought, as Nick looked mournfully after him, desperate to be part of an adventure to tell his friends back home, but thankfully not reckless enough to do anything about it.

The night ebbed and flowed, with times of quiet worry and wondering if we should just go back to bed; then we'd hear the crackle of gunfire and shouting and running from outside. The shutters were half down, ready to be pulled tightly shut in a flash. At about 2 a.m., the owner of the hostel, a large jovial Thai man, ran in from the street. He was filthy, his T-shirt ripped and stained, and his hair slicked with sweat. He was shouting, and the workers at the hostel were trying to calm him down. He shook them off, and looked at all of us, huddled on white plastic chairs and standing around nervously waiting for news.

'You people!' he shouted at us, and fear rose like sick inside me. 'Listen to me! Do not judge us! Do not think wrong of us! This is not Thailand!'

He was crying now, and a lady who may have

88

been his wife was trying to comfort him and calm him down.

'Do not leave this country and tell the world that this is Thailand! It is not! This is my country! We are good people! We are good people!'

A girl who was close to him reached out and held his arm. 'It's OK,' she said. 'We understand. This isn't your fault.'

His face crumpled and he cried into the arms of the Thai lady holding him up. Someone else patted him awkwardly as he was led into a back room.

More time passed, and we followed someone up onto the roof of our hostel. There, lying in the dark, we peered over the little backstreet separating us from the main road and the mass of police, soldiers and demonstrators. We lay until the sun came up over Bangkok, and watched the clashes, the surges back and forth, a bus driven towards the police and forced to stop in a hail of gunfire that shattered every sheet of glass. We flinched as metal bullet casings pinged onto the concrete next to us, bouncing off our heads. And we watched as one protester was shot in the leg and lay in the gutter, inching his way painfully slowly towards an alleyway where his friends waited bravely for him. Any time they ventured out to help him they were shot at; so his slow journey to safety had to be made on his own. We waited to see if he made it, and hours later, he did, and was taken into the darkness of the alleyway and out of sight.

As the sun came up things quietened down,

and everyone seemed to call it a night. We heaved ourselves onto our single beds and slept in our clothes, rucksacks close by and ready to run. A few hours later we ventured out; the street was quiet again, and we were still blocked in by the army and barbed wire. We saw for the first time that the police station on our street had somehow been burned down in the night. The phone shops were full of travellers trying to call home and tell loved ones they were safe. This was 1992; there were no such things as mobile phones, or email, so the only way to get in touch was by calling from shops with a dozen or so telephones, some on tables, some in booths, but all had to be booked and charged a fortune per minute. Charges had quadrupled and more, as the owners cashed in on the frenzy. The travel shops were jammed with people trying to get out of Bangkok, but we had no way of getting a flight or even getting to the airport. We joined a pointless queue and put our name down on a list of people willing to go anywhere.

After that, we returned to the hostel and sat tight, rucksacks ready and stomachs churning. It was a strangely quiet day. Without the noise of traffic beeping and traders shouting, there was nothing to do but sit, and wait. If it hadn't been for the churning fear it would have been quite boring.

Nothing happened during the day; there was the odd crackle of gunfire but no running or shouting. As night fell, however, I could feel the atmosphere change; people were getting geared up again. We ate our dinner and milled around with other travellers outside in the street just to stretch our legs, and soon it started. A crackle of faraway gunfire sent us scurrying back inside and the shutters were once again pulled down for our safety by our wonderful landlord, who now saw it as a personal mission to look after the young foreigners in his care. He led us up to his rooftop again, and we spent a second night watching the streets below. It was less frantic than the previous night, but nonetheless it was tense and frightening as a smaller, angrier group of protesters clashed with soldiers. The trouble seemed to have shifted to a different part of Bangkok and we seemed less in the centre of things than we had been before. At 4 a.m. I crawled into my bed, again clothed and ready to flee. I lay and listened to the music blaring from one of the other rooms, a cheesy Euro-rock ballad that was being played on repeat by a group of German girls, as the smell of dope drifted over the thin wooden walls dividing our sleeping quarters. In another room a couple were making noisy love; perhaps a now-or-never moment as gunfire popped outside.

At lunchtime on the third day we checked that our names were still on the lists of people trying to leave the city, and walked from one end of the Khao San Road to the other to see if we were still fenced in and guarded; we were. There was still no real way in or out; we could have walked, but where to? There were no buses or taxis on the streets and we didn't know which direction was safe, so it made more sense to stay where we were and hope we would be safe until this blew over.

We were sitting having a Coke when there was a sudden scrambling around us, travellers grabbing their rucksacks and running outside. What was happening? We ran upstairs and hauled our bags onto our backs, fighting our way back down the narrow stairwell as others squeezed past, going both up and down. It was chaos. No one knew what was going on, but word was that we were getting out. On the street, travellers were running in all directions while Thai men shouted and gestured. We saw our hostel owner, who recognized us and grabbed our arms, babbling as he dragged us down a tiny alleyway, 'You get out! You leave now! Come! Come!' And suddenly down another alleyway was a tiny Mazda minivan with an anxious-looking Thai man at the wheel.

'Get in! Get in!' shouted our landlord, as he pulled our rucksacks off our backs and threw them on the roof. We didn't have time to worry that all our belongings had been taken from us as we were shoved into the back seat and more travellers piled in around us. In a matter of minutes we were off, squeezing through back alleys, weaving our way in and out of side streets — towards what? Where were we going? We all sat quietly, hoping we were doing the right thing but knowing we didn't have a choice.

Some time later we approached what seemed to be the outer edge of Bangkok and our minivan indicated left to pull onto the dusty roadside. In silence, and all of us a little scared, we pulled open the door and stepped out into the heat. Alongside us sat six huge coaches, all with drivers waiting patiently at the wheel. Some entrepreneurial person had arranged for a fleet of tiny minibuses that could fit through the backstreets of Bangkok to ferry us all to a load of coaches, offering us the chance to go in whatever direction we wanted out of the city. We found a coach travelling to Surat Thani, where we could catch the ferry to Koh Samui, so paid an extortionate amount of money and climbed aboard. We were out.

When I think back on this time, the fact that I remained calm and sensible throughout it all is not what strikes me most. My love for Thailand and its wonderful people never dipped; this was an event in their history that I happened to get caught up in, and if anything I admired them, the ordinary Thai people who desperately wanted us to think well of them and their country. No; what sticks out is the fact that I thought it was perfectly OK to tell my parents that I was safe and well and out of Bangkok BY LETTER.

I didn't ring them following our all-night journey to the coast, or even after our ferry ride, or from our lovely hostel where we slept in a beach hut with electricity and even an en suite. I wrote them a long, detailed LETTER, which I took my time over and eventually posted, and didn't give it another thought. I had no idea that the BBC had been showing nightly footage of the riots, which meant they saw far more of what went on than I did from the roof of my hostel. Dozens of people had been killed, but I'd had no idea. I wasn't aware that my dad had been ringing the British embassy desperate for news of me, not knowing if I was alive or dead. Little Miss Sensible Pants lost a few Brownie points then, that's for sure.

★ ★ ★

Over the next six months we travelled safely, without any further riots or uprisings, through Malaysia, Singapore and Bali. We stayed in Cairns in northern Australia for a few months, working to save up some more money. I was fired for the first time in my life, from a tiny café, apparently for 'not being cut out for it, and not squeezing oranges fast enough'. I then got a job in the Fox and Firkin pub and stayed there for the rest of my stay — I worked in the kitchen during the day, helping the chef with his prep work, and then worked in the bar at night. I *was* cut out for that, and it was one of my happiest times.

We then moved on to Alice Springs, Coober Pedy, Melbourne and finally Sydney, the Mecca for backpackers. It was fabulous, and I didn't want to leave all the lovely friends we made during the months we lived in Coogee Bay Backpackers. It was a hostel overlooking the beautiful Coogee Bay, just a few miles along the coast from Bondi. It was nicer than Bondi, quieter and prettier, and I absolutely loved it. Eventually though, we did leave, and flew on to

Auckland, New Zealand.

We were both a bit glum when we arrived. We had been growing apart during our time in Sydney, and this was made all the more apparent now we were on our own again. Our lives had been crammed full as we worked to build up our savings; Nick was a van driver for an off-licence and I was a drinks waitress in a seafood restaurant in Darling Harbour in Sydney. When we weren't working we were hanging out with friends, partying, going to the beach and just having fun. The thing is, we weren't necessarily having fun together. Nick had really enjoyed getting close to a gang of guys again, and had been behaving more like a single man than a boyfriend. I'd felt neglected by him, but had filled my thoughts and time with having fun, and neither of us had addressed the changes that were happening between us. Things had come to a head when he hadn't wanted to take me out for Valentine's night because it was a waste of time, and I'd ended up in tears and he'd ended up in the pub.

After a long heart-to-heart, Nick admitted that he didn't want to go home to the UK just yet. But because my parents had announced while we were in Sydney that they were emigrating to Africa, I felt that I really should go home to be there for my younger sister. Nick wanted to carry on travelling, to be wild and carefree for a while longer, and I couldn't really blame him. We decided that we had become more like brother and sister, and that we would carry on travelling together as friends rather than as a couple. It felt odd, but we knew each other so well, and had our route mapped out, so it kind of made sense. Also, I think deep down we were scared of travelling on our own, of being on our own, and just having each other nearby in whatever capacity felt right.

One evening after an early dinner, we decided to go for a walk through the streets of Auckland. We were minding our own business when a young man approached us. He wasn't much older than us and looked like just another traveller, so we smiled and stopped. He said he was doing research for Oxford University to make some cash, and he had to get a certain number of people to complete a questionnaire to fulfil his quota. He was struggling to get them all, so would we mind filling one in for him? Having done all kinds of crazy jobs on our travels, we felt sorry for him and immediately said we'd help out.

We started answering his questions right there on the street, then realized it was going to take a bit longer than we thought, and he was struggling to fill in the form without anything to lean on. He said he was really sorry, but would we mind coming to the office round the corner, because we could sit at a table then and it would be quicker? We shrugged and said yes; we didn't have to be anywhere anyway.

We followed him round the corner, into a building and up some stairs, not really paying any attention to where we were heading, just chatting about our travels and what we'd been up to. He opened a door to a large office, with tables and chairs set up round the room, and a few internal offices to one end. It looked perfectly normal, and quiet, which didn't seem unusual as it was outside office hours.

He sat us down at a table and gave us the forms to fill in, and then got us a glass of water. We settled into answering sheet after sheet of questions, which seemed pretty generic: How old were we? Where were we from? Did we have siblings? What was our schooling like? How were we feeling right now? What was our relationship with our parents like? Did we have many friends? The questions seemed to go off on a bit of a tangent, but I carried on anyway, ticking A, B or C, wondering what kind of profile I was giving, and thinking it would be interesting to find out. I wondered what Oxford University was going to do with this information.

Once we had finished, the young man took our papers away, and asked if we would mind waiting while someone read over them, to make sure we had filled them in properly. Apparently he wouldn't get paid if we hadn't done it right, and he looked so friendly that we said yes, of course. We were taken into another bit of the room, an area of little separate booths, and left to read magazines and sip our water. A while later, two men appeared. They were older, and looked more official. They said they had read through our questionnaires, and the results were so interesting that would we mind talking through them? *How lovely*, I thought. *Aren't we interesting?*

Alarm bells should have rung when Nick and I

were separated into two different booths, but I thought that was so we didn't get in each other's way, so I didn't question it. The man sat down beside me rather than opposite me, and looked through my sheet. The office was subtly lit, so the mood was cocoon-like, his voice gentle. He asked me about my unusual upbringing, travelling all around the world, and my family and my sister; all pretty straightforward stuff. Then he moved on to how I felt during all those moves — did I ever get lonely? *Yes, sometimes, but didn't everyone?*

How had I coped with it all? *Pretty well; I could always see the bigger picture, so I understood why we moved.*

Did I ever feel like my parents put their needs ahead of mine? *Never.*

Did I feel like I didn't fit in, like I didn't belong? *Er, yes, but that's just the way I am.*

Did I make friends easily? *About as easily as anybody, I guess . . .*

And so it went on. He probed and prodded about my feelings, gently pushing me to admit that yes, sometimes I wished I felt more like everyone else, but I knew I was different, and though I didn't know why, I just accepted it. I'd never been one to follow a crowd.

Then he moved on to my feelings for Nick, and I told him that we were no longer a couple, but were travelling as friends. How did that make me feel, he asked? Did I feel isolated? Did I wish I had people to talk to and support me? Was I upset, let down, sad, lonely, abandoned? I welled up during this part of the chat, as of course I felt all of those things, but I would be back home soon, and would see my friends and everything would be fine. But what if my friends weren't there for me? This was something I hadn't considered. I had been away for almost a year; they could have moved on, found other friends, they may not be interested in my problems . . . Also, hadn't I said my parents were moving abroad, moving to Africa? That meant they wouldn't be there to lean on, and now I didn't have a proper boyfriend, who was I going to lean on when I got back?

He looked at me sympathetically. Surely, he said, I must feel all alone?

I wiped a tear and looked around the room as I digested what the man was saying to me. It all sounded awful, poor little me, all alone with no one to help me, on the other side of the world . . . Then I noticed the pictures on the walls. They weren't the normal pictures of bland countryside or flowers that you tend to find in an office; they seemed to be posters, but in frames. In the gentle light I looked at them more closely; they were all to do with support, and being helped to become a better person. I looked at another, and then another; there didn't seem to be anything remotely like Oxford University going on; it seemed more like a support group. Right at the back of the room, I saw a picture of John Travolta, his arm round his beautiful wife, both of them smiling and waving at the camera. Something pinged inside my head — something I had read before my year on the road, when newspapers became something to light the barbie with, not to read.

My mind replayed the last few hours in fast-forward: Nick and I walking down the street, oblivious; a young man, just like us, asking for our help with a survey; being brought off the street to a quiet, out-of-the-way place; the strange line of questioning; the probing into my feelings; the tears; the constant insinuation that no one understood me and I was alone and needed help.

Unease prickled at the back of my mind; what was going on? The man was preoccupied so I asked for a glass of water and crossed the room to get it myself from the dispenser; I wanted a closer look at those posters. As the water bubbled into my plastic cup, I read the small words at the bottom of a picture of a smiling couple and their beautiful baby: 'The Church of Scientology'.

My body was swept with cold and then heat as I took this in. *Whaaat?* Then hot anger spread from my stomach; how could we have been so *stupid?* After a year of travelling, we had been as gullible as children, led off the street by a handsome boy who looked like us, who needed our help, and was now nowhere to be seen. We were alone in a strange city, in an office with two strange men who were intent on making us feel that we needed them.

I stormed over to the booth where Nick was sitting, pouring his heart out to the man sitting beside him. They both jumped and looked up at me as I shouted, 'Come on, we're GOING! NOW!'

Nick looked flabbergasted, and then embarrassed. 'What are you doing? Sit down and let me finish.'

'No, we are GOING. These men are trying to brainwash us! Has he made you feel lonely and different and that you need someone to listen to you and help you?'

Nick flushed and looked down. The man's face remained impassive, but his eyes glinted angrily at me. My man appeared at my shoulder. 'Are you all right? Would you like to sit down? You seem to be upset.'

I shook him off and grabbed Nick by the arm, yanking him out of his seat. 'Get off me! We are leaving NOW! Nick, they are Scientologists! They want us to join them! That's what this is all about!'

My man laughed sadly, as if I had greatly mistaken their intentions.

'I'm not STUPID! I know all about you! Come ON!'

I dragged Nick away and both the men were now standing looking at me as if I had lost my mind. I didn't care. I didn't care if I looked stupid, or if I was making a mistake or a fool of myself. My alarm bells were ringing and I was listening to them; we had to get OUT.

'Show us how to get out of here!' I shouted, and my man nodded and walked in front of us, leading us to some stairs. We followed him down the narrow staircase I vaguely remembered climbing when we arrived, all those hours ago.

He unlocked the door and pushed it open to the now dark street. I shoved my way past him,

Nick still looking confused and horrified at my behaviour. We walked until we came to the main road, and didn't look back. When we got our bearings, we walked quickly back to our hostel and made our way straight to our room.

'Don't you think you overreacted?' said Nick as he plonked himself on the bed. 'It was just a bit of research.'

'I don't care,' I huffed. 'It felt all wrong. I felt like I was being sucked into something, and I didn't like it.'

'I know, but did you have to be so *rude?* I can't believe you started shouting at those men . . .'

I played it back in my head, and yes, I suppose I overreacted a bit. But I felt that they had tricked us, and hadn't been forthright about their motives, which made me feel vulnerable. If I ever feel like I have been put in a compromising situation, then I do tend to lash out, even if I have mistaken a person's intentions.

For such a short part of our overall travels, New Zealand was an important experience for us. We accepted here that we would still look out for each other even if we weren't together. I hadn't realised how vulnerable I actually felt about being on my way home to friends who might not care any more, without my boyfriend of many years, to parents who would be leaving me for the first time. It was a turning point for me, and I think it was the point when I finally started to grow up.

★ ★ ★

A few days after our little excitement, we decided to call home and let our parents know we were now in New Zealand as we were about to start hitch-hiking around the north island. In these days of Twitter and texting, emailing and blogging, it seems bizarre to think that the only way we had of speaking to someone was to walk into a phone booth, a post office or a private phone shop, pay our money and put a call in to home.

I rang first, and settled down for a lovely long chat with my mum and dad. The ringing stopped and a man's voice said, 'Hello?'

That's strange, I thought. That's not Dad's voice. Damn, I'd wasted credit dialling the wrong number. 'Oh, hello. I'm sorry, I must have the wrong number. Sorry to disturb you.'

I was about to hang up when I heard the man's voice again. I put the phone back up to my ear.

'Hello? Hello? Are you Andrea?'

*What?*

'Er, yes, this is Andrea. How do you know my name?'

'Ah! They said you would call. Hello. Now, where is their number . . . ?'

'Who said I would call? Who is this?'

'Your parents. Where did I put their number?'

This was some kind of surreal nightmare, it had to be. I could hear the familiar noises of my family kitchen. The washing machine was on, and I could hear his footsteps on our tiled floor.

'Who are you? What's going on? Where are my parents?'

103

'Ah, yes, they have moved. They said to give you their number when you rang, but I must have left it at my office. I am very sorry. Can you call back tomorrow and I will give it to you?' He sounded genuinely sorry and, I think, Dutch.

'*Moved? Where?!*'

'Oh, not far. They are going to Africa. Kenya, I think they said.'

'They've gone to Kenya already?!' I felt faint. While I was in Sydney we had spoken on the phone many times about their upcoming move, but I was sure it wasn't going to happen until I was back in the UK. Dad was so excited to be offered another chance to work in a sugar factory again, he had jumped at it. Mum had sounded less convinced, but would do whatever it took to support my dad and keep him happy. They were, and still are, a team.

'No, no, not yet. They are going in a month or so, but they let me have their house.'

'What?!'

After more confused questions and unhelpful answers I eventually hung up and burst into tears. Nick was standing next to me looking worried, and he quickly rang his parents to see if they knew what was going on. Thankfully, they did. My parents had found a tenant for their house sooner than expected, so they had moved into the little rented place they had sorted for me on my return in two months' time. They had paid eight months' rent for me, so I had somewhere to stay while I decided what I wanted to do with myself. Nick's mum gave us the number, and once he was off the phone I rang it.

The explanation of what had just happened was actually quite straightforward, but it didn't stop me crying as I was filled with the irrational fear that I would never see or hear my parents ever again.

The phone rang; it was the long burr of an international call.

'Hello?' Phew — this man's voice belonged to my dad. My tears immediately became tears of relief.

'Dad!'

'Andrea! Hello! You got the number then? Betty, it's Andrea!'

They sounded so genuinely pleased to hear from me, and the explanation seemed so benign that it felt churlish to get angry at them over the heart attack they had almost given me. It was karma, I suppose, for the letter from Bangkok. Either way, my dad joked years later that as a teenager I used to have a recurring nightmare that I would come home from school to find the key didn't fit in the lock, and a stranger would answer our front door saying that my parents had upped and left me. (This was true; I did have this dream for years, and no prizes for guessing why.) So he had decided to make my dreams come true. Ha ha. Thanks, Dad.

After we hitched a ride out of Auckland from the biggest Maori man I have ever seen, we thumbed a lift from a young guy in a pick-up, and then an old couple who were delighted to have some young British company. New Zealand was my kind of place; it was green, friendly and innocent, and was full of crazy people who liked to throw themselves off bridges with elastic bands round their feet, go white water rafting and parachuting . . . and I was one of them.

Hawaii and America were our next stops. We stayed in a Venice Beach hostel in LA and watched the street performers, the muscle men and the gorgeous people hoping to be discovered by Hollywood. We took in Las Vegas, the Grand Canyon, Niagara Falls and New York, rounding off our trip in a dodgy hostel where I was scared to go to sleep in case all our things were stolen. We walked everywhere as we couldn't afford taxis, and only caught the subway once as I was scared stiff and didn't understand how it worked.

It seems strange now, after living and working in London for so long, smacking my Oyster card down at the barriers and skipping down the escalators to the Tube, that back then I was terrified of being in a big city. New York had such a terrible reputation for crime at the time, I wouldn't go out after dark without jumping out of my skin at every siren. Even after surviving New Delhi, Bangkok and Sydney, New York's reputation preceded it, and I never quite relaxed enough to enjoy it. I have been back since, and again walked everywhere — not because I was afraid, but because I wanted to take my time to look around me and look up, not scared to stand out like a tourist enjoying the experience of a new, exciting city.

Saying goodbye to Nick as he travelled on to Mexico and I flew home was strange, and sad. We were both in tears at the airport as he headed off to catch his flight and I walked away to catch mine. We had flown out together, and had experienced so many amazing things — crazy bus drivers in India and Thailand, the wonder of climbing Ayers Rock, New Year fireworks at Sydney Harbour and the beauty of the Grand Canyon — but now we were going our separate ways. With a heavy heart I made my way to the gate and boarded my plane back to England. But where was I going to call home?

# 7

## Sunny With a Chance of Showers

Back in England I missed Nick, but I knew coming back was the right thing to do. I wanted to be in the country for my younger sister while my parents were away, to be there for her during the holiday months and if she ever wanted to come 'home' from University for a weekend. They hadn't put pressure on me to do this, it was something I decided for myself. I would have liked to have carried on travelling, but I had been lucky to have a year to do my own thing and at the age of twenty-three it was time to get back to the real world.

And I had a dream I desperately wanted to make come true. Ever since I had had my story published in *Just Seventeen* and had pestered the local paper in Market Harborough to take me on work experience, I had wanted to write. I didn't care if it was stories or features, but I enjoyed the whole process — finding an interesting story, researching it and speaking to people, and then putting it together into a piece that brought it all to life. I had been writing like crazy during that year away and had filled notebook after notebook with scribbles about our adventures. I wanted to see if I could get them published, and maybe find a way to get paid to travel and write about the experiences. Could the two things I loved doing the most possibly be combined to earn me a living?

I stayed with Mum and Dad for five days before they left — nervously in Mum's case and excitedly in Dad's — for Kenya. My friend Clare (not the one I knew from school; this was a lovely girl I met while working in The Boathouse pub in Chester, and we had been firm friends ever since) moved into the little house in Northgate Village in Chester, and as we settled into being flatmates, she got herself a job in a restaurant and I found one in a clothes shop. We were both graduates trying to figure out where we were going with our lives; Clare had studied Spanish and Portuguese, with a little French thrown in, and eventually became a languages teacher in Chester, where she is now. I still see her regularly and we laugh about those days, drinking Malibu and pineapple while getting ready for our big nights out, listening to Simply Red before heading off to Blimpers nightclub.

Nick was back in my life too. He had only lasted another month travelling on his own before coming back to Chester, and it was me and one of his best friends who met him at Heathrow to welcome him home.

There was no great song or dance; we just kind of drifted back together again. It was familiar, we were back with all our old friends in our old home town and it just kind of happened. He applied for and got a place at Cardiff University to do a postgrad in Documentary Film Making, while I worked for free for Welsh local paper the Wrexham *Leader* during my days off, covering anything that was left over from the real journalists. I wrote up travel pieces from looking through the diaries I had kept while I was away, and managed to get them published in the national magazine *19* as well. I knew I would be rubbish at hard news stories — the few times I had been asked to doorstep people for the *Leader* had proved that — but feature writing was something different. I loved it, and I thought I could do a good job of it. I approached the editor of the *Leader* nervously to ask for a job with the paper. The answer was not good: although I had a degree, and they were happy to print my work, I could not be taken on as I didn't have a postgraduate qualification in Journalism. All they could offer me was a traineeship — for £30 a week.

I was earning £100 working in the shop, and although my rent was sorted I still had bills to pay, my mum's old white Ford Fiesta to run and a life to lead. There was no way I could survive on that amount.

So I started applying for journalism courses, and eventually found one that offered what I wanted. It was in London, and it made sense to move there, as that was where the work would be too. I rang my parents and told them what had happened and how I wanted to find a way round it; that I wanted to go back to college to get more qualifications so I could do what I really wanted to do — write. They discussed it and came back to me with an offer to pay for my course, but I would have to support myself. It was fair; I was twenty-four by now, and should really have been standing on my own two feet, not asking for more after swanning round the world for a year. They were very generous, and if they hadn't helped me out I would never be in the position I am in now, so I'm very grateful to them.

I moved to London in January 1994, with everything I owned packed into the old Fiesta. I applied for and got a student loan to pay for my accommodation and spending money until I found a proper job. I slept on my best friend Jane's sofa for two weeks until I found a bedsit in nearby Clapham, and I started my journalism training at the Journalism Training Centre in Mitcham in Surrey. It wasn't exactly Oxford Uni, but I relished every moment. The work experience was the best bit, as it felt strange 'pretending' to write something when I had already been doing that. I spent a few weeks at *19* after calling them and reminding them that they had already published my work, so surely I would be capable of doing work experience? I also did a week at *Marie Claire* and was beside myself just seeing the then editor Glenda Bailey come into the office. She was a hero of mine, a normal girl who had worked her way up through the ranks to become editor of one of the most respected female magazines of the time. I was too scared to tell her this, though, and I often wish I had.

As the three-month course came to an end I applied for every job going, in every job section in every paper, as my money was running out fast. It was bound to happen that somewhere along the line I would slip up and apply for something I didn't really understand. And so it was that I replied to a tiny advert in the *UK Press Gazette* (as it was then known) asking for a 'journalist with an interest in the weather and an on-screen presence'. I saw the word 'journalist', wrote what I thought was a witty application letter about loving the sunshine when on holiday, bunged in an old photo of me in Australia and sent it off. A month or so later, by which time I was working as a staff writer/sub editor at Central Press Features in Kentish Town, I got a letter from a company called International Weather Productions, asking me to give them a call. So, at work, I dialled up and was put through to a rather pissed-off-sounding woman who asked if I was having a laugh.

'About what?' I asked, confused.

'About this job application,' she sighed. 'You have no experience, and you haven't even sent a showreel.'

'What's a showreel?'

Another sigh. 'Look, your photo isn't bad and we have decided to give you a screen test. Can you be here next Wednesday morning?'

I said yes and we hung up. I had no idea what she was talking about, but a screen test sounded interesting, and next Wednesday was my day off anyway.

I wore my 'interview suit', which had previously been a 'wedding suit', and arrived at the address I'd been given in Camden. There were five of us there, and the others were very nervous. I wasn't at all, as I had already found a job since applying for this one, and I had obviously got my wires crossed when I applied for it anyway. I just thought it sounded really interesting and unlike anything I had ever done before, so why not have a go and see what happened?

We were going to be screen-tested for one minute talking about ourselves, which I found very easy. Then we were given a fast and furious weather briefing, told to learn it, and then had to talk to time, giving a weather broadcast in front of a green screen and weather map. My shorthand came in useful as I jotted down everything the man said, then picked out what I saw as the most important facts and learned them. I confidently gave the report, every now and then waving my arm vaguely over a picture of the UK. It was just like doing an interview and telling the story in my own words, only I was saying it rather than writing it down.

The woman who had been so unfriendly on the phone sat me down and smiled at me, and that day Sally Galsworthy became the lady who changed my life. She didn't have a job to offer me there and then as I didn't have any experience, but she liked what I had done and said I had real 'potential'. I didn't want a job as a weather presenter anyway, as I was quite happy being a writer and sub, doing what I had come to London to do. But we hit it off over a cup of tea, and ended up keeping in touch.

By then, on the outside I looked and probably felt like I was coping with living in London, but inside I was small and scared. I think that's why what happened to me at Victoria Tube station one morning on my way into work had such a terrifying impact. I had been walking briskly down the escalator on the left, past my less-awake fellow commuters, and was almost at the bottom when a man in a suit pushed me from behind. I went flying, and was lucky I didn't fall onto the floor in the path of the escalator and its passengers. He shoved me out of the way and ran past to get the Tube.

'Hey!' I shouted after him, trying to keep moving so I wouldn't be swamped by the people stepping off behind me.

He ignored me and walked briskly on. I ran after him and tapped him on the shoulder.

'Hey! You nearly sent me flying back there! Have some manners!'

The man, who was in his mid-thirties to my mid-twenties, swatted my hand away and roared into my face, spittle flying, 'Why don't you just FUCK OFF, you LITTLE BITCH!'

He marched down the platform away from me.

I kept walking, carried along by the pressing flow of commuters, and only stopped when I got to the end where it was quiet, save for a few people reading their papers and ignoring the rest of the world. Nobody looked at me or noticed me; they just carried on doing what they were doing, making their way to work, not getting involved in things that had nothing to do with them.

It was such a small thing, just a grumpy man shouting at a younger woman. It had been over

114

within seconds, but something broke inside me. I stood at the end of the platform shaking. His face had been so full of ANGER and hate towards me. I hadn't even done anything wrong. I had just got in his way when he was having a bad start to the day. He had probably forgotten about it already, and on a normal day so would I, but that morning this little incident set off a chain of emotions that it would take years to get under control.

I suddenly felt powerless and small. No one had backed me up. No one had even noticed, and no one noticed me afterwards, as I stood shaking and fighting back tears, surrounded by hundreds of people in one of the busiest cities in the world.

The Tube arrived and there was a rush as people surged on and off, battering each other to get a seat, to get to the door, to get to work. Nobody made eye contact, and there was no communication; if it wasn't for the screeching of Tube brakes, the announcements over the tannoy to 'mind the gap', and the shuffling and clopping of feet, there would have been no noise at all. The enormity of all these people, moving and shoving and fighting in grim silence hit me like a wave, and I struggled not to vomit. My head started to prickle and I felt hot and like I was swelling. My heart skipped beat after beat, out of time with its usual predictable rhythm, and I choked with panic as I made my way back up the escalator to the world outside. I walked to the side of the station where it was less frantic and leaned against the wall, my eyes closed, breathing deeply through my mouth and nose until my heart slowed and I felt my skin return to normal. What had just happened?

That was just the first of my panic attacks that could creep up on me at any time. When it got to the stage where I walked out of the office because an innocent job applicant arrived for an interview to become a junior journalist, and I knew I was going to have an attack in front of him, I decided to do something about it. I saw a counsellor, who assured me that I wasn't going mad, and told me to relax more, take up yoga and focus on my breathing. So I tried to calm down when I felt myself getting stressed, and it seemed to help.

In time, of course, I did become more confident about living in London, even if the heaving masses at Victoria station still raised my stress levels every time I saw them.

When Nick finished his postgrad course he came to London to be with me full time and find a job in television. I was living in a shared house in Wimbledon, having finally got out of the bedsit. It was much nicer, but I didn't want to be living with students any more; I'd had my independence for too long to be squabbling over bread and who left the hot water on. So I found us a little flat in Earlsfield and we moved in together. The first year was tricky as Nick struggled to find work and I supported us with my meagre Central Press salary of £10,000 a year. He was working for free for various production houses and getting more and more frustrated with the whole process. The break he was waiting for did come eventually: the chance to work with Chris Packham on his new birdwatching series. Nick was in his element. As his experience grew, so did his confidence, and he has worked consistently since then on bigger and better documentaries.

I was very proud of him; he was doing something he had a passion for and was good at, and life seemed grand. We bought our own little flat and I lost myself in doing it up, decorating and tiling and 'nesting'. We made friends with Alice who lived in the flat below, and would spend contented evenings in watching telly and drinking wine, or popping to the wine bar by Earlsfield station to meet mates. Now that we were both earning we could afford to go away on holiday, and we even revisited Thailand and did a little backpacking. It was even more enjoyable because we topped and tailed it with a four-star hotel stay!

★   ★   ★

In 1996, two years after my screen test, I received a phone call from a man called Rex Roskilly, saying he had just taken over Sally's job and my tape was in a pile marked 'watch'. And, bizarrely, the same thing happened again: he asked me to come in for a chat with a potential client on a day I had booked off, this time because I already had another job interview. I messed up the one to be Production Editor at *Just Seventeen* in the morning, but that afternoon I walked out of an office knowing I was about to be offered a job at the Weather Channel.

This wasn't what I had planned to do at all . . .

A few weeks later I was travelling to the headquarters of the Weather Channel in Atlanta for training. I was *beyond* excited. Three other girls, who had been hired at the same time, and I were driven to a hotel, where we checked into our own individual *suites*. The bathroom was bigger than the bedsit I'd lived in back in London! We had fancy cars taking us to and from the studio, where we watched, learned and were trained daily in front of huge green screens in how to present a weather story, how to engage the viewer, and how to interact with the camera. It was, and still is, the only training I have ever had; no other programme that I have worked on has ever spent the time and effort that this American company did on making sure that its staff were up to speed and knew exactly what they were doing before they were put on air. It was a world away from the 'sink or swim' method I have experienced ever since, and I was so lucky that this was my first introduction to television.

The whole trip had been amazing and even the way it ended was exciting — with a limo ride to the airport! I had never been in a limo before, a proper black stretch limo, and I felt like I was in a scene from *Pretty Woman*. This, I decided, was the life for me!

I quit my staff job at Central Press Features for the offer of one month's trial at the Weather

Channel because it was the chance to try something exciting and new, and I have been working in TV ever since. My eighteen months at the Weather Channel are still one of my life's highlights. I was in my mid-twenties working with fun people, with no responsibility other than learning about the weather, remembering my briefings and talking non-stop. What was there not to like? At Central Press Features I had been promoted to Production Editor, which is one of the most thankless jobs in journalism, as you are either chasing journalists for their stories and subs for their pages, or calming down irate editors who want their pieces now, now, now! I enjoyed every minute of my time at the Weather Channel, right up until the day, one year later, when I got made redundant.

Nothing can prepare you for the shock of losing your job, especially when the week before you had been chatting with your boss about pensions and salary. That was what happened to me, and it hit me hard. Although there had been an earlier round of redundancies when the Weather Channel merged with another company, I had been told I was OK and was staying put. It was not to be. I was lucky enough to be kept on as a freelancer filling in for holidays and time off, so I still had a wage coming in while I tried to figure out what to do.

Luckily for me, fate stepped in to help me once again. I had heard through the grapevine that Sally Meen, the popular weather presenter on the country's favourite breakfast show at the time, *GMTV*, was leaving, so I sent in my show

119

reel (I had one now!) and my photo. It was the only job I applied for, and I got called in because apparently I was the spitting image of then editor Gerry Melling's girlfriend, so he and his secretary wanted to see if I was as alike in the flesh. I wasn't, but I was given a month's work covering holidays, and then a few months later, in early 1997, I started working at *GMTV* for real. It would become my home for the next eleven years.

# 8

## Here's Andrea With the Weather

When I arrived at *GMTV* in 1997, I was by then an experienced weather presenter, but had done little else on TV. I had been part of the panel show *Espresso* on Channel 5, talking about issues of the day with the host Patti Coldwell, but now I would be a weather presenter on an award-winning show as part of their team. I was terrified. What if I messed up?

I didn't sleep the night before my first shift. I was used to getting up early as I would start at 3.30 a.m. at the Weather Channel, but this was different; this felt like PROPER TELLY. I wore my smartest red jacket and black trousers, and made sure I allowed plenty of time to get lost in this new confusing building with winding corridors and split levels that seemed to lead nowhere, and to get my weather briefing from the small Met Office team housed elsewhere at ITV. It was the same team who briefed me for the Weather Channel, so at least I knew a couple of friendly faces and was at ease with what I was doing weather-wise.

Sitting in make-up the first time was terrifying. I was used to doing my own, so this was a whole new experience, sitting in a chair having my face prodded at 5 a.m., listening to the friendly banter and gossip of the people around me. Naturally on day one I wasn't yet au fait with the subtle rules of the roost. There were really only two rules to follow: the first was make sure you were out of the chair before Penny Smith wanted to get in it, otherwise she would just sit on you. And the second was to get out of the way at 6.55 a.m. when Eamonn Holmes would arrive like a whirlwind, people scattering out of his way as he rushed to get changed, powdered and on to set by 6.59.

I kept my head down and listened to the early-morning banter as Penny and the *News-hour* co-host Matthew Lorenzo chatted about the items coming up on the show. I was led into the studio and shown my spot, and left to check my graphics were in the correct order. This was so different; here the weather was just part of a much bigger picture rather than being the whole show. And I was standing next to the infamous sofa! Matt read through his script while Anne Davies clicked on her computer ready to read the news bulletins for the next hour. At 5.58 a.m. Penny sauntered in just as the titles started rolling, but no one seemed at all stressed by this. The sound girl fiddled with her mic as Penny flirted with Matt and told a rude joke to Robby the floor manager, and I could hear the gallery laughing as the PA (production assistant) counted down the seconds to going live on air. The gallery was like the *Starship Enterprise* compared to the little room we had at the Weather Channel. It was the control room, where all the camera shots came up on screens. All the outside broadcasts, all the studio cameras

— everything was there, waiting for the director to call a camera number for the vision mixer to make sure the right shot was shown on air. Everyone was relaxed and easy-going, used to each other's little ways, and there was a real feeling of camaraderie. I still couldn't quite believe that I had been invited to join this early-morning party.

At 6.01, after a brief rundown of the news headlines, Penny turned to camera one and said, 'And now it's time for our first look at the weather, and we welcome Andrea McLean. Good morning.'

When I look at that clip now on YouTube, I can't believe how calm and confident I look, smiling and replying, 'Thank you, Penny,' as if I knew her! My hair is cut into a pert professional bob, and apart from sounding a little breathless you wouldn't know that I couldn't hear what I was saying because my heart was pounding so loudly in my chest. I did my report to the time given in my ear by the team in the gallery and handed back to the sofa like I'd seen them do on the telly, then tiptoed out of the studio. I had survived my first weather report on *GMTV*!

As the morning moved on, the *Newshour* was replaced by *GMTV Today* and Eamonn Holmes and Fiona Phillips took their places on the sofa. Fiona was there early, while Eamonn rushed in and plonked himself down just as the camera cut to the first shot of them of the day. And then they were off, bantering like old buddies and making the whole thing look effortless. By the first ad break, Eamonn was joshing with the crew about the latest Manchester United score in a way that made it obvious this was a very regular occurrence.

I busied myself between bulletins, making sure I was across the weather story of the day, keeping out of everyone's way. Penny spent part of her time checking scripts and news updates and the rest of it holding court in the make-up room, telling filthy jokes and giggling. It took roughly two years before I eventually had the courage to make a joke back. Everyone else had their bit to do on the show, and once they had done it they rushed off to get home or to other jobs. Penny and I were the only ones who stayed throughout the morning to do bulletins every half an hour, so I suppose it was inevitable that we would end up spending the most time together. She was awesome.

I shared a tiny dressing room with Penny for over a decade, and after she had got used to me being around and accepted that I wasn't in any way interested in stealing her job, it was brilliant. Her ferocious tidiness, love of bad puns and ticking people off about their spelling or grammar were terrifying and fun. Just hearing her footsteps down the corridor was enough to have me clicking off our shared computer and shuffling over to the spare seat, before she had time to shout out, 'Are you off it yet, McLean?' and edge her way on to the keyboard. She tried to put me off at least one broadcast a day by pulling faces, making rude gestures in my eye line while I looked into the camera, or just casually asking — with three seconds to go

124

before we were live on air — 'Hmm, are you *really* going to wear that?' It takes a special kind of person to be so badly behaved and yet have everyone love you, but Penny managed it.

Wide-eyed, squeaky-voiced and very aware that I was now on Britain's most popular breakfast programme, I made it through my first few months, confined to the safety of my blue screen. After a couple of months I realized I'd had no feedback on how I was doing. This was very different to my previous experience at the Weather Channel, where we had a designated talent producer, who had the job of making sure we were all up to scratch, performing in the style that the channel wanted, and were generally on track. Even as a journalist, you are normally handed a style guide when you first arrive, which outlines the house style of the publication, its readership, and their likes and dislikes.

So, after the end of the programme one morning, I popped in to see one of the senior members of staff to ask how I was doing. A compact and wiry man, he looked up from his computer screen, frowning in confusion. This obviously wasn't a question he was used to answering.

'Well . . . ' he drawled eventually, swivelling round in his chair to face me on the low-level sofa in his office. Anyone who went to visit him was always sat lower down, giving them an immediate psychological disadvantage. It had windows on two sides and a glass wall to the outer office, so there was always a feeling of being in a goldfish bowl. He frowned at me and drawled, 'You're very *ordinary*. Every housewife in her dressing gown looks at you and thinks they could do a better job. But that's fine; it means you're not threatening. Let's face it, you're no Caprice . . . '

As I crawled red-faced out of the office I met Simon Keeling, the lovely plump weatherman whom I worked alongside. I told him what had happened and he roared with laughter.

'That's nothing! He called me fat!'

'Umm . . . But you *are* fat . . . '

'And you're ugly!' he replied.

We looked at one another, paused, then doubled over laughing, and have called each other Fat and Ugly ever since.

A few months later, there was a buzz in the air in the studio, as *GMTV* had been nominated for Most Popular Daytime Programme at the National Television Awards. This was a big deal, and everyone was excited, chatting about what they were going to wear, and what time they would get there for the red-carpet arrivals. I listened quietly, and realized that I hadn't been invited. After the show, I went upstairs to see Gill Stacey, a formidable and, I later learned, wonderful, warm-hearted woman who looked after the director of programmes, Peter McHugh.

I tapped on the door to Peter's office and went inside, shaking with nerves, because I knew I was being precocious. Gill was inside with another member of the production team. The two women stopped talking as I entered the room and looked at me.

'Er . . . hello, Gill,' I stammered. 'Everyone is

talking about the TV Awards tonight, and I just wondered where my invitation was?'

'Your invitation?'

'Yes. You see, it's all a bit embarrassing, as everyone else seems to be going except for me.'

'No, all the *presenters* are going . . . '

It hung in the air.

'But what am I?'

'You're the weathergirl.'

'Oh. But if I'm the weathergirl, doesn't that make Anne Davies the newsgirl? She's going?'

'That's different.'

'Why?'

'Because it's news.'

'But if you're talking about presenters, then I am the only person apart from Penny who is on air all the way through from the *Newshour* at six, *GMTV* at seven and *Lorraine* at eight thirty. Surely that makes me one of the presenting team?'

There was an awkward silence and my face went very red.

'I'll see what I can do,' said Gill.

Eight hours later I was in the back of a stinking local minicab, clutching a tatty *A-Z* and trying to direct a man who spoke no English to somewhere neither of us had ever been: the Royal Albert Hall. We eventually found our way there, and he dropped me off. It was deserted. I smoothed down my Dorothy Perkins shift dress, checked my Dolcis shoes and made my way towards what looked like an entrance. It was deathly quiet inside, and as I wandered down the long, circular corridor I wondered if I had got it

127

all wrong. No; my ticket (which had been biked over to me with a note from Gill saying, 'Enjoy!') definitely said this was the right time and place. As I walked further, I could hear a noise from up ahead. A sort of dull roar. A little further still, and it sounded like shouting. I felt a knot in my tummy — I was still a bit edgy about living in London. I hoped there wasn't some kind of riot happening outside.

Well, there was. Hundreds of people stood to one side of a smooth red carpet that led from a side road to the front steps of the Albert Hall. On the other side were hundreds of photographers, and everyone was shouting at the beautiful, glittering people slowly making their way towards me. I had been dropped off at the back door, and was gazing down at the red-carpet arrivals from the inside out.

Stars I had only ever seen on TV sashayed past me, shiny and polished and looking like this was something they did every Monday night. Most of *Coronation Street* and *EastEnders* were there, as well as Rolf Harris and the rest of *Animal Hospital*, one of my favourite shows. I stood to the side and stared, wondering where I should go, and how I was going to meet up with my fellow *GMTV* lot. Eventually I saw Penny, who took one look at my panicked face and ushered me along, introducing me with, 'This is Andrea, our new weathergirl. Isn't she lovely?' People politely agreed and then turned their backs on me, looking for someone more important to talk to.

As we made our way to our seats, it became

apparent that my ticket wasn't the same as the others, and I wasn't actually with them. I was two sections further back. I pretended not to be embarrassed, and moved away from them to sit on my own in a row of 'fillers': people who sit in empty seats so that the place looks full on TV.

Nevertheless, it was a brilliant night. My favourite Trinidadian Sir Trevor MacDonald hosted the evening, and it was so much more exciting than watching it at home. I couldn't believe I was actually there!

It was the night that Caprice arrived on stage in her magnificent skin-tight, floor-length Union Jack dress, and made all the papers the next day. What the papers didn't know was that after she came off stage, she was then taken into the auditorium to watch the rest of the show from out front. The first I knew of it was when a bouncer arrived snarling at my shoulder, growling, 'Gerrup. Caprice needs yer seat . . . ' She seemed bored as she stood behind him, flicking her blonde hair.

I looked up at him and stammered that I was with *GMTV*, that I wasn't actually a 'filler', and just when people were starting to tut and stare at me, a lovely man sitting in the row behind piped up.

'Oi! You heard her, she's with *GMTV*, and she's staying where she is. Move someone else.'

So some other red-faced 'fillers' shuffled past, and Caprice squeezed over me. I turned round and thanked the man behind me, who turned out to be Robson Green, and I've liked him for it ever since. Sitting next to the sparkling blonde

129

bombshell for the rest of the night gave me the chance to sneak some good, long sideways looks. My editor was quite right; in my plain dress and clunky shoes . . . I really was 'no Caprice'.

It was one of the most demoralizing and yet thrilling nights of my life, and I thought about it in 2010 as I made my way on stage with the other Loose Women when we won the award for Most Popular Factual Programme at the National Television Awards. Standing on the stage in the 02, where it is now held, listening to the roar of thousands of cheering *Loose Women* fans, seeing my face on the big screen as host of this award-winning show, I thought back to my twenty-seven-year-old self and did a little jig inside.

⋆   ⋆   ⋆

Learning to make tea is one of the most useful skills you can have, in any profession. Making the crew a cup of tea while you are out on a job is a decent thing to do, and I tried to do it whenever I could — sometimes with disastrous consequences.

The first time I popped from an outside weather broadcast into *GMTV* Towers (or the London Studios, as they are properly known), I hadn't realized quite how long it would take to brew up, sort out a tray, grab a plate of Danish pastries and get back down to the riverside in time for the next broadcast. As I speed-walked towards the crew, trying not to spill their milky tea, I could see by the look on the cameraman and sound man's faces that something was terribly wrong. I quickened my pace to a trot, spilling tea onto the plate of pastries, then plonked it on the ground and broke into a run, shoving my earpiece into my ear.

'Well, we would have gone to the weather now,' Fiona Phillips was saying in my ear, 'but we can't seem to find our presenter! We'll be back after the break.'

Oh. My. God. I went hot, then cold, and the two men couldn't look at me. I stood in front of the camera and waved, waiting for sound to come through from the gallery.

'Ah, Andrea. Good afternoon,' came the sarcastic voice of Simon Jasper, the overnight editor. 'How good of you to join us. Small point, but we seem to have missed your weather broadcast.'

I was beetroot, and I knew that the gallery, the studio and possibly half the building could see and hear me.

'Yes, Simon, I'm very sorry. It was my fault; I went to get the crew some tea, and I was late getting back. I'm very sorry.'

'Come and see me after class, please.'

Silence. I stepped out of camera shot and looked at the crew. They shuffled their feet and looked at the floor. They were freelance, so I had never worked with them before, and I could tell they were worried that they would never be hired again.

'It's my fault, not yours. It's me who'll get a bollocking, not you, so don't worry.'

And I did get an entirely justified bollocking,

131

which made me much quicker at getting the teas in future. It doesn't mean I didn't come close to missing any more weather reports but 90 per cent of the time it was Penny Smith's fault, not mine. Sitting in our dressing room in between bulletins, checking news and weather updates over the phone and on the computer, we still found time to look up ridiculous things on the Internet that would make us laugh so hard I'd end up sprinting down the corridor in my tights, hurling my shoes on while straightening my jacket and smoothing my hair, just in time to hear the last strains of the weather jingle. Sometimes I made it in time to catch my breath, and sometimes I didn't, and there were many times that the UK woke up to a panting, slightly hyperventilating and sweaty weather presenter, who gulped and gasped her way through her bulletin, almost passing out through lack of breath on the words, 'Here's your summary.'

A big part of my confidence came from the crew — the fact that I worked with the same wonderful cameramen, floor managers and sound girls meant coming into work was like meeting up with family. Everyone knew how everyone else worked — you could talk in shorthand — and there was joshing and joking and mickey-taking, and so much giggling behind the scenes as the Dunkirk spirit of survival kicked in to get us through the horrendous early start. We were all up at a hideous time in the morning, so we just got on with it.

'Morning, Specky,' was the first thing I heard when I walked into the studio, because I had to wear my glasses once when my lenses had played up, and the nickname stuck. I am fortunate enough still to run into the crew, as *Loose Women* is just downstairs from what is now the *Daybreak* studio, so on a daily basis I see Dave and Jon the props guys, and occasionally Nick, Richard, Carl and Darren the camera boys, Lorraine from sound and Sharon the floor manager. I'm very lucky.

I'd only been at *GMTV* for a few months when I was asked to do other little presenting jobs: first for 'Get Up and Give', a week given over every year to raising awareness for smaller and lesser-known charities around the UK. I was asked to interview people, to help make short films about their lives, and then travel the country taking part in live broadcasts linking back to the studio. It was my first go at 'proper' presenting, as other people called it. I got to mix my love of talking to people and drawing them out of themselves, with walking and talking to a camera on live television. It was daunting, and I probably made a hash of it at first, but I really enjoyed it, and I gradually got better at it. Even though I am shy myself, I get a huge buzz from making people's experience of TV an enjoyable one, especially men, women and children who have never been on TV before and probably never will again. My funniest interview for 'Get Up and Give' was with a deaf-blind man who was attempting to set a land speed record driving a three-wheeled motorbike. Through his deaf-blind interpreter, who communicated through a special sign language drawn onto his upturned hand, he flirted like mad with me, even though he had no idea what I looked or sounded like. We laughed our way through the interview, then he headed off to the end of the runway we were on at a small air strip. With a co-driver sitting behind him, tapping his left shoulder to guide him left, and right shoulder to go right, with a squeal of tyres he was off! And he did it, which put a smile on my face for the rest of the day.

Everything happens for a reason, my granny always said, and, do you know, she was right? A chance audition led me to *GMTV*, where I watched from the sidelines as legends such as Lorraine Kelly made live broadcasting look easy. I learned from her that success comes from being yourself, as well as making people feel at ease and happy to talk to you. I learned that being a good presenter means keeping your mind sharp but your manner soft. It's something I will always try to do. I was lucky enough to learn from the best.

That's not to say I haven't made massive mistakes. I once walked into the *GMTV* studio to see a boy band rehearsing during an ad break. I asked who they were. The sound girl told me they were a new band called Westlife who were managed by Ronan Keating from Boyzone.

'Chuh! That's all we need is another bloody Boyzone!' I scoffed jokingly.

The blond man standing in front of me turned round and gave me a hard stare.

'Hello, Ronan . . . ' I mumbled.

I have since interviewed him many times on *Loose Women*, and he is as sweet as pie. Luckily he's never mentioned the first time we met and I was far too embarrassed to bring it up when we had a whole *Loose Women* show dedicated to the (I now know) fabulous boys from Westlife.

# 9

## Moving Up

Getting up at 3.30 a.m. every day is hard. People say they know what it's like: 'Ooh yes, I know, I feel like that when I get up to catch a plane to go on holiday!' Well, it's not really like that, because you don't have the excitement of a holiday to look forward to. It's cold, dark and usually wet outside, and you're about to stand in it for the next four hours, *and* you've done it the day before that, the day before that, and the day before that . . . So what makes it bearable is having a routine, and working with the best crew in the world.

Every night, whether I was going to be working from the warmth of the studio or the middle of nowhere the next morning, I laid out my clothes in the order I would put them on, so there was no room for thought or error. Everything was planned out with military precision: up, shower (a MUST, or I would never wake up), teeth brushed, clothes on, hair dried, make-up on, go. No talking or fiddling about, just bam bam bam. I didn't normally speak until I got on site, either by driving myself or, if I had arrived at the edge of nowhere the night before, by local cab. I swear the editor had a map of the UK that he used to throw darts at to decide where I would do the weather from — the places were so random sometimes.

What made the job fun — and it was fun — was the crew: the cameraman, sound man and satellite engineer. Whether it was being inventive or downright daft in finding different ways to present the six reports we had to do from wherever it was we'd been sent, or just keeping cheerful despite being cold, wet and knackered, they made my day. I presented the weather in a field while a sheep gave birth right next to me, and thankfully turned round in time for us to show proud mummy and baby, without any gruesome stuff for breakfast TV viewers. 'Awww . . .' went everyone at home, at the lamb and the blue skies and the daffodils, while we retched at the smell and the blood.

I have carried on presenting while midges swarmed my face, a bird pooed on my head, a tramp threatened to pour beer over me, and numerous streakers and costume-clad pranksters ran past. I've had Donny Osmond, Meat Loaf and Jason Gardiner take over my weather map, and tried to keep an impassive face as the legend that is Donald Sutherland gazed at me from the sofa, before asking loudly, 'How does she know where she's putting her arm? That's AMAZ-ING!'

In fact, 'staying calm while Very Important People stare at me as I gesticulate at thin air' is something I should put on my CV. Helen Mirren, Gordon Brown, Tony Blair, Tony Curtis, Hugh Grant and numerous boy and girl bands have all looked on while I've done the weather, frowning as I waved my arm in front of a blank green screen. How did I do it? It's the question I get asked more than any other (well, apart from 'What is so-and-so *really* like?'). How it's done is: I looked at a monitor in the studio (a little TV) that showed what everyone at home could see, i.e. me and my map, and when I looked at the screen I could see where I was pointing. It was a bit like patting your head and rubbing your tummy while naming counties and temperatures. There was no autocue; after I'd had my briefing from the Met Office I would learn the key points they had scripted for me until it was all in my head, then off I went. Ta-da!

It all sounds very simple, and it was when it worked, but of course there were days when the computer froze and my graphics didn't move, or they went into overdrive, zipping on and off without any control by me. As the team in the gallery normally used the weather as a time to get ready for the next item, they very rarely watched or listened to me; often the only one paying attention was the PA, who was counting down the seconds until the end of my segment. So there were quite a few mornings when I was stranded in front of an uncooperative weather map, smiling and valiantly trying to keep going while willing someone to save me by cutting to the weather summary!

Things didn't always go perfectly smoothly when I was sat on the hallowed couch, either — a good example being my first day of co-hosting with Eamonn Holmes. Eamonn was, and is, one of the best broadcasters in the country today, but he can be, by his own admission, a little prickly in the mornings. And hosting a news programme sat next to a rookie co-host was probably not high on his 'to do' list. So the first morning was always going to be a tricky one. As expected (and I wouldn't have had it any other way, as I could barely speak for nerves), Eamonn would be doing the big interviews and topics of the day, while I would cover the lighter ones, and the links to news, weather and competitions. Fine by me.

Our big guest that morning was Tony Blair, then Prime Minister. He had not long started doing his now famous *GMTV* interviews, and he looked as nervous as I was. We all smiled and shook hands as he was led in during an ad break, and then Eamonn carried on scribbling his notes and checking his briefs. By the side of the sofa were the stairs dividing the room between *GMTV* and Lorraine Kelly's cosy set. Her team were busying about as it was Valentine's Day, and there were lots of romantic items coming up in her show. One of them involved Cupid, who was led to the bottom of the stairs and told to look smiling into camera as a 'cutaway' (a shot of him) was taken while Lorraine was talking. He stood sideways on to us, a young model, oiled and coiffed and dressed in tight white briefs, holding a bow and arrow. Everyone was rushing about doing their thing, and only Tony Blair and I had nothing to do, so we both glanced over to where the action was.

The cameras were lining up for the 'tease' into Lorraine's show, where she told the audience at home what was coming up later, and Cupid was told to look straight ahead at the camera in front of him. As he did, and the floor manager counted down out of the ad break, something caught my eye. And it could possibly have taken my eye out if I had been any closer.

Cupid was suddenly very, well, 'excited' about being on TV, and as he was only wearing tight white underpants, he didn't really have anywhere to hide. As he stared with a fixed grin into the camera, I glanced over at Tony Blair, and I could see by the smile on his face that he had noticed Cupid's rising problem. I looked around. Everyone was busy looking at their notes, their cameras, their computers, their autocue; no one else had noticed except for me and the Prime Minister.

Mr Blair turned to me with a glint in his eye and grinned. 'Well, he's pleased to be here!' he said, and the music started, Eamonn's head shot up and suddenly we were back on air.

Over the years I'd like to think that I have got better at interviewing people, encouraging them to tell their side of a story, but interviewing celebrities, especially really famous celebrities, is a whole different skill. On *Loose Women*, the stars have agreed to come on the show, and know what they are letting themselves in for, so they are usually lovely — but when you are sent to interview a star at a junket, it can be an entirely different story.

A junket is when a group of stars from a new film are brought to a hotel, and the nation's press is invited to meet them. That way, loads of different TV channels and programmes can interview the stars in one long, tiring day, in three-minute slots. It all runs like clockwork, and there is very little time for pleasantries; you are there to get some juicy sound bites, try and raise a smile or two and that's it. I have done many of them, and have met some wonderful Hollywood stars — Matthew McConaughey was drop-dead gorgeous and so friendly I wanted to take him to the pub to meet my friends afterwards. Beyoncé was, and is, the most beautiful person I have ever met in the flesh, and Harry Connick Jr, Michael Caine and Mike Myers were fun, friendly and down to earth. Not all celebrities *like* junkets, however, and sometimes they also seem to take a particular dislike to *me* . . .

My worst showbiz interview ever was with Verne Troyer, the actor who played Mini Me in the Austin Powers films. He has since shown himself to be a fun, likeable man when he took part in *Celebrity Big Brother*, but the day I interviewed him, he wasn't in the mood for a rather inexperienced and overawed young woman.

'So!' I breathed, full of excitement at interviewing an American star. 'This could be the first time the British public has heard you speak!'

Him, taken aback: 'What?'

Me: 'Well, you don't say much in this film, do you?'

Him, glaring: 'What do you mean?'

Me, realizing my three minutes had not got off to a good start and desperate to gain some ground and some Brownie points: 'It takes real talent to be funny and likeable on screen with a character who is essentially treated like an overgrown baby for much of the film. Was it difficult to keep quiet while working with a man as funny as Mike Myers?'

Him, now really pissed off: 'I do speak, what's the matter with you?' Looking at the assistant for help, who glances at her watch and narrows her eyes at me.

Me: 'Err . . . What was your favourite moment of making this film?'

Him: silence.

Me: 'Have you enjoyed working with Mike and Michael Caine and, of course, Beyoncé?'

Him: silence.

Assistant: 'I think that's us done now, don't you?'

Apparently the overnight editors, whose job it was to cut the piece together for the next day's show, got the biggest laugh they'd had in years when they listened to the tape recording of the 'interview'.

Following my spectacularly poor red-carpet arrival at the National Television Awards in 1997, I hadn't had much experience of award ceremonies, or indeed film premieres. All I knew was what I saw on the TV, so when I was asked to cover the premiere of *Maybe Baby* in June 2000 at the Odeon Leicester Square, I was beyond excited. I put on my best long red dress and my sparkly shoes, and tried to pin my hair up into something that looked elegant but didn't show my ears, as I hate them — they could put Prince Charles's to shame. I took my place with the crew, lovely cameraman Amos — who had

142

covered his tattoos with a smart dinner jacket — and Simon, the very droll sound man who wore a battered suit and his usual 'seen it all before' expression. We waited with the rest of the assembled press in the foyer of the Odeon, and it all seemed fairly friendly as we stood around chatting and gossiping.

Outside, hundreds of fans waited behind barriers.

Suddenly there was a roar of screaming, and we all leapt into action. Cameras were hoisted onto shoulders and everyone lunged forward to the red ropes, separating us from the stars. The men and women who had seemed so friendly just seconds before suddenly developed Wolverine-style claws jutting from their elbows, which they used to barge me to the side to claim their place.

'Push in! Push in!' muttered Amos, as he jostled his large frame and Elvis quiff through the throng. I tried to, but no amount of 'Excuse me . . . can I just . . . ? Could I possibly get through? Would you mind if I squeezed past?' would make these people budge from their rigid, in-the-trenches stance: legs apart, microphones outstretched, jaw set. I was stuck at the back, and I could see Amos looking for me as the first of the stars made their way up the carpet.

There was nothing else for it. I hitched up my dress, hunkered down, and like a goat I headbutted my way through the forest of legs. By the time I got to the front I had been trodden on, elbowed in the face and sworn at, but I had done it; I was at the red rope. I was dishevelled and most of my hair now hung over my sweaty

143

face, but I was there. The only problem now was standing up straight, and that just wasn't going to happen. All the other journalists were holding their logoed microphones out like spears, and even with Amos doing his best to film and swat people out of the way for me, the best I could manage was a half-crouch under their out-stretched arms.

Emma Thompson arrived first. 'Emma! Emma!' shouted the man from Sky, and Emma did a smiling and witty interview with him.

'Emma!' cried the woman from the BBC, and Emma duly walked over.

'Emma! Down here!' I yelled, and Emma Thompson, bless her, stooped down and did her best to catch my pathetic questions, before smiling at me pityingly and walking on.

Ben Elton was next; he thought I was hilarious, and did a jolly interview laughing down at me before carrying on to talk to the proper hacks. Most other stars walked past without even noticing me, and just as my knees and will to live were about to give out, along walked Hugh Laurie. This was before he became a huge star in the American series *House*; back then everyone knew him as the funny, bumbling man from *Blackadder* and as half of comedy duo Fry and Laurie. That night, however, I like to think I was the first to see Hugh Laurie as the absolute beauty he is.

He stood in front of me, eyes twinkling, and said, 'Hello! What are you doing down there?' Then he bent down, took my hand and helped me up. The others had no choice but to move

144

out the way, as a film star helping up a rubbish reporter is different from a rubbish reporter squirming for help on her own.

I was a bit wobbly after being hunkered down for so long, and ended up reaching out to steady myself. My hand landed on his surprisingly firm chest.

'Thank you! Gosh, aren't you muscly?' I said, and then looked up at him. 'And *tall*?' I tapped his chest. 'Crikey, you're really quite hard, aren't you?'

He laughed and walked away and I realized I hadn't asked him anything about the film . . .

Surprisingly, *GMTV* never asked me to cover another premiere again.

★  ★  ★

My encounters with internationally acclaimed stars continued during my time at *GMTV*, but there was one instance that I have never spoken about before. I didn't know how to. I figured if I refused to think about it then it never happened, and I was prepared to let it go at that.

Nick had never enjoyed celebrity parties; he wasn't a big fan of TV presenters at the best of times and thought they were overpaid, self-important, vacuous idiots who didn't appreciate the hard work that actually went into making a TV show work. He had a point, but as *I* was a TV presenter, I was expected to attend parties and award ceremonies. And, maybe because I was a vacuous idiot, I quite enjoyed them. It was fun getting dressed up, and by now I was au fait

145

with the way things were — I no longer turned up in old shift dresses and clumpy shoes; I borrowed beautiful designer clothes for the evening and accessorized them with my own high-street jewellery, handbags and shoes. I was better at putting make-up on now, too, and had learned how to style my hair. I knew the tricks of the trade when it came to looking good in the world of show business!

This night started like many others, a plush awards do at a smart hotel in London and everyone who was anyone from the world of entertainment was there. This time I arrived in a chauffeur-driven car that had been sent for me. When people start sending you cars it's a sign that you've been accepted as part of a successful TV show, which felt lovely. Tonight, I thought, I would be able to hold my head high with the best of them. Little did I know what a disastrous turn the evening would take.

The car pulled up and the milling paparazzi turned round, lifting their cameras in preparation. The driver got out and walked to my door as I gathered my bag and adjusted myself to make sure I was decent; some photographers try to get sneaky shots up your dress, but by now I was wise to this. The door opened and I stepped out onto the pavement smiling.

The flashes popped, making it difficult to see where I was going. As I made my way down the red carpet assisted by a helpful PR girl, who made sure I didn't stumble, I spotted a very well known Hollywood actor who I'd previously seen in the ITV building when he'd been over to promote one of his movies. I hadn't met him, but we'd all scrambled to the corridor to sneak a peek.

As the paps went crazy taking his shots I blinked to get rid of the white flashbulb spots in front of my eyes and made my way to the table plan to see where I was sitting, and also to have a look at who else was going to be there. Soon everyone had arrived, and after a few glasses of champagne we were led to our table, smiling and chatting.

Phone reception was always bad in this hotel, and that night was no exception; as soon as we sat down I lost all signal. Still, who did I have to call? Nick was also out that night with friends from work. After the formulaic meal — I can't really remember what we had but most of these meals seem to involve melon as a starter and a chicken main course — coffee was served and the night began.

Spirits were high; and some of the people on my table were hopeful they'd win. The host for the evening had the room in stitches as he took the mickey out of all the big stars one by one.

Then the lights dimmed, the music swelled, and the awards began in earnest. One by one they were ticked off the list, as the winners climbed to the stage to loud applause and launched into their acceptance speeches. As the night went on in much the same way, I started to wonder why I'd even come. But back then I was excited just to be included so I'd sometimes find myself in places I had no real reason to be. Now I only attend if a show I'm working on is nominated. But back to that night . . .

I looked down at my coffee cup, still half full and now lukewarm. There didn't seem much point in drinking anything to keep me awake now — there was nothing to stay awake for. I downed the rest of my wine instead and looked up at the stage, where the next category was being announced.

I stayed for a few more categories and then decided that as I needed to be up early there was no point wasting any more sleeping time. I whispered my goodbyes and made my way outside. I was about to call my car company but my phone hadn't fully regained its signal yet so I walked to the roadside looking for a black cab.

It was really dark and cold outside and I suddenly wished I'd brought my coat, but I'd only expected to be jumping in and out of waiting cars so there hadn't seemed much point. Also, my coat was the anorak that I did the weather in, so it wasn't really suited to a black-tie do like that night. Because I'd come out of the side exit to avoid the paps at the front and because it was midweek the road was quiet. I held my borrowed dress off the dirty pavement and craned my neck left and right; still not a cab in sight.

I decided to try my phone again; I was just fumbling for it in my bag, while trying to keep my dress from trailing on the pavement, when I heard a car pull up alongside me. But it wasn't a cab; it - was a luxury car with blacked-out windows, obviously dropping someone off. Disappointed, I moved out of the way as I continued rooting. The back door opened, but no one got out. I looked around; maybe someone was being picked up?

What happened next I have never told a soul until now. Not even Nick.

There was no one nearby, as everyone was inside watching the awards ceremony. I bent down and looked inside; maybe they needed me to get someone for them? My heart flipped; inside the car was the American actor. He grinned at me as I half crouched, blushing furiously.

'Hi!' he smiled.

'Er, hello,' I stuttered, hardly knowing what I was saying. 'Did you want me to get someone for you?'

I couldn't believe I was actually having a conversation with this man.

'No! I was just on my way to my hotel and I saw you standing there looking lost. Do you want a ride?'

My whole body blushed and my hands sweated against the material of my dress. It felt like something out of a movie was happening to me. The girl who'd been bullied at school, told by her TV bosses that she was certainly no Caprice, was being offered a lift home by one of the most famous men on the planet. It was at this moment my naivety and wine consumption blinded me to the reality that this was probably not a knight in shining armour.

'Oh gosh, erm, that's very nice of you, but I don't live near here. Thank you anyway,' I said and stepped back on the pavement.

The American laughed. 'C'mon! I'll get the driver to drop me at my hotel and then he can take you where you need to go. Seriously, get in. I can't leave you out here. I'd never forgive myself!'

I dithered. It seemed to make sense and, most of all, it would be an INCREDIBLE story to tell my friends. I might even see if I could get his autograph.

'Well, if it's no trouble . . . '

'It's no trouble at all.'

I got in and pulled the door closed behind me. The car smelled expensive. The leather seats squeaked under my bottom as I turned to put my seat belt on. The driver pulled away, keeping his eyes on the road, and headed off towards Knightsbridge.

'So what's your name?' he twinkled at me.

'Andrea.'

'Have you been to a party?'

'Kind of. I was at the same awards ceremony as you.'

'Oh yeah? And did you win an award tonight, An-dreya?'

'Er, no, I wasn't up for anything tonight.'

'Shame. So what do you do, An-dreya?'

'I'm a weathergirl on breakfast TV.'

'A weathergirl! I LOVE weathergirls! How do you guys do that thing where you wave your hand around and you can't see what you're looking at? That's AMAZING!'

I smiled and flushed red. 'It's not really.'

'SURE it is! It must mean you're good with

your hands, eh, An-dreya?'

I didn't know what to say so I just smiled at him.

'Are you good with your hands?' he asked. I looked at him blankly. 'Or any other part of your body?'

'Er, I don't know what you mean.'

'SURE you do!'

He was grinning at me. I suddenly felt very uncomfortable, and embarrassed, and I wished he'd stop talking like this. Even though I work in television, I always seem to believe the public image people portray is the real them — and am surprised if the reality is very different. He seemed to be an all-American hero but clearly he was an ever better actor than people gave him credit for because he was about to show his true colours and he wasn't going to be saving the girl this time.

'Is your hotel nearby?' I asked, starting to panic. 'You really don't have to make a detour for me. I'm happy to get out at your hotel and book a cab from there.'

'I'm not detouring for YOU, honey, I'm detouring for ME. I thought you'd like a little something to remember this evening by. Seeing as you didn't win an award.'

He was leaning back in his seat now and to my horror I realised he was fiddling with his trousers. Oh my God, my mind raced, this couldn't be happening.

'Look, I'm sorry, I just wanted a lift home.' I was babbling as I undid my seatbelt and reached down to get my handbag from the floor.

I don't think he was even listening as suddenly his hand was on my head, angling it towards his lap. 'Didn't I ask you if you wanted a RIDE?'

I pulled my head away and screamed, 'Let me out! Stop the car now.'

He laughed, releasing my hair. 'Relax! Let's have some fun!'

Lunging forward I banged on the window between the driver and us and shouted again, 'Stop the car now.'

The car immediately pulled up to the kerb. I scrabbled for the door handle, while the actor stared at me, astonished and getting angry.

'Why do you think I let you in here, fucking tease,' I heard him muttering, as the door swung open and I threw myself onto the pavement.

The flimsy material of my expensive borrowed dress ripped as I struggled to my feet. My bag fell off my lap and onto the floor, and in one swoop I took it and ran. My heels clipped on the wet pavement as I gathered my dress up round my knees and legged it as fast as I could. I didn't look back, I didn't hear anything more, and I didn't want to. I just wanted to get the hell out of there. I ran until I found a main road with street lights, not knowing where I was and not caring, as long as I was away from him.

What an idiot you've been, Andrea! How could you be so naive as to expect a man like that to offer you a lift out of the goodness of his heart, idiot, idiot, *idiot*, I scolded myself as I ran. My breath was coming in gasps as I gradually slowed to a trot and then a fast walk. A cab, a cab, a cab. I needed a cab. I needed to get home

152

NOW. I needed to get inside NOW.

I don't know how long I walked until eventually I saw a taxi with its yellow light on like a rescue beacon. The driver nodded when I climbed inside and croaked, 'Wimbledon,' and we pulled away as I struggled with the unyielding seat belt. To him I was just another dishevelled female on her way home.

I felt like I was in a parallel universe; I was in a normal black cab, on my way home. Only I had a thumping heart, a sick feeling in my stomach and a ripped dress. I was too numb to cry as the cab rumbled its way southwards through the streets of London.

Once I was home, I let myself in and got straight into the shower. I washed my hair, washed away the smell of the car and his aftershave. Only when I was dry and had brushed my teeth and wrapped myself in my dressing gown did I feel better. But I couldn't stop my mind reliving the night. I couldn't deny that I had thought it was exciting to climb into a strange man's car, just because he was famous. And what had actually happened? He'd been lewd, he'd pushed me into his crotch and expected I'd gladly have sex with him on the backseat, but I worried I'd given him the wrong signals by getting into his car in the first place. Maybe no one had ever said no to him before? Clearly other girls he'd invited in had been thrilled at the offer and would have relished telling their friends the story in the morning. I wasn't to know he would expect that of me, and he wasn't to know that I wasn't that kind of girl.

No, I decided, it was horrible and I wished it hadn't happened, but it had and I had to take responsibility for being so foolish. Yes I blamed myself. I was naive and stupid. Of course, if he had actually assaulted me there is no question that I would have called the police, however ashamed I felt. But he hadn't and although it was hideous, I was safe, I was home and I had learned a very valuable lesson. I will never, ever make that mistake again. Although if I ever do find myself alone with a man who tries the same trick, I like to think that instead of being frightened, he'd be limping away from our encounter.

Since then I've seen him on TV, of course, but not in person. If I ever get sent an invitation to a film he's in it goes straight in the bin. And although he may still be offering free rides to stranded females, I would say, ladies . . . just smile and say no and wait for a cab. He's not worth it, but you are.

# 10

## And Then There Were Three

Growing up, I had always said I would rather have a dog than a baby. The truth was, I just hadn't been ready even to think about starting a family. But when at twenty-eight I was diagnosed with endometriosis, everything changed. I had been suffering from pain in my lower abdomen and pelvis throughout my twenties, but had got used to it and foolishly not seen a doctor about it. Recently the pain had become sharper and more difficult to ignore, though. After an initial consultation the specialist I saw said he thought it sounded like I had endometriosis, and then a laparoscopy confirmed that one of my tubes was severely scarred and that I also had cysts on my ovaries. I was told that my chances of getting pregnant were very slim.

I felt like a dark cloud had descended over me. Instantly I knew that I had been kidding myself about the dog; I wanted a family, and I wanted to start trying for one as soon as I could. But first I wanted to be married.

Nick and I discussed it over the kitchen table in our flat and I explained how I felt. He said he would think about it. Something inside me exploded — THINK ABOUT IT?! We'd been together for eleven years, we'd bought a flat together, we were happy, we loved each other;

what was there to THINK about? So I gave him an ultimatum — marry me so we could start a family, or else I would leave him. I gave him six months to decide.

That was where I made my big mistake. I see that now. I am ashamed of forcing his hand like that; it was immature and selfish of me. He wasn't ready to get married or settle down, and I pushed too hard for something that he wasn't quite sure about.

You can't make someone love you the way you want them to, just because you love them. You can't make someone want to spend their life with you; that's not fair on them, or on you. I didn't see it that way then. It had never occurred to me after our travelling split that we would do anything else BUT get married and live happily ever after. Why would it?

So a couple of months later, on my twenty-eighth birthday on a hillside outside Barcelona, Nick got down on one knee and asked me to marry him. He pulled out a brass curtain ring and slipped it on my finger and it was the most romantic thing that had ever happened to me.

I looked at him with one knee in the mud and squealed, 'Really? *Really?* This is it? You're asking me?'

He nodded and grinned at me as I screamed, 'YES! Yes, I will!' and was heard halfway down the mountain. It was wonderful.

We got married in 1999 in the Masai Mara in Kenya. My parents were still living there, and our numerous visits to see them convinced us that it was the most special place in the world, and we wanted to tie the knot there. Helen the wardrobe lady from *GMTV* made my wedding dress from a sketch I drew myself. It was a simple sundress with a short-sleeved chiffon coat. In front of just thirty-five of our friends and family, some Masai warriors, a couple of warthogs and even a few giraffes in the distance, we said 'I do'. It was everything I hoped my wedding would be: in the sunshine, informal and surrounded by people I loved.

We started trying for a baby a few months after coming back from honeymoon. I was prepared for it to take a while, but it was still disappointing each month to see a blank window where I so hoped a blue line would appear. I started seeing a fertility specialist on the NHS who advised me to keep a detailed diary of my cycle, and told me the best times to try to conceive. Gradually the romance petered out of that side of things, as we were making love according to a calendar rather than because we felt like it. There were many times when Nick would get up to go and watch TV and leave me with my legs propped up against the wall at the back of the bed to make sure 'it all stayed in'. A guaranteed passion killer for any man, I'm sure.

Eventually, in one of the many stages before IVF, I was prescribed Clomid, the hormone drug that makes your body produce more eggs. It is a tricky drug to handle, and it made me feel very strange indeed. I could feel the hormones rushing around my body, pumping into me, making me hot and bothered, sweaty and dizzy.

157

But I kept taking them, and every month kept testing myself for that damned blue line.

And every month all I got was that same heart-wrenching disappointment . . .

★　★　★

In February 2001, almost two years after we were married, I was bridesmaid at my sister's wedding in Wales. My parents were over from Africa, and my dad was driving us around as we rushed into Cardiff for last-minute bits and bobs the day before the ceremony. I sat in the back feeling queasy, assuming it was just from Dad's driving again. Everyone was chatting about the big day tomorrow, when a thought crept into my mind . . .

We split up, arranging to meet in a coffee shop in an hour. I raced to Boots and bought a pregnancy test, hopping from one foot to the other as the woman took her time blipping it through the till. I grabbed it and raced into Debenhams, searching for the ladies' loo. It was there, in a department store in Cardiff, that the blue line finally appeared. I was pregnant! I cried in that hot little cubicle, then pulled myself together, went back down to Boots and bought three more kits from the same woman, who obviously didn't know if I was red-eyed from happiness or not. I didn't tell a soul — apart from Nick, when he arrived later on — as I didn't want to spoil Linda's moment of glory. He went pale, then a bit red, then pale again, and it was hard to say who felt the most queasy — him

158

with the terrifying realization that his life was about to change forever, or me with the arrival of instant morning sickness.

I felt ill from the moment the blue line appeared. My sense of smell went off the scale; I used to joke that the police could use me with the sniffer dogs at Heathrow, as I could pick up the smallest scent. I would make Nick run straight upstairs and change out of his moped jacket and have a shower as the smell of exhaust fumes on his clothes made me retch.

Penny knew right away that I was pregnant, because I spent every morning with my head hanging out of the window of our dressing room, desperate for some fresh air to stop the nausea. I would sit by the window while she grumbled that it was cold, then slowly creep down the corridor, trying not to lose my breakfast or get a whiff of anyone's morning breath as that would send me scurrying to the ladies'. And on breakfast telly there is a LOT of morning breath . . .

Like every pregnant woman, and especially a first timer, I spent the initial three months terrified that it was all going to go wrong. At seven weeks I had a rush of hormones that left me doubled over with pain, and I was convinced my pregnancy was ectopic. I managed to drive myself to hospital in tears, and my lovely specialist gave me an early ultrasound that showed it wasn't; I saw that the baby was forming in the right place, it was just my endometriosis scars that weren't happy with all the activity. The pain continued on and off throughout my pregnancy, but I was much calmer compared to that first, terrifying rush.

Once things subsided and I was able to move without feeling sick, I really enjoyed being pregnant. I was lucky; my baby and my bump progressed just as they should have done, and I was fit, happy and well. I loved seeing myself grow, and waited impatiently for the first little flutter of butterflies to tell me my baby was moving. I still raced around the country doing the weather, on and off trains, lugging my bag around and standing in the dark and cold in the middle of nowhere.

We had decided not to find out what our baby was going to be, so I painted our spare room yellow, and ordered a pine cot, dresser and rocking chair. We called the bump 'Britney' as a working title, but subconsciously I must have known it was a boy as I bought blue denim curtains and cushions . . .

And all the while I kept growing. As I got bigger, the comments became more frequent. 'Bloody hell! How many have you got in there?' was the most common, but they all revolved around my size. I went from eight and a bit stone to over twelve stone. By the end I'd worn holes in my trousers where my thighs rubbed together. I had to cut the insides of my sleeves to allow my huge upper arms through. My feet swelled so much that I had to wear flip-flops in October.

The day I left *GMTV* to go on maternity leave, I went to say goodbye to Peter McHugh, the director of programmes. 'Thank God you're going,' he said. 'You've been giving me a heart attack for the past month that I'd have to have

160

towels and hot water on standby. Every time you turn sideways you block out Ireland, and Wales is starting to get worried.' So, with two weeks to go until my due date, I hung up my trusty weather clicker and waddled off home.

My size was becoming a bit of an issue at home as well, as Nick could barely look at me. He didn't like putting his hand on my stomach to feel the baby kick — he said it was creepy — and I knew he didn't like how big I had become. One day as we unloaded the weekly shop he said casually, 'I suppose you've noticed I've bought these?' He held up some rice cakes. I nodded, not knowing what the point was. 'Well, that's all I've bought. They are instead of biscuits. I mean, look at the size of your arse.' I flamed red with embarrassment and quietly carried on putting the rest of the shopping away. *This will pass, I told myself. Once the baby is born and I am back to my normal size again, everything will be fine.*

The thing is, Finlay wasn't ready to be born yet; just as he is now, he decided he would arrive when he felt like it, and not before. The waiting only increased my anxiety about the birth, but I had been quietly dealing with the fear of having the baby in my own way . . .

Towards the very end of my pregnancy I began to feel a little anxious, and the panic attacks I had suffered from for the past seven years started to rear their ugly head. I kept this to myself as I didn't want to look like an idiot, even in front of Nick, and I quietly went along to see a hypnotherapist who specialized in women who

161

were happy enough to have a baby inside them, but were a bit apprehensive about getting it out . . .

One bright morning, swollen like a watermelon and feeling about as attractive, I made my way to a mansion block on a backstreet in Chelsea, just off the King's Road. That seemed like a good sign, and I had visions of lots of well-to-do mums-to-be waddling around, waiting to have their minds and lady bits put to rest. I rang the doorbell and waited, and soon a posh Englishman's voice crackled through the intercom. 'Yes?'

'Er, it's Andrea McLean. I have an appointment?'

'Ah, yes. Come up. I'm in flat number four.'

It turned out the hypnotherapist worked from his flat, not a clinic as I'd expected. This shocked me a little, and I felt uneasy at the thought of spending an hour lying on a couch on my own with a strange man in his flat. I had never met a hypnotherapist before, and I'm not sure what I expected. I had seen Paul McKenna on the telly helping people lose weight, and I'd seen guys on stage who made people eat onions thinking they were apples, but apparently there was a big difference between daft stage shows and the use of hypnotherapy as a treatment. I hoped so; I didn't want onion breath as well as everything else while I was giving birth. This man was tall and slight, with blue eyes and grey unkempt hair, and he was wearing the Chelsea uniform of cream trousers and a blue shirt.

He had black socks that were worn at the heel and he looked distracted.

Being pregnant, the first thing I did when I got there was ask to use the loo, as it had been roughly twenty seconds since the last time I had gone and my bladder was bursting. He pointed down the dark corridor and I pushed open the door. The loo was black. Not the toilet — that was a grimy, limescale-ridden beige — but the walls, floor and ceiling were painted black. The sink was cluttered with male toiletries: after-shave, deodorant, a worn-down toothbrush and a tube of toothpaste with the lid off and squeezed heartily from the middle. Along the side of the bath were half-burned candles in blackened glasses. A dried-out cleaning cloth lay on the floor by the sink, next to a dust-coated bottle of Flash. I looked in the toilet. It wasn't good. I pulled some toilet paper from the roll sitting on top of the cistern, and made myself a protective layer on top of the wooden seat, before hovering over it to wee. I flushed, washed my hands on a dried-out bit of soap and wiped them on my maternity dress.

I opened the door and walked down the corridor towards what looked like a small living area. The hall was painted dark green, and covered in paintings done either by him or an equally enthusiastic and minimally talented amateur. I think they were of people. I joined him, full of misgivings. The room was quite small; to the right, sunshine struggled in through streaky windows, and I could just make out a tree and its rippling leaves. To my side was an old

163

sofa, covered with a rumpled throw and some cushions, still dented and probably warm from his back. Behind it stood floor-to-ceiling bookshelves, crammed full of impressive-looking books that gave the impression of being heavy and difficult to read. There was another pile of books on the old wooden desk in front of me, along with papers, old coffee cups and plates. It looked and smelled like he lived in this room.

In the left corner was a green leather chair, which he asked me to sit in. I was glad it wasn't the couch, like I'd been expecting. We started by having a chat about what I'd like to get out of the session. He asked me what, in an ideal world, I would like my birth to be like. I thought of Dolly Parton. Of how when she was asked how long it took to do her hair, she chirped in her adorable drawl: 'I don't know, honey, I'm never there!' So I asked him if he could arrange a birth where I just sat in the waiting room and was handed a bright, shiny new baby that slept through the night and was potty trained. He looked at me blankly.

Feeling a bit foolish, I told him that if I could wave a magic wand, I would like to spend as much time as possible at home during my labour. I'd like to feel on top of it all, and when the time felt right, we'd drive to the hospital. Once there, I'd be taken in to get ready, and by then things would start happening quite quickly. The pain would be bad but not eye-poppingly bad, and I wouldn't feel panicky about it. Then the actual birth would start, and even through the pain I would manage to keep my head from spinning around like Linda Blair in *The Exorcist* . . . The baby would be born, it would be healthy and all would be right with the world.

He didn't throw back his head laughing, wipe the tears from his eyes and say, 'You want *WHAT*? You do realize you're going to *GIVE BIRTH*, don't you?', like I'd expected him to. He explained that he would show me how to keep myself calm during labour and help me to cope with the pain. He said that although it would probably feel like not much was happening, and I might even fall asleep during the session, hypnotherapy worked on the unconscious mind rather than the conscious, meaning that it would still be absorbed whether I remembered it or not. My mind processed this information instantly, deciding he was giving what appeared to be a get-out clause.

We began. He didn't whip out a watch on a chain and tell me that I'd soon be feeling 'verrrry sleeeeepy' like I'd seen in the movies. Instead he asked me to close my eyes and think about my breathing. He told me to imagine that instead of the air filling my lungs when I breathed in, it was coming through the walls of my heart.

I concentrated hard. My heart was swelling and shrinking in time to my breathing . . . It took a while, but I finally started to feel relaxed. Then I remembered that my mobile phone was switched on in my handbag. What if it went off? Would I have to jump up and answer it? Would he be annoyed? I sat panicking about what to do, and I have to admit I didn't really hear what he was saying for the next few minutes as I kept

165

wondering if I should open my eyes and say, 'Um, sorry, can I just switch off my phone?' But gradually his voice started drifting into my thoughts, and I forgot about my phone. He was telling me that even though I could hear noises coming from outside — the traffic going by, the builders banging away next door, aeroplanes overhead and the trees rustling — it didn't matter. *Allow those sounds to filter in, don't fight against them.* I concentrated on my heart expanding and contracting with every breath, and soon my breathing felt very deep and relaxed.

He told me to imagine the feeling I got when I saw someone I hadn't seen for ages. That warm, happy feeling you get when you say, 'Hello!' I pictured the scene in my head. Then he said, push that inner smile that you feel down to your baby, let it 'feel your hello'. I got a bit stuck then, as I couldn't figure out how to push an inner smile downwards. So I imagined what it would feel like to have my new baby put into my arms, and the rush I would feel at seeing it for the first time, and thought, *Hello there!* I don't know if I pushed the thought down or not, but it felt right anyway.

Next he told me to pick a word to focus on — any word, such as 'calm' or 'relaxed', that made me feel good. The word that popped into my head was *ushi*, which means 'sunshine' in Swahili. It's one of my favourite words, as I think it sounds as lovely as its meaning. It's also the name of a funny old dog I used to know, who always made me smile. He said, imagine you are feeling the pain of your contractions, but instead of focusing on the pain, focus on your word. Think about how that word makes you feel. Imagine clenching your fists, and all the pain you feel is being directed into your clenched hands, and when you release your hands, the pain is eased.

He went on like this for a while, and my mind meandered, half listening to him, half hearing the swishing of the trees outside, and the odd car going by. Every now and then my mind would snap back to what he was saying, and then it would drift off again, so I wasn't too sure about what was happening half the time. At one point I'm sure I fell asleep, as I haven't a clue what he was talking about when I gradually heard his voice filtering into my brain. He was telling me that I was slowly starting to wake up, slowly becoming aware of my surroundings, and I could open my eyes whenever I felt ready. I did, and from feeling like I could sleep forever, I suddenly felt completely wide awake and alert. I also felt a bit embarrassed to be sitting in this stranger's living room, having fallen asleep in front of him. I hoped I hadn't snored or dribbled.

It was a strange feeling walking down the street afterwards. I tried to replay it in my head, but I couldn't really remember what he'd said. I just knew I'd paid an exorbitant £80 to have a lovely snooze in a strange man's living room.

★　★　★

167

On my second visit to the hypnotherapist I mentioned my panic attacks, just casually, as I was sitting down. Then I wished I hadn't. He asked me how I felt when one started, and I said I'd rather not describe it in detail, as just talking about it can sometimes trigger one off. He said not to worry, it would be fine, just tell him what it felt like. So I told him, and within seconds the familiar choking feelings of absolute fear took hold.

My heart started to pound, and I could hear the blood rushing in my ears. I closed my eyes and felt the familiar sense of terror wash over me. I felt my throat tighten, my heart beat faster, and then a thick blackness started to envelop me. I tried to block it out, to think of lovely things, to breathe deeply, but the hypnotist saw what I was doing and told me to stop. He told me just to sit there, to let these feelings come to me. I told him about the thick treacle-like blackness that threatened to swamp me, and he sounded quite pleased, which annoyed me.

'What's it doing now?' he asked.

'It's all around me. I can't fight it . . . '

'Good . . . good . . . let it.' Good? Was he mad?

I felt the heaviness begin in my arms, and then creep over my legs, working inwards towards my head and torso. It was getting harder to breathe, and I was now feeling scared, even though I *knew* I wasn't in a frightening situation, and if I really wanted to I could open my eyes, have some water, go for a walk and this would pass. With my eyes still closed, I told him I wanted it

168

to stop, and he asked a really stupid question: 'Why?'

Because it was horrible, and I wanted it to go away and I wanted to feel good again, and this definitely wasn't good.

'But what's the worst thing that could happen to you if you sat here and let it carry on? You're actually just sitting in my living room. There is no blackness. You can still breathe. Try now to stand outside yourself, and see yourself as I can see you. You're just sitting in a chair, in my room; there is nothing here that can harm you.'

I tried to visualize myself, but I still kept feeling like I was being swamped, and I told him this.

'Let it come,' he urged. 'Where is it now?' *It was creeping up my arms.*

'Good. Now where is it?' *Moving over my chest and stomach.*

'Good.' How can he still think this is good?! *It was pouring down my scalp, over my face . . . once it got to my mouth I would stop breathing . . .*

And then the strangest thing happened. The thick, black feeling enveloped my whole body, coming from all sides . . . and carried on moving. It felt like it washed right over me, and just carried on its journey. I realized it was me who was holding my breath, clenching my teeth and waiting for it to crush me. As quickly as it crept over me, I felt it starting to recede. He could see by my face that it was passing, and he told me to keep my eyes closed and take a few deep breaths until I felt back to normal.

Then he started to talk me through what had just happened. He said that when my labour began and these feelings of panic started to swamp me, I would feel frightened and in pain, but that I should try to stand outside myself. I needed to see what was happening, and allow it to happen and ride it, because the more I fought it, the worse it would become.

With my eyes still closed, he talked me through my relaxing breathing techniques and told me to focus on *ushi*, my chosen word. He said that I would carry my baby to its full term for its maximum benefit, that every contraction I would feel should be welcomed not fought, as it was bringing me one step closer to meeting my unborn child.

And finally he told me that I could open my eyes.

I waited a few days before I listened to the tape he'd made of the session, and at first it was horrible to hear him talking me through it again, to hear my small, frightened voice describing how I felt. Then I thought more about what he said, about riding the fear, and riding the pain, and it kind of made sense. I also listened to the tape of the first session, and each time it sent me off into a lovely, deep sleep. I still woke up in the night to go to the loo, and with grinding pains in my legs and hips and cramp in my calf, but the tape definitely helped me to get to sleep to start with.

At my third and final session I told him I was starting to feel a bit fed up with this whole pregnancy lark. I felt so huge, and I hated the way everyone stared at my mammoth bump every time I ventured out. I also hated the way everything took so much effort: just walking to the corner shop left me breathless, and despite sleeping on top of a folded-over duvet and taking paracetamol at night, I was still waking up with terrible pains in my hips and knees. I could fall asleep OK — it was just staying asleep that was proving a problem.

He listened, and I closed my eyes. And this is where it gets rather embarrassing. I know that he talked me through the contractions, telling me to breathe deeply through each one. To welcome them as a necessary stage in my baby's arrival. To stand outside myself and see how well I was coping, and to channel any excess pain down my arm into my hand, so that whenever I squeezed the stress ball I'd bought for the big event, the pain would be eased.

But I can't remember anything else. The next thing I knew, I gave a loud snore and woke up. I felt myself go bright red and hot, and I kept my eyes closed and tried to keep my face and body looking as relaxed as possible, but I was mortified. How long had I been asleep? What on earth had he said? I could hear his voice saying that when I opened my eyes, I would feel awake and full of energy, and that my unconscious mind would remember everything he had said (which was lucky, because my conscious mind couldn't remember a thing). I opened my eyes, and he was right — I suddenly felt wide awake and perky, and a damn sight better than I had

when I walked in. I just couldn't remember what
had happened . . .

★   ★   ★

Two weeks overdue, I finally made my way to the
hospital as I was booked in for an induction. I
would have hours to test whether all that
hypno-babble really could be an alternative to
good old-fashioned prescription pain relief . . .

It was a Sunday afternoon, and Nick and I
waved a nervous goodbye to our lovely
neighbours, who grinned as they saw us go. I was
checked in and led to a room, and after a bit of
form filling and answering questions I was given
the drugs that would induce me. It was a strange
feeling, sitting on my bed, just waiting for it all to
start and feeling that *this is it!* Hours passed and
the period-type pains in my stomach became
more pronounced. I was now officially in labour.

Hour by hour the pain steadily increased, but I
was still only one centimetre dilated. The
midwife was busy and distracted, and only
popped in to check on me every now and then,
so I spent most of the night on my own. She had
told Nick that he might as well go home as this
was going to take a while, so he had decided that
there wasn't much point in both of us being tired
and he would come back when the midwife rang
to say it was going to happen.

I paced the room like a crazed tiger, up and
down, up and down. I hung on the end of the
bed and rocked back and forth. I ate a rich tea
biscuit and immediately threw up my dinner. I

switched off my plinky-plonky relaxing music because it made me want to do something violent to the CD player.

I rang the bell and asked for some pain relief, and was given two paracetamol and told to have a warm bath. Four hours later, after a bath and a useless TENS machine that only seemed to accentuate the pain rather than dull it, I rang the bell again. Thoughts of *ushi* were nowhere near the forefront of my mind. The only thing that helped to calm the pain was counting and breathing. I took a deep breath in and counted to five, then a big breath out and counted to five. Slowly in and slowly out. And it meant that I knew the pain would start to fade by at least the third or fourth breath, so I had something to aim for.

By four in the morning I couldn't sit down, or stand still, so I just paced and paced and paced, breathing in and out, and counting to five. There was no squeezing of hands, or stress balls, but I did manage to stand outside myself — and looking at myself in a nasty Mothercare nightie, clammy, red and panting, wasn't a great thing.

Eventually I was led to another room, where a lovely midwife started her morning shift and didn't leave my side. By the time Nick came back I was hanging on to the wall and inhaling gas and air like my life depended on it, unable to speak for the agony. Eventually, an epidural was put into my spine and after a night of breathtaking pain I was able to think clearly again.

I never found out if the hand-squeezing or

heart-breathing worked during an actual birth, as after seventeen hours of labour, a tank of gas and air, and gallons of epidural, my baby's heart rate started to slow dramatically. From the frantic *pat-pat-pat-pat-pat* that I could hear from the monitor strapped to my stomach, it dropped to a *pat . . . pat . . . pat . . .* To my untrained ear it sounded like his heart was slowing to the point of stopping. As I was pushed onto my side and a doctor prodded something inside me to take a blood test from the top of his head, my epidural suddenly, and with immediate effect, wore off and I was hurled into another dimension of excruciating pain.

The female doctor who had examined me looked up. 'Your baby's oxygen levels are dangerously low and he is in distress.' An oxygen mask was pushed over my mouth and nose and I was told urgently to, 'Breathe! Breathe!' What did they mean my baby was in distress? Had he been deprived of oxygen? I struggled not to cry as I was rushed into theatre, and twenty minutes later little Finlay John was delivered by emergency Caesarean section. My beautiful baby boy.

# 11

## When a Dream Dies

After three days in hospital recovering from my operation, it was time to go home. Nothing can ever prepare you for that moment when you leave the warm fuzzy security of the hospital, full of people who know what to do with a baby, and venture out into the real world again. I sat in the back while Nick fumbled with the new car seat, making sure Finlay was safe. We drove at 20 miles an hour all the way home, as every bump tore at my stomach, and I was terrified each time I saw his small head wobble that it was going to fall off. It was like arriving in a parallel universe stepping into our house for the first time.

As Finlay was placed gently on the floor in his car seat I burst into tears. The day three blues exploded inside me, and I sobbed all over Nick in exhausted, impotent rage. 'I can't believe how irresponsible the hospital are to let us bring this baby home! Can't they see that we don't know what we are doing? How can they let us look after a child on our own? It's outrageous!'

Nick took me by the shoulders, turned me round and led me upstairs. I was still crying as he pulled back the covers of our bed and told me to get in, lie down and leave everything to him. It would all be fine. And so I did, and I slept and slept until tea time in my own comfy clean bed, surrounded by the smells and sounds of home.

Soon enough I calmed down, and, with help from my cousin Heather, who'd had three children and was the font of all knowledge as far as I was concerned; from my mum, who flew over from Kenya to help me; and from my new mum books, I managed to put together a routine that worked for us. It was like having an instruction manual for Finlay, and it helped me knowing that he should be hungry by a certain time, or sleepy, because at first his cries sounded all the same and I didn't know what each one meant. When he got colic and screamed through the night for two solid weeks I thought I would die of exhaustion. Then, just like the books said, he gradually got better, stopped sicking up his milk all over me and managed to sleep for a couple of hours at a time.

The weeks passed and suddenly Christmas was coming. I wasn't able to drive because of my Caesarean, so I filled Finlay's pram with as much as I could push, and heaved it up and down the steps at Wimbledon Park Tube, going back and forth until all the presents were bought and wrapped. It was exhausting, but I loved him so much I just took him with me everywhere and got on with it. I met up with my antenatal class ladies and we swapped horror stories of feeding and sleeping, or the lack of it, and it really helped having them to talk to. We were all in the same boat — a group of women who would probably never have got together normally, and who were bound by our vulnerability.

As it does in every house around the globe,

having a baby changed everything. Nick and I adored our funny little bundle and it felt like we'd always been a gang of three. The three months I had off work were tiring but wonderful; however, my maternity leave eventually ran out and it was time to go back. There was no option to stay away longer — I wouldn't have had a job to return to. We needed my salary to pay our mortgage and to keep us afloat, so from that perspective it wasn't possible either. I found a lovely childminder who lived on the next street, and after a week of settling Finlay in with her I went back to *GMTV*.

It was horrible. I felt wretched for leaving him, and rang the childminder every minute I could. He was never there for long — Nick would drop him round at 8 a.m. and then I would pick him up at midday after I finished work — but it still felt awful. I would bring him home and settle him down for his sleep before running down the corridor to my bed to catch up with some sleep myself while I could. I was getting up at 3.30 a.m., and as he still needed a few night feeds I was shattered. Then I would spend the rest of the day doing normal 'mum' stuff: washing, ironing and cooking, all while looking after Finlay. I arranged for a cleaner to come in once a week as I needed a hand to keep on top of it. That really helped, but there was still a lot to do, as there is in any household.

Once I went back to work, things at home changed. I was very tired, and with a baby I couldn't look after Nick as well as I used to. I think he felt left out and neglected, like many new fathers, and I wish things could have been different, but they weren't. We both shut down, and the love that had pottered along since we were teenagers just ran out of steam.

When things started to go wrong in my marriage, I didn't confide in anyone. I kept thinking it would blow over, that it could all be *fixed*. And when the rough patch had grown over and become a tangled mess that neither of us were able to weed and love back to life, I withdrew further. I felt stupid; what could I tell people? We were the couple who had it all: great jobs, a lovely home, a beautiful baby boy . . . what on earth could be wrong with us? How could I explain that he had removed himself so far from me that I couldn't bring him back? That I lay beside him at night, listening to Finlay's snuffles on the baby monitor, staring into the dark feeling so alone? That some nights, I wondered, just wondered, what would happen if I slipped out of bed in my pyjamas, put Finlay in the car and drove and drove . . . to where? I lay in my bed and wondered where the sunshine had gone from my life; it just felt dark.

I was exhausted from trying to bring the light back in. My own light was being snuffed out; it was being squeezed out by the darkness of Nick's negativity, and I couldn't bring it back. Somehow over the years it had all gone wrong and I wasn't able to make it right again. And gradually I realized I didn't want to try any more. I wanted to get out.

In the last few months before I accepted that our marriage was not going to work, I put myself under so much pressure to be the 'perfect wife' and the 'perfect mother' that I spent most of my time rushing around mothering by rule-book. Finlay would be fed, bathed and put to bed screaming by 7 p.m. sharp every night. After that I'd rush round the house in a frenzy of tidying, putting away toys, folding up high chairs and putting on washing before freshening up and starting dinner. Nick found it stressful to come home to a messy house, so I liked everything to be just right when he walked in the door.

The waiting was the worst. Waiting while I stirred and poured, making dinner for two, and pureeing, mashing and spooning organic vegetable mush into ice-cube trays so that Finlay only ate the best. Hearing the key scrape in the lock — how would he be tonight? Normally Nick was just tired and distracted, but increasingly he was grumpy, distant and angry. Always so angry. He was unhappy with how things were going at work, and increasingly seemed unhappy with how they were going at home, too.

'How was your day?' I'd ask as I bent to get a beer from the fridge to hand him.

'Shit.' He'd give me a peck on the lips, take his beer and wander into the living room. I'd cringe, realizing BBC1 was still switched on (after Finlay and I had swayed along to the 'Goodnight Song' on CBeebies, and I'd taken him up to bed, I'd always flick it back to terrestrial telly). Every night was the same; but I still forgot to turn the TV off to save myself the stress.

'How can you watch this SHIT?' I'd hear from the living room, as Nick reached for the remote control to switch off *EastEnders*.

'I wasn't watching it,' I'd call from the kitchen. 'Turn it over if you like.' And I'd glance through the door to see he already had, and Sky Sports would be on, or a documentary. Nick would be slumped in front of the TV, his beer resting on the floor. I would put his dinner on a tray on his lap (I'd given up trying to get us to eat together at the table; he would just pick his dinner up and go and sit on the sofa with it, and leave me sitting alone), and he would say 'thanks' while keeping his eyes glued to the TV.

The nights took on a familiar routine: I'd get up and tidy the kitchen to give him an hour to switch off from work, then would join him to sit quietly on the couch while he watched TV. I sometimes read a book, or sewed labels onto Finlay's little clothes so they didn't get muddled with any of the other children's at the childminder's. Usually by 9.30 p.m. my head was jerking and I longed to sleep, so I crept up the stairs to check on Finlay, had a quick shower and collapsed into bed.

I'd given up trying to talk to Nick; he didn't want to hear, he didn't want to speak, and finally I understood that he didn't want to be there.

The hurt was slow to come, but deep. The more I tried to fix things, the deeper he withdrew, and the more he seemed to resent it. Nothing I did seemed right, and eventually I realized nothing he did was right either. We were simply existing; two people who used to love each other just living in the same house, not speaking, not touching, not talking.

180

The rot had taken a while, and had been so slow and corrosive that by the time I saw it was there, I didn't know how to get rid of it. Nick didn't seem to notice; he didn't seem to notice anything any more, he just lived in the house and carried on with his life. The 'last chance before the baby is born' nights out with his friends had continued, and as I was always too tired to join him, I spent a lot of time in on my own. The loneliness had started then, but soon turned into a complete blackness as I felt my marriage disintegrate around me.

By that time I knew the true meaning of loneliness. The loneliness of lying in the dark next to someone who didn't seem to care if I was there or not; the loneliness of trying to fix something that no one else would acknowledge was broken; and then the loneliness of guilt . . .

\* \* \*

I did not know that accepting a job to co-host *Our House*, a makeover show on UK Style, would change the course of my life forever. On the first day in October 2003 I was introduced to the crew and the experts I would be working with. My co-host was a builder called Steve Toms. I remember meeting him and thinking he seemed like a nice guy, but for me that was it.

Over the months that we worked together, Steve and I slowly got to know one another more and became friends. He was a big man, six foot three and broad shouldered, with dark hair and an easy smile. I thought he was cheeky and he enjoyed me putting him in his place like a naughty school boy. We made each other laugh, and I thought he was very good at what he did; he was natural and jolly in front of the cameras, and passionate about his work. Being around anyone with a passion for what they do is uplifting — whether it is writing music, performing, painting or building, it makes no difference — and uplifting was what I found him.

Nothing happened during the time we worked together, but I knew he could tell that things at home were not going well for me. He had found me standing quietly to the side of the caravan we used as our waiting area during the freezing hours we weren't needed for filming, talking urgently into my phone to Nick and then crying quietly after I'd hung up. He didn't say anything, but I knew that he understood how unhappy I was. And gradually, I could see that he cared, not just as a colleague or a friend; he cared about me, and wanted to make me happy. Selfishly, against everything I had ever believed in, I realized I wanted this man to make me happy too.

Steve and I got together after the show finished. My marriage had reached the point of no return and I found comfort elsewhere. From being a woman who was proud that I had only ever slept with one man, my husband, and had thought things would remain that way until the day I died, I did the very thing that was against everything I believed in. I knew that there would be no turning back once I had done it, but I

A natural born smiler!

On the front steps of our house, on the way to my christening. Don't Mum and Dad look glamorous?

With my lovely nanny Alison in Trinidad, 1971.

At the hospital picking up my baby sister Linda.
I don't look impressed. July 1973, Port of Spain, Trinidad.

In the children's park in front of our house, Brechin Castle, Trinidad.

On stage aged eight. I was one of Ali Baba's backing girls.

My third year class photo, St Joseph's Convent, 1983. St Joseph's was the only school I was ever truly happy at.

*Above*: This is one of my favourite photos of Linda, Mum and me at the viewpoint overlooking Maracas Bay, Trinidad. I can't remember what Dad said as he took the picture but he had us all in hysterics.

*Left*: Just look at those dodgy perms! Linda and me, 1989.

Nick and I were so excited as we set off on our round-the-world adventure.

Things seemed perfect in those early days.

Clare and me in our little house in Chester, 1993. We had some fun times there.

*Left*: My first ever photo shoot, 1996. It was for The Weather Channel. What did they do to my hair?!

*Below*: In front of my beloved *GMTV* weather map. Everyone always asked me how I knew where to point!

*Left*: Eamonn Holmes and me on the hallowed red couch. I was pregnant with Finlay at the time.

*Below*: About to go into Kingston Hospital to be induced, 28 October 2001. I was eleven days overdue and weighed nearly thirteen stone.

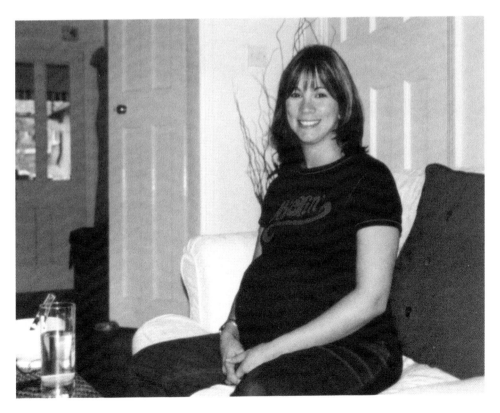

*Above*: It was the plight of fifteen-year-old Mathapelo that first caught Sue's attention and led to our trip out to Mamone.

*Left*: One of the most rewarding jobs I've ever done involved working alongside veteran news reporter Sue Jameson (pictured) helping local people in the remote village of Mamone, South Africa.

Back in South Africa to film a travel piece for *GMTV.* I decided it was a good idea to rap jump (abseil face down) off Table Mountain. But it didn't seem like such an exciting prospect when I got to the top...

My gorgeous little boy Finlay and me, 2005.

*Right*: The afternoon I took Finlay to skate at the Natural History Museum I got the call to go on *Dancing on Ice*. Who knew what a change to my life that call would make?

*Opposite*: Me, Billy (the lighting man) and Penny Smith at another brilliant *GMTV* Christmas party. They were my favourite nights of the year, where crew, production and presenters all let their hair down.

*Left*: On *Dancing On Ice* with my partner Doug Webster during the first live show. I had to smile through the excruciating pain of a cracked rib.

*Opposite*: My last day at *GMTV,* 31 Dec 2008, just before the car arrived to take me back to the studio for my surprise leaving do.

LIVE    TRAFALGAR SQUARE

gm.tv
7:57
GMTV

A typical photo of Jane and me. We have hundreds of these! Jane is much more than a best friend of thirty years; we have helped each other through tough times by talking, listening, and above all, laughing our socks off.

*Left*: On set filming *A Landscape of Lies* – my first ever film role! I played a woman with a secret dark side...

*Above right*: On the *Loose Women* set with Sally Lindsay and the fabulous Joan Collins. I'm always secretly thrilled when she comes on the show and answers one of my questions with 'Well, Andrea...' Joan Collins knows my name!

*Opposite*: The 2011 *Loose Women* Summer Party, with Lisa Maxwell, Carol McGiffin, Denise Welch, me and Jenny Eclair. I love this picture; you just know something naughty is about to happen!

*Left*: Just the girls. Me with my beautiful daughter Amy, aged four.

*Right*: Steve, me, Finlay and Amy at the local school fete, which had a cowboy theme. We love any excuse to get dressed up!

*Below*: Finlay took this picture of Steve and me relaxing at home.

At the launch of the *Christmas With The Loose Women* DVD. At the stage of forty-two I'm finally comfortable in my own skin. They say that life begins at forty and I only had to wait a little longer than that...

needed to know if this man could fix what had broken inside me, if he could give me the love I so desperately needed. I was terrified as I arranged to meet him for the first time because I knew what this meant; I was going to cross a line that could never be uncrossed.

He was quiet and calm when he held me for the first time, and my mind reeled — the arms around me belonged to someone else, the mouth kissing mine was not my husband's, but it felt right when it should have felt so wrong. It felt like coming home; *this* was where I was supposed to be. This was happiness.

I think I went a little bit mad; I was deliriously happy when I was with Steve, almost manically so. He cared for me and made me feel protected and looked after; he was my knight in shining armour. Then I was consumed with loathing, guilt and self-hatred; what was I *doing?* I lived in constant gut-churning fear that I would be found out, which of course weeks later I was, and my life changed forever. I had known it would come, you couldn't do something so awful and not expect to be found out. Someone found out and went to the papers with the story, and my world imploded. Any rational decisions about what we were going to do about the state of our marriage evaporated in the press frenzy that followed. Within months I was living on my own with Finlay, being divorced for adultery.

I had broken a dream that had begun back on the day when lightning struck me in that sixth-form common room, when I had fallen truly, madly and deeply in love for the first time.

There could be no going back from what I did, because even if Nick had found it in him to forgive me, I could never forgive myself. It was no more than I deserved.

★ ★ ★

Much has been written about my actions at the end of my marriage, some of it true but most of it speculation and hearsay. It was something out of character, and I am ashamed that I caused pain to people I loved. I could not have written the story of my life without talking about it, but rather than indulging in whys and wherefores, I point the finger of blame for my actions directly at myself. No one forced me to do it.

I betrayed my husband in the worst way that a wife can. I let him and his lovely family down, and I brought shame on my own. My parents had always been proud of me, but now I felt they were ashamed of me.

No matter how badly I felt people thought of me, though, it didn't come close to how I felt about myself — I *hated* myself. In my life my role had always been the good girl, the lovely daughter, sister and friend. I liked it that way. I knew where I was and I enjoyed being the one who tried hard to do things properly.

If any of my friends had told me they had committed adultery, I would have listened and nodded and given advice, but never really understood. 'How selfish,' the old me would have thought; 'you need to work at things, not just throw in the towel when it's all got a bit

184

much.' And I would have carried on cleaning my lovely home, feeding my lovely baby and caring for my lovely husband. I would have smugly thought that *I* would never do anything like that. But I did, and I didn't know who I was for a long while afterwards. To me I wasn't a lovely person any more; I was a selfish, evil woman and I didn't know how I could ever get back from that.

The effects of my behaviour didn't confine themselves to my family; they rippled out to friends and colleagues as well. Although I was at the epicentre, and I will never forget that. I was cast aside by people I thought knew me and cared about me, because I had thrown their world out of kilter. If someone like me could act so out of character, it rocked their faith in everything else. I was not how they had labelled, boxed and indexed me, so where should they put me now? Where did I fit? I became a stain that might contaminate them, so they slid away, out of reach so that their world stayed white and clean.

It rocked my best friend's world, too; why had I never told her how unhappy I was? And why had she not seen it coming? Jane chided herself for not being a better friend before I threw the emotional grenade into my world, and then proved herself to be superhuman in her support of me afterwards. She didn't judge or question, she just listened, and I could not have made it through that period of my life without her.

\* \* \*

It took a year for my divorce to come through, and during that time I lived two streets away from my old marital home. I felt this gave Finlay some continuity and meant he could see his father whenever he wanted. It felt like the right thing to do, and I desperately wanted to do something right. The house I bought was horrible; it had been rented out and was filthy, with drug needles on the floor and waist-high grass in the back garden. But it was all I could afford to buy, and it was in the area I needed it to be in, so I took it. Steve and his team worked tirelessly to clean it up for me. I think he saw it as penance for the situation I was now in.

My sister Linda moved in with me. Sadly, her marriage had ended too, and she had taken herself off to Australia for a year to lick her wounds and recover. Now she was back and in need of somewhere to stay, while I needed someone to stay with me, as I left the house at 4 a.m. most mornings and wanted someone I trusted to be there for Finlay, to care about him as much as I did and take him to nursery each day. Linda was a quiet, supportive rock in my wobbly world and, like Jane, I could not have survived my first year on my own without her.

Steve and I saw each other twice a week: on Wednesdays and at weekends when Finlay was with his dad. He coped with my tears and self-loathing with constant reassurance and a steady hand, and when I look back on those times, I think we must have both been slightly mad; me because my world had been turned upside down, and him for staying with me as I veered from despair to frenzied happiness, then back to my neutral setting of numb disbelief at the course my life had taken.

I needed help to get some direction in my life so I began to cut out sayings from magazines that really struck a chord with me, and one in particular, *What doesn't kill you makes you stronger*, became my mantra. It helped me make sense of the way I was feeling. *This too will pass* was another one. It was meant to make you appreciate that all moments are transient; both good and bad times end. For months I read it every day and clung to it. One day it would be over, one day I would be able to breathe again, and feel, and see, and smell. I would just be cross when someone butted in front of me in traffic, rather than filling up with tears and pulling over to sob because it seemed such a nasty thing to do. One day I'd be able to listen to the radio without feeling stabbed in the heart by the words to songs — any songs; sad, happy, nothing in particular — which all seemed to be about me. I just wanted to be numb again like the rest of the human race, who were all busy with nothing, getting wound up over nothing, being bored with the nothingness of their lives.

I went to work at *GMTV* each day, where everything carried on as normal. I remember sitting in the make-up chair one day, listening to two researchers gossiping as they worked. They seemed to go on and on, and their conversation was about *nothing*. It was all so pointless; I felt hot rage pour into me, and I wanted to scream at them, *Have you no bloody idea what life is really like? Do you really think it matters what kind of shoes you wear on a first date, when you're going to the cinema and sitting in the dark? Have you any idea what it is like to have real problems? I can't believe I have to listen to this when my life is falling apart.* Instead Simon the lovely make-up artist dabbed silently at the tears dripping down my face and squeezed my shoulder as I stared straight ahead at the mirror, unable to meet his eyes.

Most of the time during the day I held it together well; so much so that no one really noticed that I wasn't quite right. Some might have commented that I was a little quiet, but I still smiled, I still listened, I still produced. It was the nights that were hardest. Once the rush of the day was over, once Finlay was in bed and finally asleep, and toys had been tidied and dishes washed, that was when I struggled. What did I *do*? On the nights when my sister was out leading a perfectly normal life, there was no one to share my day with. No one to care that the graphics on my weather map had frozen on air that morning, or that the director had had a meltdown over talkback during one broadcast and forgot to switch me off, so I heard the whole four-lettered tirade while smiling and telling the nation that they were going to need a brolly. No one to tell how three-year-old Finlay had got on at nursery that day, or to laugh at the fact that he was refusing to answer to his name; he now insisted on being called Tarzan, and on stripping down to his underpants as soon as he walked through the front door to be just like him.

I didn't want to look needy to Steve every time he called, and I didn't want to bother him every time I had a wobble. So I drank. I opened the bottle of wine while I was preparing Finlay's supper, and gulped the first glass down while I put fish fingers in the oven. I finished the second with my dinner, sitting at the table with him, pushing fish fingers around my plate, while coaxing him to eat all of his. I got through the third after he'd gone to sleep, and the fourth while watching *Coronation Street*. Then I'd switch off the TV and just sit, and wait for the tears to come. And they did.

Sometimes I cried so loudly I thought the neighbours would come round to see if I was OK, and I hoped to God they wouldn't — I didn't want anyone seeing me like this. Sometimes, I woke up stiff and sore on the living-room floor, my face wet, needing to blow my nose and have a wee. I'd throw the empty bottles into the bin, and go to bed to sleep like the dead, and then start all over again when my alarm went off at 3.30 a.m. the next day. This was my life now.

The most difficult times were when people asked how I was. They were split into three camps, as far as I was concerned: those who just wanted to hear, 'Fine, thanks, and you?'; those who wanted all the gory details and to know exactly what had happened so they could recount the story with a sad, serious face, and talk about how 'their friend' was doing; and finally, those who cared. To those who counted, only one word would do: I was 'sad'.

189

I knew that by now I should have been feeling better; I knew people were bored of it, and of me. After a while, they stopped asking, because they didn't know what I'd say. Because some days I started talking and couldn't stop, and all this stuff came out, all this anger and grief and guilt, and I could see in their eyes that they wished they hadn't asked, and they wished I'd just said I was fine, but some days I wasn't fine. Some days I felt like my nerves had been cut and the pain was raw and I'd do anything, anything just to numb it. My head hurt.

I lost around two stone in weight because I couldn't eat. My mouth would dry up and my throat would constrict and a little voice would whisper, *You don't deserve to eat anything nice* . . . and instantly my appetite would disappear. I couldn't swallow food because I had no spit in my mouth. Have you ever tried to eat with no saliva? Everything tastes like cardboard and goes into a big lump, and in the end you have to spit it out because it just isn't going anywhere. And even if you do manage to swallow it, you think you're going to be sick, so you have to fight to keep it in.

Even when I could eat again, it felt wrong. If something tasted nice, and I liked it, and my plate was half empty, out of nowhere the little voice would reappear, just like that, and I'd have to put down my knife and fork and pretend I was full. People would say, 'Gosh, I wish I could lose weight when I get stressed, I just eat like a pig! And *look* at you,' as if having their whole world crumble around them and losing any semblance of the person they believed themselves to be was a luxury they wished they had.

I became panicky because I felt everyone was looking at me and judging. Because I had failed to keep the standards I felt we should all live up to, I thought that everyone must hate me as much as I hated myself. If I put my bin bag outside my front door, I felt as though people were whispering, 'There she is; that's the one . . . ' Because everyone knew what I had done. One particularly nasty neighbour passed me in the street one day and sneered in my face, 'Not so clever now, are we?' and laughed as she walked to her front door. I turned around, went back into my house and cried until I was sick.

I would only go out to work, the supermarket and the park with my son, and that was it. And always with my head down. Even my favourite pastime of visiting the cinema was taken away from me, as when I sat in the darkness, knowing that I was invisible, the voice would whisper in my ear again, *You don't deserve to be enjoying this*, and I would sit frozen in my seat, willing the film to end so I could go home and hide.

# 12

## Becoming a Single Mum

It was during this time that I started smoking. I wanted to punish myself by doing something that I knew was bad for me, and because I was too scared to take drugs and I'm not a big drinker, I decided that I would take up smoking instead.

No one noticed or probably cared on the afternoon that I walked into Sainsbury's Local just off Piccadilly in London and joined the queue at the cigarette counter. I had never joined this queue before and I felt quite rebellious and a little scared. I was doing a *bad thing*, but my life was one huge bad thing, so what difference would it make? The queue shuffled forward slowly, and shoppers made their way in and out, oblivious to the churning going on inside an ordinary-looking woman about to do an extraordinary thing. There was a man in front of me in the queue; one more to go and then it would be my turn. I strained to hear what he was saying. I'd never asked for cigarettes before; how did I make sure I asked for the right thing?

As the man paid for his mysterious cigarettes (I couldn't quite catch what he said, and I didn't want to get too close and look like a nutter), my hands started to shake like a drug smuggler at the airport with a cocker spaniel approaching.

There was no way out; it was my turn next. I couldn't walk away now. I was going to do this. As he walked past me, the bored shop assistant looked up and sighed, 'Next . . . '

I leaned casually on the counter and said, 'Same again, please, and a lighter.'

She turned around and grabbed a packet of cigarettes, and as she did I was convinced that at any second an army of black-clad balaclava-wearing SAS men would abseil down the front of the shop, smash through the windows, and in a hail of broken glass and impressive forward rolls would pull their guns out, point them at me and yell, 'Freeze!' I froze, and nothing happened. I paid; she put the money in the till, slammed down the change, looked over my shoulder and shouted, 'Next!'

I scuttled out the door like the dirty little rat that I was. No alarms sounded, no men in black stormed the building, nothing. I had just bought a packet of cigarettes and no one had even tried to stop me. Outrageous.

I made my way across the road to Green Park, stopping to buy an *Evening Standard* and a bottle of water. It would give me something to do while I smoked, and I'd need the water to wash the taste away. I found a spot in the sunshine and sat down. There was a couple nearby, chatting and laughing, and a man sitting on his own, reading the paper. No one was smoking; I was going to be the only one.

Feeling like I was in a *Mr Bean* sketch, I took the packet from my handbag and unwrapped the cellophane. Then, trying to look like I knew what

I was doing, I unfolded the top flap of gold paper and pulled out a cigarette. They looked all neat and orderly inside the box, not naughty at all. I placed it between my lips, flicked the lighter and sucked until I felt the smoke fill my mouth. Then I put the lighter down, leaned back and inhaled. The smoke was strong and thick, and it hurt. I held it for a few seconds then exhaled, watching the smoke coming out of my mouth. I inhaled again, too much and too fast, and I coughed as the smoke burned my throat and my eyes. I exhaled again and felt the world start to tip a little. Another drag, and then another, and another and by now I was so light-headed I was beginning to feel slightly ill. It was just what I wanted; I felt spaced-out, sick and disgusting. I lay back on the grass and watched the smoke rise from the cigarette held in the V of my two fingers. It looked cool, and a bit edgy.

I sat up and started flicking through my newspaper. My first cigarette had finished so I lit up another — I was getting quite good at this. I turned the pages and flicked my ash onto the grass. Even that felt naughty — it was like littering, but *allowed*. *Look at me, sitting in the centre of London on a hot day, just chillin' and smokin'. I'm going to be a divorced single mother soon, and this is what we do. Yeah, I'm modern. Doris Day is dead, long live . . . who?* My heart froze a little. I liked being Doris Day; who would I be if I stopped being Doris?

My mobile rang. 'Hello?' I answered, casually holding my (now third) cigarette in my left hand. 'Hello, love, just ringing to see how you are.' It was my then agent, Dave Warwick, one of the nicest men in the universe.

'Hi, Dave, I'm fine,' I said airily.

'What you up to, sweetheart?'

'I'm just sitting in the park, enjoying the sunshine, having a fag.' Oh! Even saying it out loud felt cool.

'Having a *what*? A fag? You don't smoke!'

'I've just started. I'm on my third, and I'm getting quite good at it now.'

'I see. Is this going to become a regular thing, then?'

I could hear the disappointment in Dave's soft northern voice. I blocked it out, mentally sticking my fingers in my ears and singing *la la la*.

'Oh yes, I think so. It's not as bad as I thought.'

'Right, well then, I'll be off to get you a pipe and a deerstalker hat, because if you're going to smoke you might as well have the outfit to go with it. Look after yourself, sweetheart.'

Click.

Deerstalker hat? I was thinking more slinky black dress and Trevi fountain like *La Dolce Vita*, not Sherlock Holmes.

And so I smoked on and off until I was forty, when one night, in the middle of a party while puffing away on my fag and supping my vodka and tonic, I suddenly hated the taste of it. I stubbed it out, and haven't had one since. Just like that. I think I don't smoke any more because I don't need to. My days of punishing myself are over — and if I ever start craving a packet of

Marlboro again, I'll ask myself why.

I can't deny that I miss it sometimes, especially when everyone heads outside for a ciggie, as it is a fact that all the coolest people smoke, and you hear the *best* gossip when you're huddled together outside. If only everyone would start using those white sweeties with the red tips that we used to pretend were cigarettes, I could happily wave one of them around while nibbling on the end . . .

★　★　★

Gradually, as time passed, I learned to ignore the petty things people said, and stopped looking for new, painful ways to punish myself. With the help of those close to me, the people who really mattered, I started to see that I had not changed from being a good girl into a wicked woman; I was just me. I had needed to make life-changing decisions about myself and my marriage, and my lack of life experience meant that I handled a difficult situation clumsily, and people I loved and who loved me got hurt. I will always be sorry for that, but I don't hate myself any more.

Before, I was the kind of person who thought that everything had to be perfect or else it would all crack and break. Now I see that brittle perfection is fragile and unreal, and I appreciate that life comes with bumps and grazes. I don't think that there is such a thing as a golden happily ever after. I try to appreciate what I have and do the best I can. Perfection in itself doesn't exist, in our behaviour, our daily life or in our expectations. I've realized we are allowed to make a mess of things sometimes, that it doesn't transform you from being 'good' to 'bad'; it just makes you human.

I can't put my finger on exactly when I started to heal, but bit by bit the raw, heavy, claustrophobic pain I had felt immediately after the divorce lifted, and I could feel myself rejoining the rest of the human race, becoming numb and nicely selfish and self-absorbed by the minutiae of my life, and not by its terrors. I started seeing the funny side of things again. The world was still a harsh and tragic place, but my emotions were now able to cope with that. Years earlier, I remember hearing an athlete being asked if he missed competing. His answer had struck me as strange at the time, but while I was healing it made sense. 'No, I don't miss it,' he'd said, smiling. 'I don't miss the pain, the constant pain and stress of battle. Now I can relax and just enjoy the sport.'

That's what I was doing with my life now; trying to relax and enjoy the sport. But I also began to realize that I had substituted one kind of pain for another — the pain I now felt was the constant guilt of a single mother. The guilt that I wasn't doing the best job I could, that I didn't try hard enough, that my actions had made Finlay suffer, and he would continue to suffer because he was being raised by a single parent. I had never contemplated the idea of raising a child alone before; it was off my radar. People met, fell in love, got married and lived happily ever after — wasn't that what all those books I'd read had promised? Wasn't that what my parents had done? When I'd heard of women boldly announcing that they were going to have a baby on their own, that they didn't need a *man* to complete them, I'd been bemused; I *liked* having a man beside me, loving me. It was difficult enough raising a child, but to decide to do it alone, deliberately; that was something that took real guts. Or selfishness. Or, in some cases, desperation. But to me, at that time, it wasn't a natural decision. I felt a child should be raised by its parents, and the fact that mine wasn't, despite how well I tried to do on my own, broke my heart.

I often looked at Finlay as he played with his friends, and wondered how he was, how he felt about things. It was a tough time for him too, and he coped with it as well as he could, but it makes my heart hurt to think that he might still be suffering.

Finlay has grown into a beautiful young boy, and I am proud of him every single day. He is quirky like me, and clever like his dad, and I will never stop worrying about him. He enjoys solo sports, like rock climbing and swimming — which makes me laugh now, as he used to HATE it. As a baby, he climbed on top of my head and screamed when I took him to the local tiny tots' swim class with my antenatal friends. All the other babies thrived at it, even the bit when they were submerged and made to swim to the surface. Some of the women had beautiful pictures taken of their chubby offspring, wide-eyed and bubble-nosed, swimming under the water . . . Finlay yelled like he was being murdered and had to be taken out of the pool as he was 'disturbing the other babies'. I went home, deflated and damp, wondering why he couldn't muck in like all the other little ones and just go with the flow.

He never was a 'go with the flow' kind of baby; everything was a big deal to Finlay, from teething to eating and sleeping, even bath time — that supposed time of mummy-baby bonding at the end of the day — had been a tortuous ordeal. Every night was a battle of wills, with Finlay winning pretty much every time, and me reduced to a tearful, wine-craving wreck. He was a difficult toddler: he head-banged the floor in frustration at not getting his own way, he head-butted me, bit me, scratched and screamed at me . . . within a year this delightful little bundle I'd so carefully taken home from hospital transformed into a devil child who couldn't make it through an hour without a tantrum of seismic proportions.

During that time, while I was struggling to pull myself together and get to grips with going it alone, some of my darkest moments came while worrying that I had ruined not only my ex-husband's life, but also our child's. Those moments hit me at the strangest times, usually when I was least expecting them . . .

One night when Finlay was tucked up in bed, I decided to shower before turning in. There was something so relaxing about standing under the warm water, knowing that Finlay was sound asleep; that he wasn't downstairs on his own while I rushed a quick wash. Or that he wasn't going to burst in on me while I was on the toilet, demanding to know what I was doing. I chuckled to myself while lathering my hair. He'd found an old Tampax in my handbag that evening while I was getting him ready for bed, and as a curious three-year-old he had held it up.

'What's this, Mummy?'

'Er . . . that's a tampon.'

'I like tampons,' he said happily and put it back in my bag. 'They taste funny and they stick to your tongue, but I like them.'

I had struggled to keep a straight face, and he'd carried on looking for his pyjamas. I had no idea what he was talking about, but I knew for certain what he had in his hand wasn't what *he* thought it was. *Another one for the list*, I thought as I washed. And then I realized: I had stopped keeping a list of the funny things Finlay said and did. I hadn't written anything down since . . . I stopped mid-thought, and felt the suds of shampoo trickle down my face and plop onto the shower floor. My whole life had stopped since then. I hadn't felt, seen or done anything that was normal for most of his third year. Poor, poor Finlay.

This time, the tears came quickly. I thought I would drown with grief, as I put my face under the jet of water to wash the shampoo out of my face and eyes. I gulped, and gasped in some wet air, and crouched in the bath while the water ran over me. I put my face in my hands and cried and cried and cried, the water pounding on my head and back. My poor, poor boy. He'd not had a daddy properly in his life for over a year, and I now realized he hadn't had a mummy either.

I cried until there were no more tears left. I cried for my little boy; my innocent, sweet, frustrating, exhausting little boy. How had he survived the past year? How had he managed to stay so innocent? I thought back to our conversation at bed time; he had held my face, smiling, and asked, 'Are you happy, Mummy?'

I had kissed his warm head and said, 'I'm always happy when I'm with you. Night night.'

And I'd turned out the light. Maybe he wasn't as unaware as I'd thought; maybe he had just made sense of it all in his own way, without my help or guidance. I cried thinking of him sorting it out in his own little head, without me there to help him. I had been so lost in my own sense of loss, I hadn't been able to cope with the idea of his; I had clung to the idea that he was too young — too young to remember anything, and too young to understand.

Eventually I stood up, my legs shaking, and carried on with my shower. I conditioned my hair and slowly washed my body, thinking of Finlay all the while. *Tomorrow is another day*, I thought as I washed. Tomorrow my life starts again, and so does Finlay's.

*And look at him now*, I think to myself every day. At almost ten, he is calm and happy and a joy to be around. He has come through the other side of a difficult first few years, and seems as normal and content as I could hope for. Isn't that all any mother could want? To have a happy and healthy child? That's not to say I don't feel the familiar mummy guilt trickle into my heart — maybe it *was* my fault he'd been such a terrible toddler? Maybe he'd sensed my unhappiness, and Nick's? He could have picked up on our stress; he is sensitive and aware, more so than other children his age. If he did, I am so sorry, and I hope he knows that in my own clumsy way I have tried to be a good mum, and always will.

# 13

## Bollywood or Bust

'Run!' shouted Ravi, the sound man.

I looked at him, confused. I was in the middle of walking through the colourful and iconic washing area of the Dhobi Ghat in historic Mumbai, while smiling at the cameraman filming me from the road above. I was ankle-deep in water, as all around me clothes were being bashed onto concrete and men and women squatted over their brightly coloured laundry.

Ravi was gesturing wildly at me, and the look in his eyes was desperate. He shouted something else, but by now I had grabbed his hand and was hauling myself out of the water. I hopped from one foot to another as I put on my flip-flops and was still unsteady when he pushed me in front of him and shouted again, this time louder, 'RUN!'

Looking over my shoulder, I saw a cluster of men walking briskly towards us, their brown skin wet with water. They were dressed in the international uniform of poverty: ragged trousers, torn T-shirts, and some only had loin cloths around their middle. I glanced at their faces: they were not happy. More specifically, it gradually dawned, they were not happy with ME.

I quickened my pace, and heard Ravi shouting

into his mobile phone in his native tongue. Tripping past women and children who looked up, seeming to notice me for the first time, I hurried towards the concrete steps leading to the road, my wet feet sliding in my shoes. By now the men were close and I could hear Ravi trying to placate them, in between shouting into his phone. The steps were just ahead of me and I glanced behind; the women had now joined the men in chasing us, and they too looked very, very angry. Gathering my cotton dress, I ran up the stairs two at a time, towards Abdul the cameraman, who stood at the stoop at the top of the stairs, shouting, 'Hurry! Hurry!' and waving his right arm at me. 'Come! Come! You must leave! Get in! Get in!'

*Get in what?* I gasped, my chest heaving and sweat streaming down my red face as I made it to the last step. By now a crowd had gathered at the side of the road, peering over the bridge to the laundry below to see what all the shouting was about. Now the people in front of me were as angry as those closing in from behind.

The cameraman lunged forward and grabbed my arm, pushing me roughly towards our car. The door was open and I was shoved head first, banging my head on the rear-view mirror and half landing on the driver, who had already released the clutch and was screeching forwards into the oncoming traffic. I hauled myself upright and pulled the door shut, as fists hammered down on the window and angry faces shouted words I couldn't understand. I swivelled round in my seat as we careered down the road, astounded at the sight behind me — a throng of people, shouting and waving their arms at the car, were now rounding on my crew, who were trying to get into their car with their equipment intact. How had this happened?

It had all started so differently forty-eight hours earlier, when my producer Jeremy and I buckled ourselves into our first-class seat on the Air India flight bound for Mumbai. We had congratulated ourselves on landing what had to be the assignment of the year: a visit to India and the opportunity to film a behind-the-scenes look at the thriving industry that is Bollywood. It was a trip that had been won in an auction at a ball by one of our bosses at *GMTV* and it was up to us to get ourselves out there, hook up with a local crew and get footage of the sights and sounds of the city, as well as my shining moment — a walk-on part in a Bollywood film! I was going to show what it was like behind the scenes in the biggest movie industry in the world, and give a flavour of the city that housed it. We clinked our champagne glasses and giggled as the plane took off from London. This was my first trip away from Finlay, but I knew he was perfectly happy at home with his dad.

Things took a slightly ugly turn on our arrival in India, when Jeremy — who was noted for his short temper and at times erratic behaviour — decided to shout at the top of his voice that he wasn't happy about not being able to use his bank card to get cash out as the bank was shut. I left him yelling at an official and decided to hail a taxi. I had worked with Jeremy many times, and knew from experience that it was best to let him get on with it; either the whole matter would be forgotten about in ten minutes, or he would be arrested. It was best to stand back in case it was the latter.

It was my second time visiting India, and it couldn't have been more different to my first experience when Nick and I started off our backpacking trip there. I remembered holding back the tears as we boarded a bus into the dusty city, and made our way, exhausted and terrified, to a youth hostel. Now, twelve years later, I had arrived by first class and was on my way to the infamous Taj Mahal hotel!

As I was negotiating with the driver, Jeremy bustled up and threw himself into the back seat. 'Oh, for fuck's sake! Just take us to the Taj and don't rip us off!'

The driver looked at me and I shrugged and smiled as he put the old car into gear and pulled away.

'Fucking hell, this place!'

I said nothing and looked out the window while he ranted on, waiting for Jeremy to get his venting out of his system. The night streets of Mumbai raced by. It was like being in an Indiana Jones film: the driver was weaving in and out of the traffic, cars and pedestrians hurling themselves out of the way as we dodged right, then left, then right again, shooting straight over roundabouts and causing cars to screech and brake, beeping their horns furiously at us. But the treacherous journey didn't bother me; this was nothing compared to the prospect of being locked away.

I was still irritated by Jeremy's tantrums when the car pulled up at the hotel; even the magnificent reception area and our warm welcome didn't help. Jeremy and I made our way in silence to our rooms, down centuries-old corridors past rooms that had housed visiting dignitaries and royalty. We were in the old part of the hotel, with cool whitewashed walls and tiles underfoot.

'See you in the morning,' I said cooly and shut my door.

The next day, waking up in my cream room, the wooden latticework over my window filtering the morning sunlight, I decided to start again. We were in an amazing hotel, this was an amazing opportunity and this was going to be an amazing day. I showered and changed, getting myself ready for my day on set as an extra in a Bollywood movie. Amazing.

Jeremy was waiting for me at breakfast, and in unspoken agreement we ignored his bad mood of the previous day.

It was a short taxi ride to the location; we were going to be joining the Indian film crew on site at a local café, where the day's story revolved around the hero of the film meeting up with a beautiful girl. Sadly there was to be no singing or dancing today, always a vibrant and beautiful spectacle. I grew up watching Bollywood movies while living in the Caribbean. With the large Indian population of Trinidad, and the fact that there was only ever one channel to watch, the TV was a mixture of American comedy, Afro-Caribbean talent shows and Indian movies. Every Sunday my sister and I would let my parents have a lie-in as we watched improbable plots unfold, reading the subtitles as best we could. I've had a soft spot for them ever since.

We arrived, both a little excited and unsure what was going to happen next. Well, the quick answer was . . . not much. No one had a clue that we were coming; they knew nothing about it. Jeremy showed the small nervous-looking assistant his papers, which outlined in detail the auction prize, and explained that we had flown all the way from England just to do this. There was shrugging. So Jeremy changed tack, and pointed at me, as I sucked in my tummy and gave my brightest smile.

'She is a HUGE STAR back in England! She was chosen especially by the head of the biggest television station in the UK to star in YOUR film! How do I explain to our boss that you have snubbed her? The press in the UK are going to go crazy over this!'

Our own film crew got it all on camera; they were filming everything I did, which made us look a little more impressive.

The assistant frowned and looked a little rattled. Jeremy shook his head, and I hoped he hadn't brought anything with him to 'relax'. There was a huddle around the director, a bit of gesticulation, some nodding, and then the assistant came back all smiles. I was to get my shining moment after all. And so, it would seem, would Jeremy.

We were led together to a table at the front of the café and ushered to our seats. And over the course of a morning, the scene was shot. It took a couple of hours, but eventually everyone was happy and it was in the bag. My role? Well, as the assistant shouted, 'ACTION!' everyone in the café started chatting quietly among themselves. As the camera slowly tracked past a small bush, I had to lift my cup of (now cold) coffee to my lips and laugh at something that Jeremy said. The camera focused on my laughing face and then slowly passed me, to the handsome star of the movie sat at the table behind us. He had a bit of dialogue with a beautiful Indian girl, then they both got up and left. After roughly one hundred takes, which I'm sure was not because of me (my smiling was genuine because Jeremy was being hilarious and VERY rude, knowing I couldn't react), they got what they wanted.

'So,' he whispered to me, knowing we weren't mic'd for sound so he could get away with it, 'the last time I shagged this guy . . . '

I almost spat my coffee all over him.

' . . . he was so fucking huge I thought I was going to end up in hospital. Seriously. I'd never seen anything like it!'

I tried to keep my face impassive as the camera swept by for my close up.

Somewhere out there, in one of the hundreds of movies released in 2004, is one where a British girl sits in the foreground of a café scene, giggling into her cold coffee as her secret dreams of overnight Bollywood stardom dissolve like the leftover sugar in her cup — sweet and pointless.

209

We had allowed a full day, as we hadn't been sure exactly what was expected of us, which left Jeremy and I with an afternoon free. We used the time well, and booked a taxi to take us around the city, allowing us to put together a filming schedule for the next day. We scribbled notes and listed places of interest, cobbling together a running order and script between us, the basic premise being my arrival in Mumbai and my take on this amazing city. It would take in the sights that people would expect — the beautiful and historic hotel where we were staying (which made filming there very easy), the sights around the harbour, the city itself, the local washing area where people gathered every day to wash their clothes, and finally the beach at sunset, where people came to see and be seen. We congratulated ourselves on being so organized and headed back to the hotel. After a shower and a freshen-up, Jeremy and I met for dinner.

'I think we should celebrate your starring role!' he said, and he ordered a bottle of wine with our starters.

'I think we should celebrate yours!' I said as I ordered another bottle with our main course.

'I think we should toast our success!' we giggled as we made our way to the bar and ordered some tequila slammers.

The disco was calling and we answered, two badly dancing British visitors in one of the poshest hotels in India, hopping and bopping and laughing like lunatics to bhangra among the Mumbai elite. It was one of the funniest nights of my life; I have never, ever laughed so much.

The next day I crawled out of bed at 8 a.m. after what felt like four minutes' sleep. I looked and felt disgusting. I showered and dressed, then made my way to Jeremy's room. I knocked, swaying slightly and wondering if he felt as terrible as I did. The door opened and Jeremy stood in the doorway, his fluffy dressing gown open over his boxer shorts. He looked worse.

He turned away and I followed him into the room. It looked like it had exploded. Jeremy bolted to the left, and his bathroom door slammed. The room was filled with the unmistakable sounds of a very sick man. When he eventually came back into the bedroom, Jeremy was shaking.

'I think I'm dying,' he said, and laid himself down. He certainly didn't look very well. 'I've been sick all night,' he gasped, 'and all that's coming out is blood.'

Shock bolted through me. 'Blood? Oh my God, Jeremy, you need to see a doctor.'

'I know.' He was lying with his eyes shut on the bed. 'I've called down to reception and they're sending one over.'

'Is there anything I can do? Can I get you anything?'

'I don't need anything, but you are going to have to do today's filming on your own. There is no way I can do anything today.'

Alarm made sickness rise in me, but I squashed it down. Jeremy was very ill, I could see that. 'OK. Well, we plotted it all out yesterday, so it should be fine. Do you have all the paperwork?'

He gestured to the table in the corner of the room. There was a folder with 'Bollywood' written on it in blue biro. I picked it up and looked inside.

'There are the numbers of the crew we're meeting at ten o'clock in reception. I've sent them over the details of today, so they know what we want to film. They've told me it's all sorted.'

'Do we have filming permits?'

'They said we don't need any, but I have the general permit I arranged before we left the UK. That should get us out of trouble.'

There was a knock at the door, and I let in the smartly dressed receptionist and what looked like a doctor.

'Thank you so much for getting here so quickly,' I said, and stood quietly out of the way as the doctor began his examinations. Jeremy explained about his sickness, and the doctor asked him to breathe in and out while he listened through a stethoscope. By now Jeremy was a strange grey colour.

'He needs to be tested in a hospital,' he told us. 'I will arrange it, and the hotel will sort out a car to collect you. For now, take this to stop the sickness.' He opened his bag and brought out a packet of tablets, scribbling on them. He nodded seriously at us, and let himself out. It was over in minutes.

'Hospital? Oh my God!' Jeremy started to cry, and then curled up in pain. The receptionist picked up the hotel phone and dialled quickly, speaking calmly but firmly in Gujarati.

I patted his head. 'I'll come with you.'

'No! We have to get this filming done, we can't go back with nothing!'

He had a point. Our guts would be made into *GMTV* garters if we went back empty-handed.

The receptionist looked at both of us. 'I will be with him,' she said. 'He has become ill in our hotel, it is our responsibility to look after him.'

Crikey. I couldn't imagine *that* happening back home.

'You've got the notes. Just do what we talked about yesterday. It will be fine. It's all arranged. It'll be fine.'

Two hours later, I was standing by the harbour at the Gateway to India, setting up my first piece to camera. The crew, when they arrived, were different from the previous day. They were a lovely group of men: a combination of enthusiastic amateur students and an older experienced cameraman. The sound man, Ravi, was a student who hadn't worked on a real filming project before, and had never even used a radio mic, (which is clipped on to a presenter's clothes and picked up by radio frequency), so didn't have one as part of his kit. Actually, he didn't have a kit, he just had a boom and a very long wire attaching him to the cameraman, but he was very enthusiastic and spoke good, if broken, English.

Ravi explained to the cameraman in Gujarati that I wanted him to pan down from the blue Indian sky as I walked into shot in front of the Gateway to India, say my piece and then keep walking as he panned away. It would mean coordinating it so he and I moved together, and if it worked, I could be filmed speaking while close enough to the boom to be heard. Normally I could do a 'walkie-talkie' piece to camera from as far away as I liked with a radio mic, but this wasn't an option.

The first few run-throughs were clumsy, but eventually I managed to make the team understand what I was after. We were just getting the hang of it when we were approached by an official-looking man. He spoke to the crew as I rooted in my bag for our filming permit, the one that had been emailed over from Mumbai before we left the UK. I handed it to Ravi; it is quite normal to be stopped by officials asking for filming permits, no matter where you are. I have been stopped in St James's Park in London, five minutes before I was about to go live with a weather broadcast. Luckily I only had one piece to camera left to do, so the smiling officers on horseback allowed me to do it standing next to them, and I let them say hello to their wives at home. That might have worked in the UK, but it cut no ice here, as the unsmiling man handed back the papers and said the word I really didn't want to hear: 'No.'

We packed up and headed back into the coolness of the hotel to have a drink and regroup. OK. So it seemed that the permit I had wasn't valid for filming in public places, which pretty much meant the whole of Mumbai. As the others drank their cold Cokes, I called Ravi and the cameraman over.

'So,' I began, 'what is the worst thing that

could happen if we get caught filming without the right papers in Mumbai?'

'We will be moved on,' said a nervous-looking Ravi. He was so obviously a rookie; I was sorry that I was breaking him in this way, but there was no time and I had a film to make and only a few hours left in which to film it.

'Is that the worst thing that could happen? Can we be arrested?'

Ravi swallowed, and asked the cameraman, who smiled knowingly. They rattled back and forth a bit in their native tongue, and I may not have understood the words, but I understood the sentiment. Not if we didn't get caught.

Ten minutes later I was in the front seat of a car being driven across Mumbai with a handful of men I had just met, only one of whom could communicate with me. I frowned as I read through the notes Jeremy and I had scribbled the previous day, scoring lines through proposed pieces to camera and scrawling 'Voice Over' in the margin. Without a radio mic the chances of surreptitiously walking and talking to a camera a discreet distance away were nil. That reduced our filming opportunities by two thirds.

We arrived at a street market, and from the passenger seat of the car I twisted round to instruct the men. The cameraman, who I now knew was called Abdul, was instructed to get as many 'GVs' (general views) as possible before I got out of the car and drew attention to them; a white girl would stand out more than a cameraman in Bollywood. He nodded and grinned as Ravi explained what I wanted, and I

215

got the impression this was the most fun he'd had in a long time. The others — I never really ascertained what they were there for — were deployed as lookouts, to let us know if an official was coming so we could get into our cars and get out of there.

With shots of sari stalls, spice sellers and tat pedlars in the bag, it was my turn. We would probably only get one shot at it before I was surrounded by children and adults trying to sell me something, so I got my lines straight in my head, smoothed down my sweaty hair as best I could and got out of the car, wandering away from the men and pretending to look at the wares on display. In the corner of my eye I saw Ravi nod to me that the camera was up to speed and that sound was ready. I turned slowly and walked towards them, looking gently to my left and right until Ravi was close to me with his furry boom outstretched. Hoping it wasn't in shot, I stopped and gave a brief description of where I was and how lovely it was, then turned and carried on walking.

As soon as I was five steps away I turned round and hurried back. Then Abdul shook his head — the boom was in shot.

'Keep rolling,' I said, and trotted back to my starting point. By now curious children had gathered round, bringing unwanted attention. He nodded and I did it again, this time with a dozen children in tow, tugging at my dress and laughing. Ravi looked nervous and jerked his head towards the car — we had better not push our luck.

We laughed as we drove on to our next spot: the train station, the Chhatrapati Shivaji Terminus, which used to be called Victoria Terminus. It's a beautiful building, and reminded me of St Pancras in London. We filmed quickly around it, mainly of me walking with the camera a long way away so we managed to get what we needed quickly and without bother. As we were en route to our next location, Ravi said quietly to me that the men were hungry and wanted their lunch break; they were used to an hour off at lunchtimes!

'OK,' I said, silently looking at my watch and calculating how much we had to film and how much time was left until the sun went down; we had no lights with us, and the crew were only booked for a day shoot. The cars headed to the edge of the city, where we stopped at the side of a dusty road. To our right was a queue of men, standing patiently in line in front of tables groaning under the weight of huge pots of curry that were being filled from steaming vats bubbling away behind them.

'This is where we eat,' said Ravi, and we got out. I joined the queue and stood at the back, watching what they did. Each man took a stainless-steel tray with a series of hollows for each dish, whatever it was. What looked like red lentil curry was slopped into the first hollow, then something brown, and then two neat chapattis. We moved along the line, holding out our trays, and then made our way to a plastic table and chairs away from the road but still in the harsh sunlight. I gave Ravi the money to pay for us and he returned with change. Everyone tucked in heartily, using chapattis and fingers as cutlery. As I dipped mine into the brown sauce I calculated that by the time the food poisoning kicked in I would be 36,000 feet in the air, and hopefully there would be a doctor on board. I swallowed.

A woman approached the table, scowling, and took our drinks order. Another brought our tray of chai and Pepsi, and threw me a filthy look. I looked back at her in surprise. What was her problem? Ravi saw what had happened and laughed.

'They think you are taking their business,' he smiled.

'How would I do that? I don't work here.'

'No, but you are a woman, and the men are looking at you rather than them, and that is bad for their business.'

'How can I have anything to do with what people have to drink?'

'The women here are not just for bringing chai.'

I looked around me, and for the first time noticed that I was indeed the only woman there, apart from the waitresses, who seemed to be smiling and flirting with their hungry customers. To the right was a small shack, roughly put together with wood and with a series of doors. I had assumed they were the toilets. The dawn of my realization was slow.

'You mean, they offer . . . other services?'

Ravi smiled at my astonishment. 'Yes.' He

218

calmly carried on eating his curry, and I looked around me with fresh eyes. Wow, did this happen on the M6, too?

Lunch sorted, I now had a job on my hands getting the men back into the cars. They were snoozy and ready for a post-lunch nap; no one else had the stress of not completing this job to keep them moving. Eventually I cajoled them onwards, with promises of an early finish and cold beer. Dhobi Ghat, apparently the world's largest open-air laundry was our next stop . . . and as we've seen, that did not go well.

We screeched away from the angry mob with my head reeling; how had I offended them? The driver didn't speak English, and was babbling into his phone at the others in the car behind.

'Tell them to meet us at Marine Drive!' I told him, scrabbling through my notes again.

Ravi never told me why I upset the men in the open air laundry, and I have looked into it since and found that it is a regular tourist haunt. Perhaps I ventured too far in, away from the periphery where visitors usually go. I hope my presence there didn't offend and that there was another more benign reason for the upset.

When we arrived at Marine Drive, the mood was subdued. I apologized sincerely to all the men for causing them such trouble, but promised them that this was the last bit of filming for the day. I just needed an end piece walking along the famous promenade where tourists and locals alike flocked to see the sunset, watching Mumbai by day go to sleep as the city nightlife awoke. They looked at the floor and

219

shuffled their feet. They were fading, and so was the sun — fast. I didn't have long.

With Abdul perched on the wall ahead of me, the camera steady on his shoulder, and Ravi crawling on his haunches below me, his boom wobbling just out of view, I managed to get my only 'walkie-talkie' of the day. Filthy, sweaty and with the light fading, I said my goodbye to Bollywood. Before they got too excited that their working day had finished, I put Ravi's headphones to my ears and instructed Abdul to rewind the tape, so I could hear for myself that we had a take. I could feel them holding their breath as I frowned into the tiny monitor, waiting for the final piece to start. There I was, walking along the wall in the pink dusky light, smiling and telling the world about my wonderful day in this colourful city of dreams . . . I could be seen, and I could be heard. The rest could be done in editing, with music, voiceovers and, if necessary, stock film of Mumbai. It was a wrap.

★   ★   ★

The car was quiet as the men drove me in convoy back to my hotel. We had started the day as strangers, and I still wasn't sure they quite understood what it was I'd been trying to do, but they had stuck by me and tried their damnedest to give what I asked of them. As we pulled up I invited them in, but Ravi shook his head and said the men would rather go to where they were comfortable to relax, and I understood. The Taj

220

was a wonderful hotel, but perhaps not the best place for a dusty Indian crew to knock back a few beers and talk about the strange British girl they had spent their day with.

I held out my hand and solemnly shook Ravi's. I took out the envelope that held all the rupees I possessed and I gave it to him.

'Take them all out and get them a drink for me,' I said. 'It's been a pleasure to work with you, and thank you.'

Ravi smiled shyly at me and got back into the car.

Back in the hotel, I allowed myself a smile as I knocked on Jeremy's door, then I dropped to my knees so I was on all fours when he opened the door.

'What the . . . ?'

I crawled towards him, filthy with dust, streaked with grime and sweat-stained, my hair flopped over my face. He couldn't see it, but I was smiling as I struggled past him into his room, dragging my bag behind me.

'I . . . did . . . it . . . ' I gasped and collapsed onto the floor.

'Fuck!' shouted Jeremy, and I could feel him shaking my shoulder. I rolled over, grinning up at him and holding out my bag of tapes.

'I got it. We have a film.' I laughed and got to my feet.

'You cow! I thought you'd been mugged!' Jeremy grinned back at me. He looked much better than when I'd left him that morning.

'Ha! That was just the half of it!' I laughed again and flopped down onto his bed. 'How are

221

you? What did the doctors say?'

'They said I've torn my oesophagus from vomiting so violently.'

I sat up. 'You're kidding!'

'No.' He looked almost proud.

'Bloody hell.' I looked up at him. 'Will you be OK?'

'Apparently I may need an operation when we get back home, but they've given me a load of tablets until then. They're fucking good, actually. I feel amazing.'

'You're a nightmare.'

'I know.'

We grinned at each other across the room, him in a dressing gown with a torn oesophagus and me in a filthy dress clutching a bag full of tapes.

'What a ride, eh?'

Yup, that's telly. What a ride.

★   ★   ★

People who know me for my job on *Loose Women* maybe don't realize that I have *GMTV* to thank for giving me the opportunity to try my hand at so many different types of presenting. I have mastered most formats of live TV: from studio-based hosting, live 'walkie-talkie' broadcasts and in-depth interviews for news packages, to corresponding from wonderful events such as the Queen Mother's 100th birthday celebrations.

One of the most challenging and enjoyable presenting jobs I have ever had was the week in 2004 when I did live broadcasts every day from the village of Mamone in South Africa for

*GMTV*. By then my divorce had come through and I was a single mother, building a new life for myself in Wimbledon. Finlay was three years old, and while I was away my mum once again made the long journey over from Uganda, where they now lived, to take care of him. I could not have done half the things I have done without my mum constantly hopping on a plane to be by my side, treating it like a quick trip on a bus to help out her daughter. She still does it now that they have returned to the UK, but with the company of Dad who is now retired. Miles have made little difference in their unwavering support of me and my sister, and I know we both feel blessed to have them as our parents.

The *GMTV* team provided the village with its only supply of free running water, kitted out the local school with computers and built two extra classrooms. It was wonderful to be part of something that made such a difference to people's lives, and it was the people of Mamone, as well as the inspiring crew, who made it such a rewarding experience.

Sue Jameson, the veteran news reporter who has been part of the morning news team for over two decades, was responsible for the trip coming about. She had heard about a desperately poor but bright young girl called Mathapelo from a South African crew member while filming in the country a few months before. Hugely touched by Mathapelo's story, she had contacted the teenager, and after surmounting various logistical problems had succeeded in helping to arrange for computers and bicycles to be delivered and for building work to be done at her school. Working alongside the experienced producer Michelle Porter, they arranged for a week of live broadcasts from her village of Mamone, showing the delivery of these gifts and the difference it would make. It was viewers' support and donations and the hard work and determination of Michelle and Sue that made the whole experience possible.

The village was small, mainly just one street with a local shop and a few houses dotted around. There was electricity and the buildings were made of concrete, so there was a feeling that some sort of infrastructure was in place, it just lacked the funds to push it further. Mathapelo's home was a decent size compared to others I have seen on my trips to Africa, but inside it was almost empty. There was a sparsely furnished living room, a kitchen with just a stove and some cupboards and a dark bedroom with one bed for her mother and a mat on the floor for Mathapelo. After our live broadcasts to London every morning, Sue, the crew and I all mucked in to help paint Mathapelo's home, sew curtains and make her a bed so she didn't have to sleep on her mother's floor. There was another room in the house that was empty and bare with rough concrete walls and floor, so we painted it, and transformed it into a room any young girl would be thrilled with. Most importantly, we gave her some space of her own, where she could live in comfort. We spent one whole day blowing up the tyres on bicycles that were to be delivered to the schoolchildren the next morning, to help ease their long journey to school. Sue is an example of journalism at its finest; she doesn't just report on a story, she thinks about it, and cares enough to want to return to its point of origin to help. She is still in touch with Mathapelo, who is now at college, something that would have been impossible without the help and support of Sue, *GMTV* and its viewers.

I got so much out of my week in South Africa with Sue; she didn't patronize me as a young presenter, but let me into her gang and, by example, reinforced my already strong belief that being part of the team and working together are the most fundamental element of working in television. We are all cogs in a wheel; some may be smaller and unseen and some may appear bigger and brighter, but without one of them, none of it works.

A year after my trip to Mamone, and having left Finlay in the capable hands of my mum once more, I was on my way to South Africa again. This time, it would be for my last ever travel series for *GMTV*. I actually slept on the overnight flight to Cape Town, which I was never normally able to do, so I took that as a good omen. I woke up as the captain told us to look out the window to our right . . . and there it was, Table Mountain. I'd seen it a hundred times in photos, but it still made me gawp; I don't think anything can prepare you for just how big it is compared to the flat landscape surrounding it. Or how strange-looking it is; it's as if a giant with a scythe got bored one day, scratched his chin and thought, *I wonder what would happen if I*

225

*just chopped a bit off there . . . ?*

The crew and I had some amazing, and eye-opening, experiences there that I'll never forget. We witnessed the stark contrast between the luxury of central Cape Town and the complete poverty of the outlying townships; we visited Robben Island, the penal settlement that once housed Nelson Mandela; and we camped in the middle of the Kruger National Park, with nothing separating us from lions, elephants and hyenas but a few little strands of electric fence. But one part of the trip in particular became a real turning point in my life when it didn't go quite the way I'd planned . . .

It was the bit I had been looking forward to the most. In fact, it was me who'd suggested it to the producer. She'd looked at me like I was insane, then said, 'OK, if you're sure, but you don't have to . . .'

'No, trust me! I really want to! I've ALWAYS wanted to do this!' I cried. And that was how I found myself standing on the edge of Table Mountain, in a helmet and attached to ropes preparing myself to jump off *face first*. It's called rap jumping, whereby you rapidly abseil down a cliff, facing forwards, and ever since I'd heard about it as a young backpacker in Australia, I'd been desperate to try it. I did. And it was horrible. It was a sad moment in the history of Andrea McLean, because it was then I realized that a) I was no longer a fit and strong twenty-two-year-old. I was a very unfit thirty-five-year-old mother of one, who quite frankly should have known better; and b) some dreams are best left unfulfilled. I was apprehensive but excited as I stood at the cliff edge, listening to the instructor telling me what to do. Then I held the rope as he told me to, and leaned over the side of Table Mountain staring down at the sea in front of me and the jagged yellow rocks and scrubby bushes below. But then I took my first step. It was awful. I was terrible at it. The rope wobbled and shook, and I had no strength in my arms, so I just kept falling over and crashing into Table Mountain. Bottom first. Table Mountain is hard. It hurts. And the next time anyone suggests I try something like this again (including myself), I will pull out this book and remind myself that I am no longer 'up for it'. I am now 'past it'. It's a painful truth, but not as painful as my bum, shoulders, back, neck and head were by the time I got to the bottom . . .

As we got on our bus back to the airport, we chatted about what we'd made of South Africa. It was everything and nothing like I'd expected it to be. It was just as beautiful, and then more so. A First World country in a Third World environment, it is a country on its way up; it has had its chance to be reborn and has taken it. It's something I have tried to take on board too, and over the years, as I have been offered opportunities to make positive changes in my life, to be reborn in my own way, I have grasped them with both hands. You only get one chance at life, and I intend to make the most of it.

# 14

## Dancing on Ice Melts Me

Sometimes things just happen. Normal things, that you have no idea how important they are until afterwards, and you look back and think, *Wow, I nearly didn't do that, and look what I'd have missed out on . . .*

It was a normal, cold, early-December morning in 2005 when I was sent to do a weather report from the ice rink at the Natural History Museum in London. I left Finlay sleeping at home under the care of our much-loved French au pair Emilie, and at 5.30 a.m. was pulling on some blue rented skates and about to wobble my way around the rink for the entertainment of early-morning viewers. I had only ice skated a couple of times before, but as a young teen had been the proud owner of a pair of white roller-skating boots with a bright orange stopper. I would spend hours whirling and twirling on the smooth road outside our house in sunny Trinidad. Ice skating couldn't be that much different — could it?

I opened the door and let myself out onto the ice. The crew were busy setting up, making sure the satellite link was up and running, that the camera was working properly and that the gallery back at the studio could hear us all OK. I held on tightly to the side and put my blue-clad foot down on the slippery surface, glowing in the half-light. With two feet down I pushed off falteringly, first with my right, then with my left. I made my way slowly round the rink, concentrating on putting one foot in front of the other. I muttered under my breath as I did so, learning my weather notes and the order of my graphics, as I would be talking over pictures I couldn't see and if I got them out of sequence it would look ridiculous.

★ ★ ★

At 6.01 a.m. I did my first live broadcast from the ice rink, telling the country what kind of weather they could expect as they headed out the door. By 7.30 a.m. I was feeling a little more daring, and managed to do half a circuit. By 8.25 a.m. I was able to show off a little bit, and like a woolly-hatted Bambi I completed a half turn, and managed to go backwards while doing a live weather broadcast! The hosts back in the warmth of the studio laughed and clapped as I signed off for the day, wobbling out of vision with a 'See you tomorrowwww . . . '

It had been good fun, and as it was the first day the rink was open to the public, I decided to bring four-year-old Finlay back in the afternoon. He had never been skating before, and it was a lovely rink, just a short Tube ride away from Wimbledon where we were still living. It was while I was pulling him gently round later that day that I had a missed call on my mobile. It was my agent. A new programme was being launched called *Dancing on Ice*, where celebrities were taught to skate with professional partners, and in a few weeks' time they would be judged both in the studio and by the viewers at home. Apparently, an actress from *Footballers' Wives* had just found out that she was pregnant the day before and had had to pull out, leaving them a female celebrity short. That morning, Christopher Dean, the British Olympic ice-skating champion, had happened to switch on his TV and saw me wobbling backwards across the ice. He put a call in to the producers, saying, 'I don't know who she is, but I've just seen a weathergirl on TV and she can skate. Get her in.'

And that was how I got on to the first series of *Dancing on Ice*. At the time I just thought it was exciting and would be fun for me to be part of a new show where I would learn how to ice skate; I had no idea it would grow into the huge prime-time show it later became.

Three days later I was on an ice rink in north London, with a film crew, being introduced to the legendary Jayne Torvill and the man who had got me on the show, Christopher Dean. They were as lovely as you could hope for, twinkling and friendly, and, as I would learn later, supportive too. Chris and Jayne led me onto the ice and showed me a few steps, laughing as I stumbled and wobbled. Then I heard, 'Well, *hello!*' and I turned to meet my new ice-skating partner, Douglas Webster. Doug was an American skating champion and choreographer, well used to putting together professional skaters in the *Holiday on Ice* spectaculars. He was just taller than me, with dark hair, hazel eyes and a wide smile, and I liked him instantly.

For the next few weeks I squeezed in training where I could, in between running round the country doing the weather for *GMTV* in the build-up to Christmas, and looking after Finlay. Everyone stepped in to help me keep things running; my sister Linda, Steve and Emilie, my au pair, who had become a close member of our family. Nick, my now ex-husband, helped as well; as we were living so close to each other, he had Finlay over when he could, and every weekend that the show was on, so I knew he was in safe hands.

What felt like a handful of weeks later, Christmas was over and we were getting ready to launch the show. It seems strange now, as it has become such a major part of the winter schedule, but at the time, no one had any idea how successful *Dancing on Ice* would become. As we all trained separately when our different work schedules allowed, I didn't get to meet any of the other celebrities until we showcased our first numbers in front of each other a couple of weeks before we were due to go on air with the live shows. Suddenly it seemed real; we went from messing about on the ice and learning a few faltering steps to seeing just how good everyone else was. Falling over no longer seemed funny; it would make you look bad, so we knuckled down to business. It was during one of these tough training sessions that my first disaster happened.

Chris and Jayne were in charge of our routines

and it was their role to give us more advanced manoeuvres as our confidence and abilities grew to make the show more exciting. My first song was Beyoncé's 'Crazy in Love', which had always been a favourite, but I was now hearing it over and over in my head at night while I slept, subconsciously running through my routine during down time. Even between weather bulletins at work, I would find a quiet corner and try to work through my moves in my mind, singing quietly and counting in my head. It was impossible to comprehend that I'd had a month to learn this routine and I was still struggling with it, but if I got through to the next round, I would only have six days to learn another one — and go to work and be a mum as well!

Most mornings if I was doing the weather from the studio I headed straight over to Lee Valley ice rink in north-east London to practise with Doug. Karen Barber, the champion ice skater and former dance partner of *Dancing on Ice* judge Nicky Slater, oversaw our training sessions, and with her gentle encouragement I grew more confident. Confidence was my main obstacle, and it was proving to be a problem, not only with my skating, but in my relationship with Doug as well. I didn't feel I could live up to the standards he was expecting of me, which was incredibly frustrating for him. He was used to working with professionals; this was his first time working alongside a raw recruit like me, and after my initial thrill at being able to go backwards all those weeks ago while doing the weather, that skill was small fry compared to what was expected of me now. Maybe I had set my sights too high; maybe there are some things that people just cannot do? Doubts had set in, and we hadn't even started the show yet.

One morning, Chris and Jayne came to see how we were getting on, and Doug and I took to the ice in front of them. They watched closely, Chris frowning with concentration, and Jayne smiling encouragingly.

'Hmm,' said Chris once we had finished and returned breathless to the side of the rink.

'You need to get your speed up, Andrea. You're still too slow and it's not showing your moves off to their best.'

He saw my face and laughed. 'I know it feels like you are flying along, but you're really not. You need to learn not to be afraid of speed.'

He stepped out onto the ice and took my hand. 'Come on, let me show you.'

So there I was being led onto the middle of the ice rink by the legend that is Christopher Dean, his hand warm, dry and confident in my damp, shaking one. 'Just trust me,' he smiled, and he quickened his pace, pulling me along with him. We did a lap of the rink, then another, building up speed as we went. It was exhilarating, our skates knifing over the cold surface in unison. 'You see?' he said. 'You can do it. Just have faith in your blades and in Doug and you will be fine. We are looking after you.'

He swooped round and swept me into his arms, startling me. 'You're going to have to get used to this, Andrea,' he laughed. 'Relax!' We soared over the rink in a clinch, with him pushing me backwards over the ice. 'That's good,' he said. 'You have to be able to do this if you are ever going to go up a level. Don't be afraid.'

We did another lap, and as I grew more confident, he increased his speed, pushing us faster, and faster. It was all starting to make sense, and then he pushed on a little more. The fear only lasted a split second, but it was long enough to prove catastrophic. My feet, which moments earlier had been solid and strong on the slippery surface, wobbled. That tiny movement, like the jerking of a steering wheel in a car travelling at speed, had momentous consequences. My skate nudged Chris's, causing him to stumble, and as he tried to right himself I panicked, sending my feet once more into his path.

The fall seemed to happen in slow motion. Chris tried his hardest to keep us upright, but the combination of speed and my inability to control it was too much for even a professional to rectify. I landed backwards with a thud on the ice, pulling Chris down with me. My head bounced off the ice with the initial impact, and then Chris's weight crushed down onto my ribs. His face smashed into the ice, cutting his lip, and we skidded in an icy heap in silence. When we finally slid to a stop, Chris rolled off me, groaning. We both lay with our eyes closed, as my track 'Crazy in Love' boomed out through the loudspeakers. Karen and Jayne appeared in seconds, followed by Doug, their worried faces looming above us.

'You OK?' Chris said, as we lay side by side. I couldn't speak. I was winded, and I felt like I had been shot in the side. We were helped to our feet and led to the side of the rink, where Chris held a tissue to his bleeding lip and I struggled not to cry. Once everyone was sure that we were OK, we decided that the best thing to do was to get straight back on the ice again, before fear set in to stay.

Doug and I skated to our positions, and waited for the music to start. I was wobbly, but determined to put the fall behind me; it was bound to happen, it had only been a matter of time. It was just my turn, I kept telling myself, and I felt awful that my turn had coincided with bashing the lip of an Olympic champion. I skated tentatively through each move, and Doug took it very easy with me, quietly encouraging me on. Then came the last lift, the cartwheel to end the routine, where Doug grabbed me and flipped me over. I skated into position, took a deep breath and launched myself into the air.

As Doug lifted me, there was a noise like a whip cracking and I crumpled into his arms. The pressure of his strong hands on my ribs had been too much — the crack caused by my fall with Chris gave way and my rib snapped in two. The pain was incredible. Doug led me gently off the ice and called for Sharon the physio, who came running. She supported me up the stairs to her tiny room, and helped me onto her bed, concern on her face. She lifted up my layers of warm clothes and gently felt around my ribs as I lay on my front, tears dripping silently off my nose onto the floor.

'I'm sorry, Andrea, I know this hurts,' she said quietly, as she moved her hands expertly over me, feeling down my spine and along each rib. I winced and jolted as she pressed on my right side. 'I'm afraid a rib has popped out and it looks like it's broken. There's nothing we can do apart from strap you up and make you comfortable. It will eventually heal itself.' She patted me. 'What a shame.'

That night, sleep was impossible, as I struggled to find a comfortable way to lie. What felt like minutes later, the alarm went and it was 3.30 a.m.: time to get up and go to work.

With only a week to go until the series launch, there was no time to mope around. Unfortunately, in rehearsals I was now afraid of every step, every moment on the ice that involved speed or letting go of Doug's hand, but excitement among the crew and skaters was building as we headed towards that first Saturday night and it was impossible not to get caught up in it. My costume had been made; it was a beautiful pale-green dress that sparkled, and Doug had black trousers and a matching green shirt.

The day of the first show dawned, and a taxi arrived at 8 a.m. to take me from home to Elstree Studios in Borehamwood. I was scared; my ribs throbbed and I couldn't remember a single step. Feeling sick with nerves, I switched on my iPod and clicked onto the soothing tones of Jack Johnson — if anyone's voice could calm me, his could.

The day seemed to last forever. We were all given an allotted time to perform our routine twice through, to get used to the small space of the rink compared to where we had been training, and to doing it in our costumes for the first time. This also gave the camera crew their first look, and the director his chance to plot through his shots of each couple's routine. It was a long day for the team, to get through each dance and quickly sort the lighting, camera angles and timing for a dozen celebrities and their partners. Everyone was professional and did what was asked of them, and bit by bit the green room filled with couples who had done their technical run-through; now all we had to do was wait. Our routine had gone as well as I'd hoped; I didn't cock it up too badly, so I saw that as a success!

There was a monitor in the room, on which we could watch whomever was doing their run through on the ice, and it soon became clear that some were much better than others. John Barrowman was a natural showman, as you'd expect, and Bonnie Langford looked like a dancing fairy as she was effortlessly lifted over the ice by her handsome partner Matt Evers. We were all at different levels of ability; some celebs had taken to the ice like naturals, and were enjoying the chance to show off their new skills. Others had found it a little more difficult and were beside themselves with nerves at the thought of skating in front of a live audience. And then there were the ones like me: a bit battered and bruised and not hugely confident, but excited to be a part of it all.

It helped being in the room with the others. Spirits were nervously high as none of us knew what to expect and we all seemed to have the same worries. Would we do OK? Would the audience like us? Would we fall over? In fairness, it was this element of danger that had the nation tuning in, and of course there were enough dramas to keep the people at home glued to their sets for the entire run. David Seaman and his partner Pam provided most of them, as she was very badly hurt during one particular routine when she landed on her chin with her arms behind her back. Ouch. Everyone tumbled at one point or another, though.

Finally we were called down into make-up, and the long process of transforming us into stars of the ice began. Our hair was tousled and teased into shape; mine was scraped off my face into a bun at the back of my head; always a worry as my ears are my most hated feature, and now they were on show to the world. Foundation was applied, as were sparkly eye shadow and false lashes . . . we were unrecognizable by the time they had finished with us! Loo trips became more frequent, and more difficult, especially once we had our costumes on, as someone had to come in to undo us then put us back together again.

We were ushered into the 'holding area', a room behind the rink where we would be filmed throughout the show, limbering up and getting ourselves ready. The audience were in; they sounded excited and up for a good night, as the

238

warm-up man whipped them into a frenzy. We could see glimpses of them as we made our way backstage, all of us craning our necks to see loved ones. Then, after what felt like an eternity, the theme tune to *Dancing on Ice* began. We were off!

We all hovered in a line, waiting to hear the unseen announcer call our name. Most of us were nervous and giggly, but some people who were more used to performing on stage were making jokes and couldn't wait to get out there. Work-wise, I was used to doing my thing in a little room full of people I knew, doing something that I was confident in, and not thinking too much about the millions of people sitting at home judging me. But now I was standing in a little skating dress, waiting to hurl myself onto a frozen stage in front of millions of people. I was absolutely terrified.

All of a sudden I could hear my name being announced. My knees knocked so hard I could barely stand, and I thought I was going to be sick. I focused on my breathing, tried to smile and *whoosh!* — Doug led me out onto the ice. The noise was deafening — music, clapping, cheering — but I barely heard any of it, I was so scared. Doug led me into my opening swoop, we joined the line-up of waving celebrities, and then Phillip Schofield and Holly Willoughby announced the first couple to take to the ice. The rest of us crept backstage as the video footage of their training began. I didn't look; we were third up, and I could barely stand upright with fear. I went into the quiet corridor behind the green room and breathed in and out in the darkness, trying to block out the cheering and music coming from the ice. The next couple went up, then there was an advert break and I heard Phillip say, 'Coming up next, will our weathergirl put on a brave front when it comes to her turn on the ice? Find out, after this break.'

I was led back into the room behind the rink, where there was a cameraman waiting. It was quiet despite the couples waiting nervously for their turn, everyone focused on fiddling with their skates, counting through their routine or just sitting with their eyes closed. Doug and I stood close together, pretending to limber up as the show came back on air, and then Phillip linked to the video of my training. We made our way to the entrance to the ice, unable to see the video, but I could hear it being played on the huge screen. I touched the tape holding my broken rib in place; my side was throbbing, but it was barely noticeable compared to the pounding of my anxious heart. I couldn't hear any reference to my fall, so the public had no idea I was skating with a serious injury. Before I had time to compute that information, the announcer called my name and Doug and I were on the ice — it was our turn!

I was shaking so hard I don't know how I managed to make it through the routine, never mind smile, move my arms and legs and stay upright. We did our back flip, our twirl and even our cartwheel, which sent a spasm of pain through my body as Doug held me by my strapped-up sides. We'd done everything, almost perfectly, so I foolishly began to relax, thinking we were nearly done, I had made it. And that was when my skate collided with Doug's and the two of us rocked violently to the side before righting ourselves. We managed an awkward spin, and finished with a limp 'tada!' rather than the flourish we had choreographed. Laughing with relief that it was all over and I had survived in one piece, we skated to the side to get our points and hear the judges' verdicts. We got fifteen points out of a possible thirty; not bad, and what we deserved. The judges were very nice, even Jason Gardner, and they said I had 'potential'. I was happy with that!

The rest of the show passed in a blur. Tamara Beckwith ended up in the skate-off and was the first celebrity to leave the show. I didn't know her that well, but she had seemed friendly and full of naughty fun, so it was a shame to see her go. Then it was off to the bar, to meet up with friends and family, judges and skaters, and drink until the wee hours and till our nerves, pain and excitement were all gone.

The following Monday we were back at training again, and this time, they had managed to get me a space at Streatham ice rink, as it was so much closer to home. After work at *GMTV* I picked up Finlay and Emilie and took them along, so that Finlay could see what Mummy had been up to. It was a big mistake, as he of course wanted to skate too, and as a three-year-old he wasn't able to understand why he couldn't stay on the ice with Mummy. We let him come round with me for a bit, and Doug spun him in the air, which he thought was brilliant, but then it was time to start practising my new routine. He didn't take it well, and he wailed and thrashed at the side, with Emilie unable to calm him. Andi Peters was also at the rink, so I decided to let him use my time so I could hopefully calm Finlay down. I headed off the ice, still in my skates, and took him down to where the skate hire part was, to hand his skates in and try and find something else to amuse him. I got his shoes back on, and chattered to him the whole time, trying to take his mind off things, while wondering whether to put him and Emilie in a cab back to the house, as this wasn't really working.

That's why I was looking at him rather than where I was going as we made our way up the concrete steps back towards the rink. And why I didn't notice until it was too late that the front of my skate had caught the edge of the step, and next thing I knew I was flung forward, cracking my temple, cheek and jaw on the stairs. The noise inside my head was incredible; it was the bang of two cars colliding, followed by darkness and silence. I have no idea how long I lay on the steps, but I eventually became aware of Finlay's hand hitting me on my back, telling me to wake up. 'Come on, Mummy!' he was shouting. 'Wake up!' He didn't sound scared, just confused, and a bit cross that he had been stopped mid-conversation. In the distance I heard Andi Peters' voice saying, 'Hello, Finlay, what is it? Oh my God! Andrea's fallen!'

I could hear people running over and Finlay

saying, 'I can't wake Mummy up,' but for the life of me I couldn't open my eyes to let them know I could hear everything that was going on around me. I just couldn't move.

Andi's voice was closer now, and he shook me gently. 'Andrea. Can you hear me?' He patted my back and asked someone, 'What should we do?'

There was muttering as people decided what to do with me, and finally I forced my eyes to open. I was lying on the steps of Streatham ice rink, and it didn't smell very nice. 'Mummy!' Finlay was still shouting, as Andi bent over to help me to sit up. My head hurt, but I was scared to open my mouth in case all my teeth fell out like something out of a *Tom and Jerry* cartoon. After checking my head, which surprisingly wasn't bleeding, it was decided that I should call it a day. A taxi was ordered, and someone helped me take off my skates, while someone else helped us to the car.

'I'm sure it's fine.' I smiled weakly, and lowered myself into the front seat. On the way home, I got the taxi driver to drop me off at A&E at St George's Hospital in Tooting, telling Finlay I just needed to stop here for a bit, and that Emilie would take him home where he could watch *Shrek*. Once he was safely on his way, and I was sat alone on a hard metal chair waiting to be seen, the shock hit me. I had bashed myself again. What on earth must everyone on the show think of me?

Many hours later, after I had been checked over and told that if I started vomiting or seeing double I was to come back immediately, I had a shower and crawled into bed. It was then that I allowed tears of self-pity to pour down my face. Every part of me hurt. My legs and arms were covered in bruises from either falling down or being lifted. My ribs throbbed every time I breathed. My head, jaw and teeth hurt. Why was I doing this?

Two days later, Doug asked me the same question. By now his patience with me had worn thin, and he was grasping the reality of having to deal with a frightened, injured amateur. I watched sadly as Gaynor Faye and her lovely partner Dan rehearsed, scooting across the ice, laughing and smiling at each other. Doug just seemed tired, fed up and very, very irritated with me. I felt as if I couldn't do anything right, and the more I tried the clumsier I became, which sent both of us into a tailspin — me of apprehension and him of anger born out of frustration. It didn't help that as time had gone on I realized that he looked very like Nick, and every time Doug got angry with me, all my feelings of guilt at the way I had hurt Nick came flooding back. In my head it became Nick who was shouting at me, telling me I'd messed up *again*, that I needed to pull myself together.

I decided that maybe if Doug got to know me as a person rather than just a skating partner, we might work better together, so I invited him over for Sunday lunch. Steve tried his best to reason with him man to man, to tell him that shouting at me wasn't the best way to handle me. I could see that Doug didn't want to hurt me, that he was a nice guy, but he couldn't handle the frustration of working with a klutz like me, who kept making mistakes and messing up and apologizing over and over again. It wasn't working any more.

The following Saturday I had my ribs bound up and my bruises covered in fake tan and make-up. My hair was put into two bundles on the side of my head, and my midnight-blue costume splayed out like a crazy tutu. We were dancing to Björk's 'It's Oh So Quiet', so I had to look a bit kooky. I felt it as we waited backstage, as my nerves and nausea gripped me. It was like a strange sort of *Groundhog Day*; we waited for our names to be called, the audience and music went mad and we did our thing. This time, I managed to get through it without falling over, and Doug looked pleased with me, at last.

We made our way over to the side stage, where we waited for our scores and comments: sixteen. Not bad. The judges again were very kind; Karen said I had done very well, and Robin Cousins said I could push myself further, which was fair. Then it was Jason Gardner's turn.

'Well,' he sighed in exasperation, 'I don't know if it's because you've had too much Botox, or you were too close to the ice, but your face was devoid of any expression. You were stiff, your arms were all wrong and your legs looked like a Great Dane's. Not good, sweetheart.' There was a gasp from the audience, and a few 'boo's of support for me. I felt Doug stiffen, but after the initial shock of being accused of using Botox, I thought Jason was hilarious. And when I looked back at myself the following week, he was absolutely right — grace and extension of limbs weren't a strong point.

The production team sent me to a ballet class, where I was filmed flailing around and looking generally gawky. By now Doug seemed to have lost the will to live as far as I was concerned, and could barely contain his irritation. Our next routine was to a beautiful Eva Cassidy version of the song 'Time After Time', and involved not only long, flowing limbs, but a particularly tricky move where I had to throw myself over his back and land on my feet, while making it look elegant. It was never going to work.

The eight weeks of training, working and performing had started to take their toll, and both Doug and I came down with heavy colds. There was no time to rest, however, so we dosed ourselves up with Lemsip and carried on. My rib was starting to feel better at least, and the bruises on my face were fading, but my confidence was sliding. Doug's pained expression at my paltry attempts at grace on the ice were demoralizing me, and at one point he stormed off the ice shouting, 'This is impossible!' I waited quietly in the stands for him to return, fighting back tears. When he returned, we started again as if nothing had happened, but not looking each other in the eye. It was horrible.

The day of the show came round again, and everyone was fighting some kind of injury or illness. David Seaman's lovely partner Pam had taken a battering on the ice, but was bravely carrying on, so none of us wanted to moan about the odd bruise or our injured pride, as she had really hurt herself but was behaving like a true pro.

When we were called to the rink for our rehearsal, I was dressed and ready in my flowing red dress. Doug was waiting for me, skating slowly round in circles, and already in a bad mood by the looks of it. I skated round him and got warmed up, then we got the signal that the gallery were ready for us to go through our routine. We skated to opposite sides of the rink and stood ready, waiting for the music to begin. The lights dimmed and everyone stood still in the darkness. The song began, and I slowly skated towards him, counting my steps silently in my head. *A crossover, a turn, remember to use my outside edge* . . . I was focused entirely on the routine and what steps were coming next, my brow creased with concentration.

The rehearsal was going smoothly, or so I thought, and I was gearing myself up for the next move — the high point of the routine, which was designed to make the audience 'ooh' and 'aah'. I had to get my timing right or I wouldn't have the momentum I needed to flip myself over Doug's back. *One, two, three* . . . I quickened my pace as I moved over the ice towards him. *Four, five, six* . . . I was about three feet away from him when suddenly Doug stood up straight, threw his arms in the air and shouted, 'Oh, what's the fucking point?!' and skated off the rink. Just like that he was gone, leaving me to slow to a halt and stand looking a fool while the music played. Eventually somebody switched it off, and then the lights came back on. I was on my own in the middle of the rink with everyone looking at me, not sure what they should do next.

I skated slowly to the side of the rink, where David Seaman was putting on his boots as he was on next. I sat down next to him, embarrassed as tears welled up. This wasn't fun any more. I just wanted it to be over so I could go home.

'Don't worry,' muttered David, and he put his big arm round me in a brotherly hug. Dave the floor manager came over, his schedule in his hand, looking worried.

'Sweetheart, are you all right? What happened out there?'

'I honestly don't know,' I answered, because I didn't.

'What a wanker. Um, do you think he's coming back? Because we need to get the next couple on, and we're running a bit behind.'

'I don't know, Dave, but I don't think I could do it again anyway. I know we didn't finish; are the lighting and camera guys OK if we leave it here?'

'Don't you worry about that, love. You go and get some lunch and we'll see you later. I'm sorry he's been such a tosser to you. We've all seen it, and you've handled it really well.'

Tears sprang up again and I fought them back.

'Thanks, Dave,' I said, and made my way back to my dressing room. I couldn't face the green room; I knew everyone would have been watching, and would have seen what happened and be full of curious questions that I couldn't answer. Instead I rang Steve and poured my heart out to him, glad at least that I had someone I could talk to, who knew how much Doug's behaviour had been upsetting me.

The day seemed to stretch on forever, and Doug, when I eventually saw him again, acted like nothing had happened. I couldn't look at him, so we kept out of each other's way until it was time for the show to begin. I knew he was also feeling poorly, and he had a nasty cold sore on his lip, so he was obviously very run down. Eventually, once the audience had been whipped into a frenzy, the familiar strains of the theme tune began. My nerves were now frayed and raw, and I wished I had a nip of brandy to hand to calm myself down. I felt close to tears, full of cold, tired and in pain, and I knew that Doug didn't want to do this at all. We stood next to each other and forced ourselves to smile whenever the cameras focused in on us.

Our turn, when it came, was over in a flash. As I skated towards him for our opening sequence, I looked at his left ear, as I knew I would falter and stumble if I tried to look into his eyes. The big move, when I did it, was clumsy and not at all graceful, but I didn't fall over so I considered it to be a success. So did the judges, and we were awarded our highest points so far: twenty out of thirty. Even Jason said I had taken on board what he had said, which was good.

Doug and I kept out of each other's way during the hour's break between the main show and the results. I could see my family and friends in the audience; my mum had made it over from

Africa to come and see me, and she had no idea how hideous an evening I was having. I could see them all smiling and texting my voting number furiously, all wearing the 'Andrea's Angels' T-shirts they'd had specially made.

At the results show everyone was on edge. We were now three shows in, and people were getting into the rhythm of it all, and those who were rising to the challenge were enjoying it and didn't want it to end. I didn't want to leave the show, but I did want things to change. Maybe I just needed some more Lemsip and a good night's sleep. Maybe next week things would be better.

Well, that's something I will never know, as that night it was my turn to leave *Dancing on Ice*. I was in the bottom two, and when my name was called I felt a moment of shock, and then a certain inevitability. It seemed to jolt Doug to his senses, as he looked crestfallen and sorry as we made our way to the side of the ice to prepare for the skate-off. The last skate we did was lovely, and I enjoyed every move, every turn and every dip of it. It wasn't perfect, but it was perfect for me, as it was my goodbye dance with Doug. I was sad as I linked into his arms, listening to Eva Cassidy wash over the silent studio. I wished things had been different; I wished I hadn't got injured, and had been better at this, and had been tougher. But I wasn't, and it was entirely right that Stefan Booth and his partner went through to the next round.

As I said, sometimes things just happen and

250

you have no idea how important they are until after the event, when you think, *Wow, I nearly missed out on that.* You see, fate was watching, and was waiting to hand me something fantastic.

★ ★ ★

In the weeks that I had been frantically practising and working, Paul O'Grady had suddenly announced that he was not going to be renewing his contract with ITV. This left a gaping hole in the afternoon schedule, which needed to be filled with something, and a rumour had swept round that it was to be filled with a show to do with *Dancing on Ice*, as that was proving to be such a ratings success for the network. The next day, after waking up with a beautiful and well-deserved hangover, it popped into my head. Why couldn't I do something on this new show? I was an experienced live presenter, I knew all about *Dancing on Ice* as I'd been in it, and I was now available — surely it made sense? Well, of course, it wasn't quite as simple as that, so I rang one of the lovely video editors at *GMTV* called Nick Thomas and asked him to quickly put together a showreel for me of the latest things I had done at *GMTV*, showing me doing live reporting, not the weather. He worked at lightning speed and between us we managed to get a reel done and dusted and over to the head of ITV Daytime within twenty-four hours, made easier by the fact that we all worked in the same building and could use internal mail. At the same time I rang my agent and begged her to put a good word in for me. No matter what came of it, at least I would know I'd given it my best shot.

A nail-biting two days later I got the call. The network were going to replace the Paul O'Grady slot with a new show called *Dancing on Ice Extra*, hosted by myself and Andi Peters! It was the biggest break I could get. As much as I enjoyed presenting the weather every day, I was ready for a new challenge work-wise and I knew this would give me the chance to show both the public and potential employers that I was capable of doing much more. I was so excited.

Every day after doing *GMTV* I would race over to the studios at Elstree and watch all the new friends I'd made on *Dancing on Ice* practising and training. I still met up with the lovely crew filming behind the scenes, and I now also had the thrill of doing my own show with Andi. He was fantastic, as you'd expect of someone who has been in the business, both in front of and behind the camera, for as long as he has. Andi and I hosted *Dancing on Ice Extra* every afternoon at 5 p.m. on ITV1 for four brilliant weeks, interviewing the skaters, inviting celebrities on to chat about their favourite parts of the show, running competitions and generally having fun. Every Saturday I got to go to the live show to film inserts for ours, enjoying the thrill of the spectacle without enduring a single bruise or fall.

Doug and I went to lunch a few days after we were voted off, before he returned to New York. He apologized for not being supportive and for being rude and impatient, and explained that he had not fully appreciated how difficult it would be for a novice to learn to skate in such a short space of time. We had a drink and said our goodbyes, and have actually kept in touch. I met up with him only a few weeks ago, and it was genuinely lovely to see him again. I see it as fate that we didn't gel on the ice, because if we hadn't been voted off that week, I would never have got the job on *Dancing on Ice Extra*, a job I absolutely adored, and one that would in turn lead to me hosting *Loose Women* further down the line. As far as I was concerned, it had all ended perfectly.

In fact, *Dancing on Ice* gave me something that I never could have expected. For the evening of the wrap party, after lovely Gaynor Faye had been crowned champion, champagne had been quaffed, the vodka bar had been drunk dry and John Barrowman and I had thrown some impressive shapes on the dance floor, Steve and I made our way back to his house, not a little merry. One thing inevitably led to another, and nine months later my own little Ice Ice Baby arrived, and she was to change my life for ever.

# 15

## Amy

I can remember exactly where I was when I discovered I was pregnant again: in the Earl Spencer pub in Wimbledon on a Sunday afternoon with Steve, staring down at a stomach-churning plate of mussels and complaining about how horrible everything smelled. Realization dawned, prompting us to make a mad dash to the chemist.

When we got home I ran to the bathroom and found myself staring in disbelief at the blue line on the stick. I still had endometriosis, had barely had a period due to my hormone imbalance and there had been no planning and no fertility drugs, just a fun end to a night, and BANG — I was pregnant. I was stunned and, to be honest, scared. What would happen now? I was shaking as I made my way downstairs to Steve, who was waiting in my tiny kitchen.

'Remember how I said not to worry, that it would take a miracle for me to get pregnant?'

He looked at me, confused and tense. 'Yes.'

'Well, this must be the second coming, because guess what? You're going to be a daddy.'

The words hung in the air and we stared at each other in disbelief, neither of us knowing how to react. I was desperate to know what was going through his mind. Was he pleased? Did he want to have a baby? We had spoken about children in an abstract way and I knew that he wanted to be a father at some point in his life, but did he want it now? With me? And what did I want? I was just finding my feet again a year after a painful divorce, work was going well and I was happy living with Finlay and seeing Steve a few nights a week. What happened now?

Steve's face was a picture of conflicting emotions and I knew he was fighting to think of the right thing to say. What *was* the right thing to say?

I stood still, feeling small and scared and in a state of shock. Steve walked across the room in three easy strides and hugged me tight, tears in his eyes.

'Well, I don't know how you feel about it, but I'm happy. But we can do whatever you want, OK?'

We hugged each other as my mind raced. I was pregnant. I was a newly divorced single mum seeing a man I loved very much, but was I ready to have his baby? My life was skidding completely into right angles — how had Doris Day ended up like this? Good girls don't find themselves in this situation! Well, this good girl did, and once again the course of my life took a new and unexpected turn.

There was no talk of not keeping the baby; it was not an option that either of us was prepared to consider. We sat and talked for most of the night, and agreed that this was sudden, and unplanned, but it must have happened for a reason. It was a blessing and we should see it as such, and we would work through whatever this change of circumstances brought to our relationship. We would see it as a new beginning.

★ ★ ★

My second pregnancy, physically speaking, was normal: feeling dreadful for the first trimester, like a rocket of energy for the second, and like a big fat lump for the third — nothing unusual about any of that at all! What was unusual was that Steve and I didn't live together; he stayed in Watford and I was still in Wimbledon. We saw each other often, and were looking forward to the baby coming, but a tiny part of me wasn't ready yet to have him fully move in. And Steve needed time to adjust to the fact that he was going to become a father, and also a stepfather to Finlay. We didn't want to jump into moving in together as soon as we found out I was pregnant; we needed a period of adjustment before taking the next inevitable step.

It sounds insane now, but it made perfect sense at the time; I was still working, Finlay and I were fine and it all seemed to work. Then one day I came home from Sainsbury's with a car loaded with shopping. As ever, there was nowhere to park near the house, so I double parked on our narrow street and began lugging all the shopping to the front door. I was about six months pregnant, my belly was huge and I was huffing and puffing when a driver pulled up and beeped angrily. I smiled apologetically and waved to show I would be finished soon, and he beeped again.

'Get out of the bloody way!' he raged, banging his hand on the steering wheel in frustration.

He could see I was pregnant and unloading a weekly shop — I hadn't blocked the road down a quiet side street just for the. hell of it. He sat in his car and watched me trudge back and forth, tutting and gesticulating at me until I finished and drove round the corner to a parking space, leaving all my shopping on the front doorstep. I lugged it all into the house and had just unpacked it when the doorbell went. It was a delivery man with the pram, all boxed up and waiting to be assembled. I dragged the box into the living room and sat on the floor to put it together. It took the rest of the morning, and I was very proud that I had done it myself. I pushed it towards the living-room door to give it a little go up and down the hall to see what it felt like. Bump. I tried again. Bump. The bloody thing wouldn't fit through the narrow doorway; the pram was stuck in the living room.

Cue furious tapping of number into mobile and livid hormonal ranting about the day I was having. Steve listened patiently until I had worn myself out and then suggested quietly that maybe now was the time to start looking for a place we could live in *together*. He found Wimbledon too crowded and hated the fact that my tiny garden was overlooked by rows of terraced houses. He felt penned in whenever he came to stay and couldn't face the thought of living in a cramped Victorian terrace. Maybe, he suggested hopefully, we should look for a bigger place. After all, wouldn't it be nice to have a driveway, rather than blocking the road and having someone shout at me for doing the weekly shop? Imagine having a garden big enough for five-year-old Finlay to run around in and gather momentum, rather than running in circles like a chimp at the zoo? To have a kitchen big enough to fit a family-sized table, rather than the IKEA fold-out Finlay and I had been squeezed round for the past two years?

He was right, of course, but for me the decision to leave Wimbledon was more than just a practical one; it was an emotional one. I had lived in South London for twelve years, since I first arrived in my mother's old Fiesta, having driven from Cheshire down to the bright lights of Clapham, car crammed with all my worldly possessions. I'd had highs and lows within my little three-mile radius ... living alone in a bedsit, saving fifty-pence pieces for the meter to keep the electricity going; moving into a house share with three young music students who enjoyed a rich and varied social life while I traipsed across London every day to my first job in journalism; buying my first flat with my first boyfriend; carrying my baby home for the first time; getting divorced and the anguish that followed; then pulling myself together and starting again. There were ghosts on every corner, and memories that were both happy and sad; but was I really ready to leave? I knew every shopkeeper down our little parade, the man at the barrier at my Tube stop, the lady at the dry cleaner's. I was on nodding terms with scores of mums who stood every day at the sand pit in the park waiting for their little ones to wear themselves out. I was on wine-drinking, tear-wiping terms with some lovely neighbours who had supported me and made me laugh and handed me tissues as I'd cried at their kitchen table, while our children ran and screamed and played. Was I ready to leave all this behind?

We talked it through carefully and sensibly and I decided that the time was right to move on. I was about to start a new chapter in my life, and it made sense to start afresh, somewhere I wouldn't be haunted by the memories of my past life, and the hopes and dreams that had been both realized and dashed here. It would be good to start again somewhere neutral for both of us, where we had no history apart from the new one we were making together. We couldn't move far, as I wanted Finlay to be in easy reach of his dad, so we searched directly south of Wimbledon, in Surrey. It was here that we came across Ashtead, a small, quiet village near the Epsom Downs that had a direct train service into Waterloo, which was good for getting to ITV; and was just down the A3 from Wimbledon, which was good for Nick. We bought a small bungalow that needed renovating and decided that together, with this fresh start for both of us, we would transform it into our dream home. It had a big south-facing garden that Finlay gasped at and said, 'Wow! It's like the park!' and we were able to put swings and a trampoline in it for him. Our neighbours were, and are, lovely: an elderly father and son called Alan and Michael who welcomed us to the street with open arms. I found a great infant school for Finlay, which was only a short walk from our house, and managed to get him enrolled there, ready to start in a few months' time.

★ ★ ★

In November 2006, two weeks before the baby was due, we had a nice night in with Steve's sister Lisa and her fiancé Clive, and got a Chinese takeaway. Steve had now moved in with me, as he had sold his house in readiness for our move to Ashtead. We got to bed at about midnight, and I woke with a start at 2 a.m. thinking I'd wet the bed. I got up and went to the loo, and there it was: a 'show'. I felt hot and cold at the same time, and quite scared. I'd gone two weeks overdue with Finlay and had to be induced; I'd never gone into natural labour before. I got my *What to Expect When You're Expecting* book out, and sat on the loo with shaking hands reading about the signs of 'false labour' and 'real labour'. I thought I was in the real labour bit, but I wasn't sure. I felt a bit period-painy, but nothing too bad. I decided to time them, to see if the pains came and went. I put a towel over the wet bit, and got back into bed.

Ten long minutes passed, and then I could feel it. A rumbling of pain in my back. Not much, but definitely there. I lay still and waited. Ten minutes later, there it was again, a little stronger.

I timed them for an hour, and by then was breathing through them, as they were really starting to kick up a bit. I got out of bed and crept to the bathroom again, this time with my phone and my hospital book. I felt stupid and teary and shaky when I rang the labour ward, and described to the lady what I was feeling, and that my waters had broken. She told me to give it another hour, then to call again. I did, and by then the pains were still every ten minutes, but really smarting. I rang the hospital again, and they said to come in when they were five minutes apart. I hung up and dialled my sister's number, praying she'd be in, and sober, as it was Saturday night, and she actually HAD a social life. Since the end of her marriage she had left Wales, gone travelling and lived with me for a while, but now she was living in North London with her new partner Rory. She sounded croaky as she picked up the phone and I just burst into tears, babbling and making no sense at all. Thank God she worked out what I was saying, and she and her lovely boyfriend jumped in the car and headed straight over. They did the drive from north London to south in thirty-five minutes — unheard of.

By then I had woken Steve. He was in the spare room, as I was sleeping so lightly because of my bump, and it made sense for at least one of us to get a good night's rest. I shook him gently, and said his name, just like you see in the movies. He jumped out of his skin, rolled over and shouted, 'What? What is it? What's happening?!' I burst into tears again, and didn't make any sense, so he carried on shouting, 'What?! WHAT?!' like a man possessed, and I ended up sobbing, 'Stop shouting! The baby is coming!' and he shouted, 'OH MY GOD!' like he hadn't had nine months to get his head around the idea. Once he'd managed to calm down, he gave me a cuddle and told me we needed to ring the hospital and sort out someone to look after Finlay, but I told him not to worry — I'd done it already. There was now nothing to do apart from get ready for when it was time to go to the hospital. We both stopped and looked at each other in the dark, hanging on to each other, excited and scared.

We lay down and carried on timing the contractions, and within half an hour they had gone from ten minutes, to six, to five. My sister arrived, with red-eyed boyfriend in tow, who looked at me lying in bed as if he was terrified I'd have the baby there and then and he'd have to get involved. I got up, had a shower, hanging on to the wall every few minutes, and we made our way downstairs. I kissed a sleeping Finlay goodbye and hobbled to the car, and that was just like you see in the movies.

It was 7 a.m. when we arrived at the hospital, and by then I had to stop every couple of minutes to hang on to something. By 8 a.m. my best friend Jane had arrived (she was enlisted as my birth partner, as well as Steve, because I was so frightened of being left alone while in labour like I had been last time). By 9 a.m. I was mooing in agony as I was whisked into theatre, not even giving the hypnotherapy a second thought, and at 9.34 a.m. baby Amy Jane (named after my lovely friend) arrived in this world.

And that was that. An early-morning flit to the hospital and another emergency C-section, as yet again after hours of labour and fierce contractions I was still only one centimetre dilated and my baby was in distress. Steve was by my side throughout it all, holding my hand and encouraging me. He stood by the table as they cut me open and was the first to see our daughter as she was pulled from me, red and screaming. He held her gently in his huge arms and showed her proudly to me while I cried with relief that she was healthy and strong and that I hadn't had to spend a minute on my own and terrified. He even snuck out with her to see Jane, who was waiting like an expectant father in the corridor to proudly show off her namesake. And then later that day he arrived with the biggest bunch of lilies I have ever seen for me, and a pink balloon for Amy. It was so different to the half-dead bunch of garage flowers I'd been presented with at Finlay's birth, because, as his dad put it, 'you'll be getting loads from everyone else anyway'. As with Finlay, all it took was one look at my scrunched-up newborn's face and I was smitten. I had been worried that I wouldn't be able to love another child as much as I loved my beautiful son, but I needn't have. I realized then that a mother's heart is made from the strongest elastic, capable of stretching to fill with love for all her children. I adored her instantly.

# 16

## A Show Full of Women
## Shouting at Each Other

If I thought things were difficult after my
marriage ended, they were to take a whole
new direction after Amy's birth. I struggled
with a list of post-baby complications that left
me exhausted, tearful and in constant pain. I
felt worthless and useless and over the hill. I
was physically weaker than I had ever been in
my life, just at the time when I needed to be
strong.

It's been well documented how big I became
during both my pregnancies; I gained four stone
with each child, mainly with water retention but
also, to be honest, with a bit of biscuit retention.
Becoming so large was understandably bad
for my self esteem, as it was *loved* by other
women during this time, who squealed with
delight when they saw me both during
pregnancy and in the two years it took me to lose
my weight after each child. 'Aren't you *big*!' they
cooed with delight, eyeing up my swollen tummy
and thick thighs. But my size also left me with a
series of painful health problems.

Some women slink out of hospital in their
pre-pregnancy jeans, newborn baby cradled
casually in their slim arms. I wasn't one of them.
I waddled into hospital a huffing, puffing

heffalump, and hobbled out after each Caesarean, having lost my dignity but very little baby weight. After having Amy, however, I was also left with a large painful stomach and a huge bump under my belly button. It was so painful I couldn't bear the weight of clothing on it; even a T-shirt brushing against it hurt. The best way to relieve it was wearing something firm and supportive, like a girdle, which held the bump in place and felt like a protective hand over my belly. The doctors assured me that this would all settle down in time as my stomach muscles joined together again, but sadly this wasn't to happen. However, as we had completed the sale on our new home while I was still in hospital, I didn't have time to mooch about and feel sorry for myself. We had a couple of weeks to make it ship-shape before we moved in, so while Finlay was at school, I chipped in with the painting and scrubbing as Amy snoozed in a corner of the room in her carrycot.

It was while I was climbing up onto the kitchen counter to paint a wall that I felt, and I swear even *heard*, the rip in my abdominal muscle. I gasped and sat down hard, paintbrush in hand, and waited for the pain to ease. Mum and Dad were now living in Spain, and had come over to help us move and settle in. They and Steve were busy in another room, and I didn't want to tell them what had happened as I knew it was my own stupid fault for not taking it easy, but I'm not really a 'take it easy' kind of person. I quietly made my way to the bathroom, and sure enough, I had popped a couple of stitches in my C-section, and something felt very wrong in my abdomen. I foolishly told no one what had happened as I didn't want to make a fuss, and I thought it would all just sort itself out. I had no idea that years later that decision would almost cost me my life, and my body would never be the same again.

Rather than slowing down, life only seemed to become more and more hectic. We moved house a week before Christmas, with a four-week-old baby girl, a five-year-old little boy, and two sixty-something parents who were a godsend with their energy and helpfulness. We also decided, insanely, that we didn't need removal men and did it on our own. Then twelve weeks after the birth I was back at *GMTV* and I started hosting *Loose Women*. This job had come out of the blue. A few weeks before going back to work I had popped into London to see a producer friend of mine to ask her for some career advice. I had been working on live terrestrial television for over a decade, but although I was put up for other jobs and had come close a few times to getting some good prime-time co-hosting work, with the exception of *Dancing on Ice Extra* I was always pipped at the post, coming a close second. I was seen as a 'safe pair of hands' in terms of my ability, but people weren't that interested in me.

Sue Walton had hired me to work on *Our House*, the show on UK Style where I had met Steve. She knew me and what I was capable of, and had become enough of a friend that I trusted her judgement. I didn't expect anything

266

other than some advice when we met up that day in the bar at ITV, but our chat was to change the course of my career forever.

'Have you ever thought of working on *Loose Women*?' she asked me, her blue eyes twinkling. Sue had now moved to ITV and was the executive producer of the lunchtime chat show.

'Absolutely not!' I laughed. 'That's a show full of women shouting at each other and rowing! I'd be rubbish!' I had been a guest on the show a couple of years earlier and had been so intimidated that I'd hardly said a word. I've never liked confrontation, or telling the world about my private life, so I didn't think it was my kind of thing at all. We carried on talking and Sue told me I needed to have more confidence in myself and be more outgoing, and that would help me work-wise. We said a cheery goodbye and I didn't think about *Loose Women* until I got a call from my agent on my first day back at work.

'Sue Walton has just been on the phone. She's seen that you are back at work now and wants to try you out on *Loose Women*.'

I was shocked. 'But I'd be terrible! I'd never get a word in and I don't have anything to say compared to the other women!'

'That's OK, you could just come in where you wanted to. The rest of it will be fine.'

'But surely that's your job on *Loose Women*, to have strong opinions and not be afraid to fight for them?'

'Not if you're the anchor. You have to be balanced and fair if you're the anchor and let the others speak. You just need to lead the discussion and make sure it has covered all sides, you don't have to *take* sides.'

'The anchor?' *Hmm, that's quite a different prospect,* I thought to myself. 'I'd LOVE to try it!'

And so three days later, after doing the weather on *GMTV*, I made my way downstairs at ITV to the *Loose Women* meeting room. I sat quietly and made notes while the ladies gave their opinions on the topics the producers and researchers had thought up for the day, and then went into make-up, and then into the studio for a read-through and to voice over the day's competition. Suddenly the hours had passed, it was 12.30 and I was smiling into a camera in front of a studio audience, about to present a live TV show with four feisty women. I was terrified. As the music faded out I wiped my sweaty palms on my seat, smiled brightly and pretended I was Kaye Adams. I'd always been a fan of hers, and I tried to copy her calm air of authority and look like I knew what the hell I was doing. The ladies were kind to me and did their thing without much guidance from me, talking brightly and arguing spiritedly among themselves while I sat rooted to the spot. The sweat was running down my back by the time we finished an hour later, and I was exhausted, but I had done it! Then I was in the car on my way home and it was all finished. By the time I got home my agent was on the phone.

'They want you to do it again next week!' she said, sounding thrilled. I felt sick; I had fooled them into thinking I could do it once, but could I pull it off a second time?

Somehow I did, and gradually I got asked to do a few more days, then a few more days, and then I was asked to stand in for Jackie Brambles when she went on maternity leave.

It was all quite straightforward, as I was in the building anyway so could easily pop down after my last weather slot at 8.30 a.m. The only problems came when I was sent away to do an outside broadcast, as I would have to hightail it from one end of the country to the other just to get back in time to be on air by 12.30. Sometimes I made it with lots of time to spare, other times it was a bit hairy, like when I raced back from being live at Ascot and ended up just brushing my hair and rushing on in the same clothes I'd been wearing all morning. The viewers didn't seem to notice and the production team didn't mind, so I carried on. As time went by I became more confident, and stopped crying on my way home because I felt I wasn't strong enough to handle the ladies. I was younger than them, less experienced in terms of life stories and was much too soft. I knew I had to butch up, but I didn't know how. How did I stop myself from being such an irritatingly nice girl?

Well, I did. It took time and a few run-ins along the way, but over the years I learned to stand up for myself. I learned not to take it to heart when someone shouted down my opinion or laughed at my ideas. I can count the times I have lost my temper on one hand, which is saying something, but each of those times made me stronger for it. I may have quivered inside, but I stood tall and held my ground, and gradually I have been accepted into the pack. There have been snarls and raised hackles, and possibly a few nips and squeals, but with each one my skin has grown tougher. And I have lasted on the show for five years because of it. I used to be the good girl, afraid to cause a fuss or defend myself, but not any more. I'm proud to be a host of that show, and will fight for my job because I love it! I know I am good at it and I deserve to be there.

★   ★   ★

For my first year as a Loose Woman I was still holding down my weather job on *GMTV*. Much as I enjoyed both jobs, it was tiring trying to keep cheerful while being sent around the country at a moment's notice, lugging my suitcase on and off trains late at night. I wore my maternity trousers for the first six months after having Amy, so they were high enough to protect my bulging stomach, but it didn't help when people patted me and told me 'congratulations' . . . not for the baby I'd had, but the one they thought I was expecting. My belly button was by now the size of a child's elbow, and was tender and sore. I could barely carry Amy as the strain was so great on my stomach, and I also had another smaller, but just as painful, bulge between my belly button and breast bone. At times it looked like I had a little Loch Ness monster poking his head out of my belly.

I had left it for far too long — I'd been too busy with two jobs and a family to look after myself — but when Amy was ten months old I decided to get it looked at. The specialist told me that I had a large umbilical hernia, a complication following on from *diastasis recti*, or the separation of the left and right sides of my abdominal muscles, which had allowed part of my intestines to protrude.

I didn't want to wait any longer as it was now incredibly painful and unsightly, so I paid to have the umbilical hernia repaired. It was a straightforward operation where the surgeon pushed the lump back in, and inserted a mesh over the top to stop it bulging through again. It was hoped that my abdominal walls would in time return to normal, which would push back my second hernia, but this wasn't the case.

Rather than healing me, my operation seemed to create problems of its own, not least the shock of discovering I had contracted MRSA. A swab taken before I had gone in for surgery had come back positive, and a curt letter arrived telling me that I needed to go to my GP and get a prescription to stop it infecting my wound. I had no symptoms, which meant my wound was clear, but it was still a shock. I felt like a shadow had passed over me that I hadn't been aware of, as if I had brushed past Death in a corridor and felt its chill, not knowing that he had been looking for me but my time hadn't come. An over-dramatic reaction, I'm sure, but it was my reaction nonetheless, and it was was enough to send me into a tailspin of sorting out wills and life insurance so that my children would be provided for if anything happened to me. My mortality and fragility shocked me; I was not the fighter I thought I was, and the realization that I was fallible didn't sit well. My already hormonal brain struggled with this, and I have to say it was one of my lowest points.

Mentally, I had not returned to my normal happy self after having Amy, something I denied for a long time until the blackness became too big to cover with a cheery smile. As one of life's 'copers', it was hard to admit to myself that I was struggling. When I broached the subject with Steve his reaction wasn't good; he didn't have much time for people who said they were feeling depressed and he didn't want to know. He felt it was weak, and that I should just pull myself together, which I tried desperately hard to do. I went to work every day, I held down two demanding jobs with a cheery smile and didn't let anything ruffle me. I organized my house and made sure that things ran smoothly and that the children were happy. But quietly, on my own, I felt like I was cracking up.

Sometimes it would happen without warning: I'd pop to the loo in the middle of the morning meeting and suddenly find myself overwhelmed with sadness and grief, tears pouring down my face and my hand over my mouth to stifle the sobs. After a few minutes of holding my breath and trying to pull myself together I'd flush the loo, wash my hands and wipe my face with a tissue, then walk back into the meeting room, smile in place and ready for work.

At home I did the same thing. I tidied and smiled and hugged and coped while feeling that if someone poked me just a little too hard, I would shatter into a thousand pieces. I was capable, and was a loving mum and partner and I was good at my job, so there couldn't be that much wrong with me, could there? I was doing what I always did: I was coping and being good, not bothering anyone with the fact that underneath I felt hopeless and worthless and exhausted.

Then one night in bed I started crying and couldn't stop. Everything was awful; everything. Amy was so beautiful, I didn't deserve her. Finlay was being difficult and had said he didn't like me. Steve was finding the whole shift from life as a single man to life as a new dad of two with a hormonal partner a bit of a shock to the system and had done the man thing of shutting down. I felt like everyone would be better off without me hanging around, and that night I tentatively mentioned it to him.

Steve was livid. 'What a stupid thing to say!' he snapped and threw the covers back and got out of bed. 'I won't have you saying things like that. Just sort yourself out and deal with it.' He stomped off to watch TV in the living room, unable to cope. I cried and cried, and lay awake after the tears had dried wondering what I should do. Where had the old me gone? Would I ever have the physical and mental strength I'd once had? Where was the girl who felt like she could grab hold of her dreams and make them a reality, who thought that anything was possible?

Then out of the blue something clicked. I finally acknowledged that I would never get back to my old self, either mentally or physically, so I would have to live with a new me. It was not necessarily an improved me, but it was what I had become, and that was that. I would learn to love this new person for the sake of my children and Steve. I would do as he said and take control of this and never mention it again.

So the next day, without telling Steve, I went to my doctor and tearfully said I thought I was suffering from postnatal depression. I described how I had been feeling, how I was able to put on a façade in public but in private I felt like I was drowning. My doctor was wonderful. She told me not to see this as a failing in myself, or a weakness or lack of strength; it was just something that many women went through after having a baby because of hormonal imbalance. I briefly explained what had been going on in my life: my marriage ending, a surprise pregnancy, moving house, starting a new job . . . all within the space of two and a half years. She smiled and said that it was a wonder I had coped for so long without needing any kind of help, and she gave me some tablets that changed everything.

For years I didn't tell anyone that I had been prescribed antidepressants. I felt ashamed that I hadn't been able to 'pull myself together' and be strong enough on my own to cope. I know that some people think antidepressants are a modern crutch for pathetic people who can't deal with what life throws at them, and I respect their opinion. But they are wrong. Within a month of taking my tablets I woke up one day and felt like someone had flicked a switch in my brain. The best way I can describe it is that a brain is like a fuse board — when a fuse blows in your home, you have to flick the one switch that is down to make things work again, and suddenly you can hear the fridge start to hum as it comes back to life, and the lights flicker on and everything is back as it was. That is what it felt like.

I didn't go from being in tears one day to bouncing around full of the joys the next; I just felt normal again. I'm not ashamed any more that I need help to cope, because you know what? Life is hard, and sometimes we all need something to help us get through. I don't care if people think I am weak, because I know I'm not. I am strong enough to know when I need help and brave enough to ask for it. What's weak about that?

The day after I went to the doctor I joined a gym; I saw this as something constructive, something positive. I couldn't find any local postnatal classes so I decided to go to a 'Nice and Easy' aerobics class. I had never been to aerobics in my life, but I thought it might be the kick start I needed. I went along, and was the youngest by at least twenty years. I stood at the back, lost and fat and pale, while these energetic fifty- and sixty-year-old women leapt and clapped and grapevined and box-stepped around me. It was like the instructor was speaking in tongues; I had no idea what he was talking about. I crawled home, humiliated and stiff, but a few days later I decided to swallow my pride and go again. And this time I kind of understood what he was on about, and could almost keep up.

After that I went to the class twice a week for four weeks, always at the back, always the youngest and nearly always the slowest. But eventually something clicked. The class ended and I was hot and sweaty as always, but I felt like I had more in me, like I wasn't quite done. So I went into the gym and rode on the bike for a while, and did some weights. And I looked in the mirror, and I kind of saw myself. For the first time since Amy was born, I saw someone who looked a bit like me. It was still a big me, with a flabby round tummy that looked suspiciously maternity-like, with widened hips and pale bingo-winged arms . . . but I was in there somewhere; I was starting to break through, and that was enough. I realized then that nothing could take away what makes me me, and that I had taken my first tentative steps on the road to recovery.

★   ★   ★

About a year after moving out of London and settling into our new life in Surrey, Finlay was happy in his school and Amy was happy with Lin — a wonderful woman who we hired to help me with childcare and much, much more after Emilie, our lovely au-pair, went travelling round America. I was starting to settle into my life as a Loose Woman and was managing to juggle *GMTV* as well. So we decided the time was right to do what we had always set out to do . . . we knocked our house down.

The biggest practical undertaking of my life began with little sketches on scraps of paper showing what my 'dream home' would look like. Every night I thrust them under Steve's nose, and he gently told me that this room wasn't possible as a support wall was needed; and that room wasn't possible due to the laws of physics . . . and as we combined his building know-how with my ideas, our sketches turned into drawings, and eventually these became proper architect's plans. We'd also obtained planning permission to demolish the old house (bar one existing wall) and build the new one, so before long we were ready to start making our dream home a reality.

We packed everyone up again, and moved into a rented house with the idea that we could be in there for a year, but hoping it would be quicker as the budget, our bank manager and, of course, we would be happier that way. Two weeks later our home was a pile of rubble; there was no going back.

The first few weeks were very exciting as our little house was knocked down and the site was levelled and cleared, before the ground workers moved in to dig out the foundations. Then came the first problem; we had been waiting for it. I had watched enough episodes of *Grand Designs* to know that things never went smoothly on a house build, and although Kevin McCloud wasn't around to talk in posh, hushed tones about our first hiccup, to me it was no less dramatic. Steve sighed and took it in his stride; he had been expecting something too, but not this. Our home had a cellar . . . a big cellar — which wasn't listed on any of our deeds and meant that there was a gaping hole where our foundations were meant to be. I panicked that there could be bodies inside and told Steve not to go anywhere near it, and he quite sensibly ignored me and discovered it was empty; there weren't even any ridiculously expensive bottles of wine that we could have sold to help pay for the cost of filling up the hole. The building work stopped, the council was called and the site was checked over. Eventually we were given permission to carry on, which meant filling a great big hole in the ground with enough dirt to support a house — *after* we had got rid of several skips full of useful rubble.

That drama over, the foundations were dug and concreted and the walls started to creep upwards. Rooms were measured out, and the bare bones of our house appeared. I visited the site most days, picking my way through the piles of rough sand and setting concrete, snapping away like a brick-crazed paparazzi so that I had a log of what our house looked like at every stage. By May, three months after we had begun, the floors had been concreted over, and the walls were high enough for Steve to step in and do his thing. His team of builders arrived to guide in the series of steel supports that would eventually hold up our first floor, skipping over joists like circus acts, shouting orders and laughing as they stood fearlessly on lengths of wood above my head. It was amazing to see, as steel after steel was craned in and lowered onto our growing house, then pushed, pulled and finally screwed into place. I had my eyes shut through most of it, convinced someone was going to fall and land on their head. Steve smiled at me: 'It's fine, Andrea . . . this is what I do . . . ' I'm only glad I'm not around to see this every day, or I would have them all dressed as Mr Blobby just so they'd bounce if they hit the floor.

With the steels in place, the work cranked up a gear, and the house seemed to grow by the day. *At this rate we'll be in by summer*, I thought, but Steve warned me not to get over-excited — this was the fast bit, he said; things start slowing down near the end of a build, and that's when nerves get frayed. It went in one ear and out the other; it was sunny, our house was being built, and I was convinced he was just being a spoilsport! By June, the whole of the upstairs had taken shape, and I could pick my way around the skeleton of each room. In my mind the end was most definitely in sight.

But time raced on and before we knew it autumn was upon us. And while the outside of the house looked as it should, inside was a different story, with dangling wires, unfinished plumbing and wet plaster. Everyone seemed to be waiting for everyone else to finish before they could start, and to the untrained eye, the whole thing seemed to have ground to a halt. This was the bit Steve had warned me about, when decisions had to be made on an almost daily basis on heights for plugs and positioning of toilets; when orders needed to be in on time, otherwise people were standing around waiting, and time was money.

And that was another thing . . . money. What had started out as a fairly healthy pot had vanished within roughly three minutes of starting the building work. Savings were plundered, bank loans begged for, and a remortgage applied for just as the world went into global economic meltdown. There were men inside and outside the house, all busy doing necessary work, all needing to be paid. We *had* to get out of the rental house as soon as possible to save some money. Steve had promised we would be in for Christmas, and he changed the goalposts to aim for November to save some cash.

Everyone pulled out all the stops, and just as quickly things began to speed up again. Steve and I had long discussions into the night about every little decision, and every decision we made ultimately came down to two things: what I thought looked good, and what he said we could afford — a pretty normal situation for most couples. I had folders dedicated to types of sliding doors, windows, roof tiles, brickwork and render. I wanted the look of the outside to match my vision for the inside, but also to be in keeping with the area we lived in.

I didn't want a *Grand Designs* special, all modern white cube and floor-to-roof glass; I wanted a family home that looked traditional from the front, but gave a nod to modernism at the back, away from prying eyes. I wanted huge sliding doors that allowed the south-facing garden to be seen and enjoyed, and which made the large patio feel like it swept out from the kitchen. I wanted it to flow from inside to out and outside to in, so that on bright days the doors could slide back and the children could play in the sun and still feel like they were in part of the house, but on cold winter days the glass doors would mean we didn't feel hemmed in, we were still part of the garden, without actually having to be cold and wet.

I lay awake at night fretting over the details. Not a day went by without some decision or another needing to be made. Plug sockets: where did I want them, and how many? Bathroom suites: had they been chosen and ordered? Tiles? Lights? Skirting? Architrave? Doors? Door handles? The kitchen! I scoured beautiful designer shops looking for ideas, and I got loads of them. The thing was, I would have had to sell the house to be able to buy them. And a beautiful hand-finished silver velvet love seat is not really what you need if you're forced to live in a box under a bridge to finance it. So, I kept myself frantically busy searching for things that *looked like* they were designer but were actually off the high street, while Steve pushed and cajoled and laughed and bantered in a desperate bid to get the project finished. And he did. I don't know how he did it, but in the last week of November we moved into our dream house.

Our wonderful home is all thanks to Steve, who like an articulated lorry cranked up the gears and powered all of us through. He pushed and bullied and kept us going. There were times when he was horrible to live with and he drove me mad every time he said, 'This is how it is when you build a house; get over it.' But he was right. We needed someone to keep the vision in sight and keep on trucking until we got there, come what may — and he did it.

By the time we moved in, a month before Christmas in 2008, we were at breaking point, exhausted both mentally and physically, emotionally and financially drained and, to be honest, sick of the sight of 'the bloody house'. The stress of constant decision-making, of needing answers, solutions, more answers, more money, more money, more money had reduced us to the point where we could barely speak to each other. Then one night about two weeks after we moved in, we sat in our beautiful living room, watching our beautiful TV, and we both looked around and said, 'We did it. Look at our beautiful home. We did it.' And we both burst into tears.

It was an amazing experience to build our own home, and when people come to visit and say it's lovely, we know that they don't know the half of it. They have no idea of the blood, sweat, tears and tantrums that went into making our dream a reality. We didn't just choose this house; we built it, from scratch. Every single inch of it was decided by us, some of it through choice, some through compromise. We had an idea, one that started out as a drawing on a scrap of paper, and now we are living in it; what's better than that? Every time I put my key in the lock I feel a sense of pride that I chose our front door and had it specially made, so it is just how I had pictured it. Every time we visit our local pub I laugh to myself because our house is painted the same colour; I'd had a 'eureka!' moment when we drove by one day and I realized it was the exact shade of cream I wanted. The landlord managed to track down the company that painted it and we ordered our paint from the same suppliers!

There is a story behind every part of the house, and even if we don't end up living there until the end of our days, we will always be able to say, 'See that house? We built that.' And it feels good.

# 17

## I Am Grateful

Despite all my wonderful experiences at *GMTV*, and there were many, my main job there was to present the weather, and there came a time when I decided that eleven years of standing in the rain was really long enough. Being a weather presenter had its drawbacks when bad weather was not only expected but, in some cases, relished. To a welly-clad festival-goer, rain is a foregone conclusion. To a broadcaster, it's a chance to show people sliding in mud, and is a *good thing*, which is why in 2008, I found myself heading off to another muddy field. This time it was Glastonbury. Torrential rain had been predicted, and boy did it deliver, all over me and an unlucky young producer as we struggled in the dark to pitch a tent in the mud next to a satellite truck. We lay for four hours while music thumped, people raved and the rain came down. In the morning, while Glastonbury slept, I tiptoed between the tents and told the nation that the heavens had delivered and the welly-fest could begin. And as I made my way home on the train, slightly damp, and very tired and sore from my sleepless night on stony wet ground, I made a decision. I was getting too old and too tired for this; it was time for someone else to take *GMTV*'s weather reins.

I handed in my resignation and worked out my six months' notice. It was pretty long, but knowing that there was an end in sight made things easier. Nothing really changed during that time; I just carried on as normal, quietly counting down the months until I didn't have to set my alarm for 3.30 a.m.

My last day was New Year's Eve 2008, when I was asked to present the weather from Trafalgar Square — the day would be spent in the cold and wet, just like old times. Then, as I was about to do my 8 a.m. broadcast, my lovely fellow weathergirl Clare Nasir arrived in a blacked-out Mercedes and announced she was taking me back into the warmth of the studio! She bundled me into the back of the car, and next thing I knew I was being rushed in to do my last ever weather broadcast for *GMTV* in front of the green screen in the studio dressed in jeans and thermals. It was not the best look, especially as I'd been wearing a bobble hat all morning and had hat hair, but I was so happy to have the chance to see the crew one last time that I didn't care how I looked. I joked and giggled my way through the broadcast, my heart warming to the laughter coming from the gallery and the smiles from behind the cameras.

Then I was led over to the infamous red sofa, presented with a huge bunch of flowers and invited to watch a montage of my 'best bits'. It included footage of me doing a loop the loop strapped to the top of a biplane and screaming loudly enough to be heard in at least three counties. It showed me doing the weather in snow, rain, wind and sun, from all parts of the UK and from all around the world. It showed me slim, it showed me fat, with long hair and short, all the while smiling and laughing through eleven years of live breakfast television. I was choked with emotion when it finished. I'd forgotten just how much I had done in those years, and how much fun I'd had along the way. I started as a rookie girl and left that day as a confident, capable woman, and much of it was thanks to the fantastic people who worked there and gave me the chance to try new things and to improve on the job. Before the last few seconds of the show ticked to a close, I managed to thank live on air the people who had made my time at *GMTV* so amazing: the crew.

And then as everyone rushed off home to start their New Year celebrations, I loaded up my taxi with flowers and gifts and said goodbye for the final time to the studio that had been my home for so long. It felt like a chapter was ending, but for all the right reasons. It was time to move on and face new challenges, and who knew what exciting things lay in store for me now?

★ ★ ★

I missed the first two days of 2009 as I slept right through them. I took to my bed in the early hours of 1 January after announcing that I didn't know when I would be getting up, having been awake for over twenty-four hours, but I intended to sleep for a VERY long time. And I did; I caught up on eleven years' worth of sleep! When

I woke up on 3 January I was excited and raring to go. I wasn't a weathergirl any more, I was now a Loose Woman!

It is not an exaggeration to say that getting the job on *Loose Women* changed my life. I was sharing the role with Jackie Brambles, who had returned from maternity leave, and was working two or three days a week. I was now able to go to bed at the same time as the rest of the adult population, something I hadn't been able to do for over a decade. I wasn't permanently exhausted after early starts, or stressed out every time my phone rang that I was going to be sent to the furthest reaches of the UK without any notice. My life became my own. I knew where I was going to be, and for how long, and it meant I could drop the children to school and nursery in the mornings if I wasn't working, and even be around to pick them up in the afternoon if I was, while still being awake enough to enjoy their company rather than counting the hours until they went to bed. It gave me the energy to be a better mum to them and a better partner to Steve. It is a perfect job for a working mum, and all the mums who work on it are thankful for that.

Once I had left *GMTV* I felt like I was really able to relax and be myself on *Loose Women*. I wasn't having to worry that anything I said on the show might upset someone at my other job; this was where I worked now, and I settled in with a renewed enthusiasm. I didn't think about the show in terms of furthering my career; it was just something that fulfilled me, that worked for me as a woman and a mother as well as a presenter.

It was at this time that I started to loosen up and enjoy myself more on the show, not just because I had the confidence to do so, but also because I had more energy as I was getting more sleep. It sounds like such a small thing, but even with Amy still not sleeping through every night, I am more awake in my forties than I was right through my thirties working in breakfast television!

To me, the magic of *Loose Women* is its simplicity. Like a master chef who uses fresh ingredients that complement each other, all the women bring something different to the table. Together, they are spicy, warm and homely, all at the same time, and definitely saucy!

One of the charms of the show is that it looks so effortless, but there is a lot more going on behind the scenes than people think. The most important part of our day is the morning meeting, as this is where the topics are thrashed out. Our editor Emily Humphries begins by introducing each subject and, depending on the ladies' reaction to it, we either use it on the show, or ditch it and move on to another.

This is the part of the show that it took me the longest to get used to. The other ladies were accustomed to the setup when I first joined, and threw themselves into each topic with relish while I held back. Now I am used to it and I can easily spill the beans about my personal thoughts and feelings, as we all know and trust each other implicitly. What is said in the room stays in the

288

room, unless we have announced that a certain story or revelation is for public consumption. If the walls of our meeting room had ears, the stories it could tell!

Each morning starts with the delivery of coffee, tea and sometimes toast, as we settle down on three comfy sofas around a small table and gossip about what we've been up to the night before or what we've seen on telly. Carol McGiffin is always dressed from head to toe in an 'outfit'; everything matches and has been thought through from the underwear outwards, so she looks fabulous. Lisa Maxwell looks like a sleepy little blonde dormouse when she arrives, having snoozed in the back of a car all the way from Gloucestershire to London. Denise Welch is normally full of fabulous gossip, Janet Street Porter has usually got something exciting to say about her friend Elton John, which we are all secretly hugely impressed with, and Jenny Eclair tucks in heartily to a Pret A Manger sandwich as the meeting begins, preparing to say something that will have us all giggling. It's like coming to school and waiting for the teacher to start assembly, although we are not as well behaved as schoolchildren, and probably get told off more . . .

The biggest change for me when I started on *Loose Women* was an editorial one. I was used to sitting in meetings with an editor and discussing the stories of the day; I had done that since my days in journalism, and through my time in breakfast TV when I was covering stories other than the weather. This time, however, rather than deciding on an interesting story, then discussing how we were going to report on it, I had to be prepared to give my opinion on it, something I'd never been expected to do before. And as someone with splinters in her bum from a lifetime of sitting on the fence, I am relieved that as anchor, I am mainly expected to steer the others through their range of opinions, rather than necessarily give one of my own. This is where the ladies really come into their own, and it's something that both viewers and wannabe Loose Women think is easy. It's not. It's actually incredibly difficult to be open and honest about parts of your life that your family or friends would prefer you kept to yourself. There will always be someone on the show whom viewers will agree or disagree with — that's the whole point of it — but it's this honesty, when women at home sit up and think, *I feel like that too*, that makes the show so special, and makes my job so interesting and so much fun.

★　★　★

I have been lucky to interview some fabulous people since I first joined *Loose Women*, people I would never previously have imagined I'd even lay eyes on during my lifetime — Andy García, Enrique Inglesias, Russell Brand, David Hassel-hoff, Joan Collins and Cilla Black, who has now become a Loose Woman herself! We even finally got Ant and Dec on the show to promote their autobiography, after years of drunken cajoling by us at TV parties. The picture on the front of their book shows the two of them in a grinning clinch. Well, Dec is grinning, Ant looks rather odd. I pointed this out to them on the show, and offered a possible solution to Ant's rather strained expression.

'Where's your hand?' I asked Dec. 'Because you're smiling, but Ant looks like, well . . . where's your hand?!'

They both looked at the picture quizzically, and then roared with laughter.

'I was trying to look, you know, dashing! I was trying to do that eyebrow thing!' Ant said.

And instead he looks like he's being goosed by his best mate, which wasn't quite what they'd been after.

Usher, the man behind the pop whirlwind that is Justin Bieber, was a recent guest, and the one that sparked the most texted requests I've ever had from friends and acquaintances asking for seats on the show — I've never been so popular! I wasn't sure what to expect from him — maybe shades on and a huge entourage — but he couldn't have been nicer. He took us ladies all in his stride, laughed at himself, and even sang in the lift for one of our favourite runners, Anthony, which made his year. Some stars are way beyond expectation.

Alex Zane is another who is much more than he seems. After a minute and a half of chatting to him about film, which is a real passion of mine, I wanted to take him home. Obviously to talk about film, and maybe help around the house a bit, possibly even walk the dog for me, but come home nonetheless. I think my husband would

291

have understood, as he is as mad about films as I am — as long as we all had entertaining conversations about the merits of Spanish director Pedro Almodovar versus the dumbing-down of Hollywood, I think he'd be happy to put him up in the spare room.

I usually base my opinions on our star guests around two things: how they behave behind the scenes, and whether I'd like to go to the pub with them afterwards. The question I get asked by people more than any other is, 'Who's the worst guest you've had on the show?' and it's a really difficult one to answer. Interviewing someone on television is a completely different ball game to interviewing them for a newspaper or magazine, for one specific reason: they are on show. If you are given a one-to-one interview with a star that involves just the two of you and a tape recorder, they can behave exactly as they like. A flick of the hair, a roll of the eyes and an explosive sigh before trotting out a stock answer that looks fine on paper but has been uttered without a shred of sincerity is easy to do when you are not on camera.

I have interviewed one female in particular who is hugely famous around the world, whom I have met many times in TV circles, who never twigged that I was the same person she'd fawned over while on the show a week before, and then ignored me as I sat in front of her with my notebook in hand, waiting until she was 'ready' to talk. Even though I was introduced as *Loose Women*'s Andrea McLean, because it was out of context she didn't get it, and was bored, rude and dismissive. When interviewing people for the show, I don't usually get to see that side of them, as I meet them when they are primed and ready with something to sell. So when people ask me who is the worst person we've had on the show, I would tell them to ask one of the team behind the scenes. Because they are the ones who have to deal with the diva demands, the sulks and tantrums of men and women who don't know what side their bread is buttered. They may be smiling and jovial and game for a laugh during their six minutes of air time, but their behaviour off stage can be quite different.

Some stars do come for a drink after the show — not so much now that we are live every day, but a few years ago when we used to record a couple of programmes in a day and would head straight to the bar next door for a cheeky half afterwards, we were sometimes joined by the guests. It was mainly the boys, to be honest: Andy García and Max Beesley are just two who stayed for a drink and were great company.

Jackie Collins is someone we all WANT to take for a drink, but she hasn't come along as yet. She is always wonderful when she comes on the show, full of twinkle and mischief, and you just know that she would have fabulous gossip to share. Her sister Joan has also been on the show many times, and I think she quite enjoys it now, after an initial and understandable wariness. There is always a palpable air of fear before Joan arrives, as the runners tuck in their shirts, pull up their ridiculously low-slung trousers and sometimes even produce a jacket and tie. 'Miss

Collins' likes people around her to look smart, and is the only person I have ever seen who can reduce a runner to a quivering wreck with the power of one perfectly plucked raised eyebrow. She is always impeccably dressed, unfailingly courteous and absolutely terrifying to those charged with making her visit run smoothly. I have never heard of any untoward behaviour on her part and I admire that she doesn't need it; one look is enough! Joan has always been a pleasure to have on the show, and there is a part of me that is secretly thrilled when she turns to me on camera, replies to my prompting with a glossy red smile and purrs, 'Well, Andrea, I'm *so* glad you asked me that . . . ' The legendary Joan Collins knows my name. It doesn't get better than that.

Nights out with the Loose ladies are something I often get asked about, and yes, we've had some fantastic times. Before joining *Loose Women*, I had spent over a decade working in breakfast television and getting up at 3.30 a.m., so my social life had hardly been a whirl. I had also fitted in a marriage, a baby, a divorce, a new partner and a new baby, so I hadn't had much time for crazy nights out. Suddenly, I found myself thrown into in a world where you *could* go for a drink after work (as it wasn't 9.30 a.m.), and having a few 'to take the edge off' was actually embraced! It was liberating and really helped me to gel with the ladies and the rest of the team on the show.

One of the most fun nights I've had with the ladies was at the launch of *Calendar Girls* in

London, starring our very own Lynda Bellingham. We all went along to support Bellers, and suddenly it turned into a night of Women on the Loose! At least that's how the press saw it. I had turned up wearing black, my hair in a ponytail and my glasses on, not quite realizing the fuss that would be made. After the wonderful show, we were introduced to the *real* Calendar Girls, which was such an honour, before we all headed out of the theatre. There was a frenzy of flashbulbs — it must have been a deathly quiet night on the London social scene as every paparazzi in the city was trying to get a picture of us! At first it was funny, because we'd never experienced anything like it before, but then they started to chase us down the street. Denise and I ended up separated from the rest of the ladies, so we decided to make a break for it by jumping into one of those pedal taxis. Well, we couldn't breathe for laughing as the paps chased us through London while our poor little cyclist pedalled like the clappers. We eventually pulled up outside the Groucho Club and dashed inside (very exciting for me as I'd only been in there once before), and the next day the papers were full of pictures of Denise's 'drunken night on the town', showing her fighting through the crowds outside the theatre, jumping into the rickshaw and laughing. Even though I was by her side through the whole journey, and we hadn't even seen a bar yet, never mind had a drink, the papers made out that it was another 'crazy night out on the lash'. So don't believe everything you read . . .

I remember one particular awards do early on, where we had been nominated but hadn't won, and because our award had been one of the first to be announced and I had *GMTV* the next day, I snuck out early. In fact I was at home in bed by eleven. That night, Carol flashed her lovely black frilly pants, and Denise flashed her not-so-lovely Spanx. It was a quick-as-a-flash joke that was forgotten about minutes later, but in the papers the next day — knickergate. And apparently I had left as sozzled as the next man, flashing my boobs on the way. The picture they showed was actually of me blinking because of the flash bulbs, leaning forward to shut the taxi door, and accidentally flashing a bit more boob than I'd intended. But why let that get in the way of a good story? After that night the Loose Women became known as party animals, just because we showed a bit of lycra and perhaps a little too much flesh. The press sneered at us, while everyone else wanted to go out on the town with us, and they still do!

In actual fact, most of our nights out are great fun but low key. They don't involve flash parties or awards ceremonies; they are just nights in the bar next door to work, sitting outside so people can smoke, sharing bottles of wine and nibbles while laughing and talking rubbish. The production team are far funnier than we are anyway, so most of the night revolves around them! What starts off as a 'quick half' occasionally leads to everyone being turfed out at closing time, wobbly and hugging and heading off on our merry way, but not getting up to anything more unusual than that. Just as the best parties always end up in the kitchen, our best nights out are usually unplanned and not flash at all, and just involve us and the lovely people we work with. Oh, and quite a few bottles of Chardonnay . . .

★ ★ ★

My family and friends have all noticed a change in me since I joined *Loose Women* — hopefully for the better. I have learned that it is healthy to have your own opinion and express it, that to disagree with someone doesn't mean falling out with them, and that you can move on to another subject and start completely afresh. My blinkered 'Snow White' views on life have been robustly challenged, at times even shot down in flames, and bit by bit I have come out of my shell.

Very little shocks me now. We have all revealed parts of our lives that are deeply personal in that meeting room, and every morning is like a tiny bit of therapy, where we can openly say how we feel about whatever is bothering us, either in the world, ourselves or our home life. I have opened up more in those four walls than I have probably ever done to my family and friends, and have had my thoughts dissected and my opinions machine-gunned. Because of my talks with the Loose Women I have re-evaluated just about every part of my life, and I will always be glad that the show came into my life when it did.

It amazes me how life can be taking you in one

particular direction, and then something tiny happens that redirects you along a completely different path. It was a chance cup of coffee that led to me hosting *Loose Women*. I've now been there for almost five wonderful years, during which time the show has gone on to win many wonderful awards. Coincidence? Absolutely, but I am thrilled and grateful that I have been there while it has been at its peak. I'm a firm believer that you have to take every opportunity life throws you, and the chance to host *Loose Women* is most definitely one I'm glad I grabbed hold of with both hands.

# 18

## Back to Life

At the beginning of 2009, Steve and I took the kids away to Egypt for a break and a chance to soak up some sunshine. It was one evening while we were there, the kids asleep and us lying in bed watching *Forrest Gump*, that Steve asked me to marry him. He got up and fiddled about in the cupboard while I sat teary-eyed (it's one of my favourite films) and then dropped down on one knee by the side of the bed, wearing nothing but his underpants. I looked round to see him holding out a box with a beautiful diamond ring inside, just as he said, 'Will you marry me?' It was so ridiculous it was perfect.

We got married later that year in front of friends and family in a small hotel in Surrey. Amy and Finlay were flower girl and pageboy, Jane was 'best woman' and Steve's friend (also called Steve) was best man. We did everything *our* way, including having two little figurines of Snow White and Bob the Builder on the top tier of a stack of white and silver cupcakes. We danced to Take That 2, a tribute band who not only were fantastic, but were also really good sports when Steve stormed the stage and demanded to be Robbie.

Everyone mucked in and had a great time. Penny Smith and Clare Nasir from *GMTV*

299

chatted with Lisa from *Loose Women*, while Denise enthusiastically danced with the groom on the dance floor. She then twirled me around, wedding dress and all, and I was only saved from landing on my back by my sister who was standing behind me! Phil Turner (whom we'd become friendly with during our time on UK Style) danced with his husband, make-up artist Gary Cockerill. My cousins spent long hours chatting to Denise's husband Tim Healy at the bar, Jane did handstands with our friend 'yoga' Tony at 3 a.m., and my friend Sarah laughed at the size of Steve's friend's unfeasibly large head. All in all it was a pretty normal wedding and to me it couldn't have gone any better.

With everything going so well at *Loose Women* and Steve and I having settled into married life, it felt as though things were pretty much perfect. Well, apart from one thing: my little 'monster' was still rearing its head. Each morning as I got dressed I would look down at my tender protruding belly in disgust, before pulling my Spanx up to cover it as best I could. It was making me so miserable; I wanted it fixed — NOW! The last operation had only patched over the one hernia and had done nothing about the gaping hole that allowed another to protrude above it, leaving me with a doughnut-shaped mound of stomach with a large, flat belly button in the middle. By spring 2011 I knew it was time to take a different approach — and a drastic one at that.

The surgeon I decided to use was lovely. Rather than simply talking me through the technicalities of my operation and why I needed it, I could see he cared about me looking and feeling good afterwards, not just being 'made better'. I would still need to be cut open from the pubic bone to just under my breast bone, as well as hip to hip for him to be able to pull together and connect my failing stomach muscles, but he would try and create a new belly button for me and get rid of the excess skin as well. For him it wasn't simply about fixing the hole the hernias kept popping through, cutting me open, stitching me up and sending me on my way. It was about helping me to look in the mirror and like what I see.

★   ★   ★

So when the big day arrived, in the summer, I went to four-year-old Amy's last day at nursery to hear her sing and see her perform in a little show they put on for us parents, then I made my way to the hospital. The surgeon drew on me with a large black magic marker. He smiled at me reassuringly and then said, 'Don't worry. I'll see you down there when you're ready.' I walked down to theatre with my gown flapping at the back, lay down and chatted nervously to the anaesthetist, a bearded man who wasn't interested in chitchat. And then I woke up.

I had joked before I went in that it was worth having an operation just for the good sleep; at least if I was knocked out then Amy couldn't wake me up. When I came round I felt strange, kind of floaty, and in quite a bit of pain, but I

301

don't remember much more about the first night. I know Steve came in to see me and I kept falling asleep. I slept for most of the next day, and then the following morning I felt a little clearer, just incredibly sore and tight, as if I had been sawn in half and put back together with a bit missing in the middle. I managed to walk like Mrs Overall in *Acorn Antiques* to the bathroom and have a shower, then had to lie down for the rest of the day to recover.

I was still feeling strange when Steve came to visit me that evening. The kids had been and gone, picked up by a friend and taken back home, so luckily it was just the two of us in the room when it happened. The nurse bustled in and gave me my tablets: a selection of different-coloured little pills in a white paper cup.

Steve chatted as he settled into the chair by the window, telling me about his day, how work had been, how the kids were, what he had planned for tomorrow . . . I coughed; my throat felt a little strange. I listened as he fiddled with the remote control, talking me through what was on the telly, then I coughed again. My throat was feeling quite tight and . . . was it me or was the room getting hotter? As he flicked through the channels, I closed my eyes and lay back against the pillows, trying desperately to take a deep breath; I couldn't seem to get enough air inside me. My breath made a strange wheezing sound as I inhaled, and whistled as I pushed the air out. Steve turned round and looked at me, remote control in hand.

'Are you OK?'

I tried to take another breath, but this time the noise was louder and more forced. My face felt like it was on fire and my chest was tight. 'I can't seem to catch my breath . . . ' I saw a look of concern creep onto Steve's face.

I took another wheezing breath in; it felt like I was inhaling through a broken straw. My throat was closing.

'Andrea! What's happening?!'

I tried to answer him, straining hard to suck air into my lungs. It was as if I was being strangled from the inside. Panic rose in me as I gasped for air. I could hear a high-pitched wheezing noise filling the room. Was that coming from me? Then all of a sudden I began to feel really sleepy . . .

The next thing I knew a female voice was shouting my name, and other voices were barking orders at each other. It sounded urgent, but disconnected, nothing to do with me. Someone grabbed my wrist and wrestled with the needles already inserted in my veins and taped to my hand. I felt cold liquid snake into my body through the tiny hole in my skin. A clear mask was pressed over my nose and mouth and oxygen hissed into my strangulated airways. More orders, more urgent voices, but they were far away from me. I was just so sleepy . . .

My breath was shallow now, coming in tiny gasps, but at last I felt as if air was arriving in my lungs. With each tiny breath of oxygen and steroids my chest opened and a little more trickled in, reaching into the crevices of my deprived lungs. The swelling was receding and my throat was opening, allowing air, wonderful air, inside me. I lay still and quiet on my hospital bed, breathing slowly in and out, grateful for each inhalation.

I don't know how much longer I lay there but eventually I felt strong enough to open my eyes and look around. A nurse stood at the foot of my bed, frowning at me. Steve sat to my right, elbows on his knees, his face grim. I looked at him and croaked through my oxygen mask, which was still hissing into my mouth and nose, 'Hi. Sorry about that.'

He held my hand in a vice-like grip, his strong fingers crushing mine. 'Will you stop scaring me, please!' He smiled, but I heard the catch in his voice. 'Bloody hell, Mrs. Don't do that to me. One minute you were there, then you couldn't get your breath, then you were gone. I thought you'd died . . . ' His voice trailed off as his eyes filled with tears. 'I kept thinking, 'I told her it was OK to have this operation, to go for it, and now I've killed her.'' He exhaled noisily through pursed lips, looking at the floor. 'I don't know what I'd do if I lost you. Don't do that again.'

'What happened?'

'They think you had a bad reaction to your medication,' he told me.

I closed my eyes as he left the room to have a calming cigarette, and the nurse checked my mask and drips then closed the door quietly behind her. I lay still, listening to the hiss of life-giving air rushing cold and metallic into my airwaves. I could hear chatter from the corridor as somebody walked past, talking on their mobile phone. Their life was carrying on as normal; popping in to pay a loved one a visit before nipping to the pub for a drink before home, TV and bed. In the past hour they had sat in traffic, listening to the radio and thinking of nothing in particular, while my life had choked in my throat and then been forced back into me by the expertise of hospital staff. At that moment, something inside me changed, and it is fair to say that I would never be the same person again after that day. I may not be religious, but I thanked God for giving me another chance. Forty-one had almost been my end, but from that day forward it was going to be my beginning.

★   ★   ★

I would have given anything not to go through the experience again. But I did, less than a week later. I was home by now, sleeping around twenty hours a day and spending my waking hours hobbling to and from the kitchen to get glasses of water and soup. I had waited until Steve was home from work before having a shower; with the kids at school and nursery I spent most of the day on my own, and I wanted a grown-up in the house before I got out of bed for any period of time.

The water was warm and soothing as it ran over my tired body, and I was able to carefully wash my hair, although I was exhausted by the effort of raising my arms up. As the suds flopped onto the shower tray I closed my eyes, feeling a wave of faintness. I put out my hand to steady myself on the shower wall as it came over me again. Frightened, I stood still under the spray, waiting for the room to stop spinning. The water dribbled into my mouth as I inhaled slowly, and I could feel my face getting hotter. My throat was closing again; I needed to get out.

I turned off the shower while leaning heavily on the wall, opened the shower door and felt for my towel. My hair was matted and sopping wet, suds embedded in the tangles. The blood roared in my ears as I felt my way to the bedroom door and called for Steve. He was watching *Come Dine With Me*, and I heard him turn the volume down before shouting back, 'Yes?'

'Can you come, please? Now.'

I felt my way over to the bed and lay down, my drenched hair and body soaking the duvet and pillow. With my eyes shut tight I fought to breathe slowly, but the air wouldn't come. Tears trickled out of my eyes and ran into my ears as I heard Steve's footsteps pounding up the stairs.

'Everything OK? Oh my God, is it happening again?'

With my eyes still closed I tried to explain about the shower, my breath coming in rasping gasps. 'Can you raise my legs, please? I feel very weak.'

Steve shoved a rolled-up pillow under my calves, and pulled the rest of the duvet over my now shaking body. Finlay has suffered with asthma since he was three, and we always have inhalers to hand, so Steve raced into his room to grab one. As he held it to my lips and pressed the cylinder, a blast of sharp, cold air rushed into my throat. He did it again, then again, and I lay back against the pillow, my breath shallow and wheezy. I couldn't believe it was happening again. Why? Why?

Steve grabbed my phone and dialled my surgeon's secretary, pacing the room. He was in surgery, so she advised us to contact the hospital and see if I could go straight in. Steve was becoming agitated, and I heard a sharp exchange of words with whomever was on duty at the hospital. Then silence, then mutterings, then he came striding back into the room. I felt like I was shrinking, becoming smaller with each tiny breath. Nothing mattered.

Steve gently pulled me into a sitting position, and I don't know how, but managed to put some knickers and a dress on me as I hung off him. Then he led me to the front door, half dragging me, his voice quiet but urgent in my ear.

'Come on, Andrea, one foot in front of the other. That's it. Lin's on her way. The kids are watching TV, they don't know what's happening. It's all OK. Keep going.'

We got to the front door, then down the step and to the car. He struggled to open it while propping me up; I was a life-sized rag doll, struggling for air. He put me in the front seat, and I heard him talking again. Lin, our right-hand woman and honorary member of our family, had dropped what she was doing and raced round to our house to look after the children while he took me to hospital. I knew none of this as I slumped in the front seat, my head lolling against the headrest, my breath in wheezy, shallow gasps.

As we pulled out of the drive I slumped sideways onto Steve, and didn't have the strength or wherewithal to pull myself away. Somehow we arrived at the hospital, I don't remember how, and Steve pushed me gently back into my seat before jumping out of the car.

'I can't breathe, I can't breathe, it's happening again, don't leave me, don't leave me . . . ' I don't know if I was saying these things out loud, but they roared inside my head. Suddenly he was by my side again.

'Andrea, you have to get out of the car now. I'll help you. Swing your legs round.'

I tried, but nothing would do what I wanted it to do; my legs, my arms, my lungs . . .

'Come on, Andrea! I have to get you inside!'

My head lolled sideways, unable to keep steady, and the momentum sent me sprawling into the driver's seat. I was barely conscious.

'Fuck!'

Steve reached into the car and grabbed me under my arms, dragging me like a fireman out of a burning building. Then I was up in his arms as he staggered towards the front door of the hospital, leaving the car where it was, doors wide open and keys inside. My shoes fell off as we made our way inside, Steve shouting to the receptionist, 'I need a doctor NOW! I need a wheelchair NOW!' There was more shouting, and movement and I think a wheelchair, and by the time they got me into a room and the doctor

308

came I was hyperventilating, my breath coming in ragged gasps.

'I can't feel my hands . . . ' I sobbed quietly, my eyes squeezed shut. Then my legs began to convulse and my whole body shook uncontrollably. 'What's happening to me?' My teeth were grinding with the effort of forcing my body to keep still, but by now my whole body had gone into spasm.

'Help me!'

'Andrea!' barked the doctor from somewhere above my head in a strong German accent. 'You are hyperventilating. You must take even breaths before we can examine you. You are making this worse for yourself, you must calm down.'

I wanted to scream at him and rip the skin off his face, even though I couldn't see him as my eyes were squeezed shut and my face contorted with the agony of my convulsions.

'Just make it stop!' I gasped, gripping the edge of the bed.

'Only you can make it stop. You MUST calm down.'

'I can't! I can't make my legs stop shaking. I can't feel my hands. I can't breathe! I don't know what's happening to me!'

Another spasm rippled through me and I groaned in pain as my whole body went rigid and my head jerked back against the pillow.

'Can't you give her something to make this stop?' I heard Steve ask the doctor, his voice sounding strained.

'Not now, she needs to calm down first.'

'Can't you give her something to calm down?'

'No, because then we can't test her properly.'

'But look at her!'

I was jerking on the bed as if I was having electric shock treatment, as each convulsion brought another wave of pain and panic. I groaned.

'Andrea!' the doctor's voice was sharp. 'Listen to me. You must slow your breathing down. Try and take a deep breath in, and then a deep breath out.'

'But I can't breathe!' My teeth had started to chatter and I clenched them to make them stop.

Then Steve's voice: 'Come on, Andrea. Breathe with me. One . . . two . . . three . . . four . . . five . . . '

'I can't!'

'You can! Breathe with me. One . . . two . . . three . . . four . . . five . . . '

I tried to breathe in time with him, to listen to his voice and believe that everything was going to be all right. I forced my breath to lengthen, bit by bit.

I don't know how long it took, but gradually, just listening to Steve's voice and keeping my eyes squeezed tightly shut, my breathing started to regulate and I began to calm down. It was a slow process, and even though my legs were still jerking in spasm every couple of minutes, eventually the pins and needles receded from my hands and my brain started to function properly. I was dramatically calmer than when I'd arrived, but still very groggy and not quite sure what was going on.

I opened my eyes. I was in a little treatment

room, and Steve hovered over me anxiously. To my left, a tall, unsmiling doctor stood by, frowning in concern.

'How are you now?' he asked.

'I don't know. I still feel very strange.'

'You hyperventilated. That's why you couldn't feel your hands and you felt light-headed.'

'Oh.'

Steve and the doctor then talked about me like I wasn't there, and to be fair, although I was there in body, in mind I wasn't much use to anyone. After a murmured discussion it was decided that I should stay the night for 'observation' as they weren't sure exactly what had happened and would like to keep an eye on me. I was helped, painfully, to a sitting position, my damp and tangled hair flopping over my pale face. Between them, they hoisted me up and then lowered me gently into the wheelchair. I hadn't an ounce of energy left in me. I sagged in the chair, my head flopping forward so my chin was resting on my chest, matted hair stuck to my face, my dress stuck to me and my feet bare.

After being wheeled into a lift, then down a corridor, I was helped onto a bed. My chest hurt from the exertion of forcing air into my tired body, and my legs kept going into painful spasm. Over the next few hours I was checked over by another nurse and then the doctor came back to see me. I felt like I was looking at him properly for the first time; I couldn't remember what he looked like from our earlier encounter, only the German accent was the same. He seemed less stern now, and smiled down at me in my bed.

311

'You are feeling better now?' It was more of a statement than a question, but yes, comparatively, I did feel better than before.

'Good. You will stay here so we can check on you, but I think it would be good for you to take some medication to help you sleep, then you will feel much better in the morning.'

I couldn't agree more; the thought of a full night's sleep always appealed, especially as I was still in a great deal of pain from my operation. I took the paper cup the nurse handed me and gratefully gulped down the magic little pill with some water. Steve hugged me tight as the sleepiness took hold and promised to be back in the morning. And then I was gone.

The next morning was like waking in a stranger's house, knowing there had been a party of some kind the night before, but everything was a little hazy, and the details took a while to come back to me. My hair was a tangled mop, I was sleeping in my clothes and I could tell I hadn't brushed my teeth. I was in hospital; I had been poorly . . . I lay in bed under the stiff sheet and blanket waiting for someone to come and tell me what was going on, drifting in and out of a drugged sleep. A while later a nurse appeared, followed by my impeccably dressed surgeon. His blue eyes crinkled down at me as he smiled.

'Well, you've been in the wars, haven't you? What happened yesterday?'

I told him I couldn't quite remember, but I'd felt like I was having a funny turn again and had been struggling to breathe. He listened solemnly, and then told me of the feedback he had been given by the doctor on duty last night. He said that he agreed with him, that it sounded like I had got into trouble then had a massive panic attack because of what had happened before. All my tests had come back fine; there was nothing wrong with my wound or my chest, so I didn't have an infection. He told me to take it VERY easy and to call him if it happened again. He also suggested that I get tested for asthma by my GP, something I had last had done as a teenager but hadn't suffered from since.

I was embarrassed when Steve came to collect me, tottering through the hospital to our car, smelly and scruffy. That proved I was feeling better; the day before I had been carried in wailing and soaking wet, without a thought about how I looked.

I had to take more time off work than I expected, but everyone at *Loose Women* was incredibly supportive; Kate Thornton gamely covered all my shifts and the ladies sent me texts of support and beautiful flowers. I didn't go into detail about what happened, I just said there had been complications and I'd had a 'funny turn' but would hopefully be back soon.

I wasn't embarrassed that my second episode had turned out to be a severe panic attack; the first had been frightening and real enough to make it entirely justified that I had panicked when I felt faint again. Touch wood, I have not had another since then, and hopefully it will stay that way, as I have realized that the only person who has the power to make sure that I never feel that frightened again is me.

313

★ ★ ★

With just two weeks until the end of the series, and despite feeling sore and tired, I managed to hit the ground running and fitted in the rest of my *Loose Women* shifts alongside taking part in my first ever proper movie role. This one didn't involve running around Mumbai; I had been given a main part in an upcoming Brit flick, and I wasn't going to let something like a 'funny turn' stop me!

The email had come in a few weeks before my operation, asking me if I would like to read for a role in a small independent film called *A Landscape of Lies*. I had read the request and put it to one side, seeing it as one of many things I would get round to dealing with at some point. My enforced bed rest provided me with the opportunity, and as I scrolled down my emails on my phone I saw it again. This time I replied to the director and we arranged to meet him after my first day back on *Loose Women*. It was quite surreal and yet very straightforward. I had been through the script and knew which part he wanted me to read for, and Amanda in my agent's office had sat with me for a couple of hours, going through the lines and the character so that I was past any kind of embarrassment by the time it came to my audition. I hadn't done any acting since I was at Coventry, but the 'new me' wasn't going to let an opportunity like this slip by without trying my best!

I auditioned for the role of Audrey Grey, the sinister psychiatrist with a dark secret . . . and I

314

got it! The next few weeks were a flurry of sorting out filming dates alongside my television duties, and I managed to squeeze everything in by filming in the afternoons and evenings on my *Loose Women* days, and on weekends in between. I didn't mention anything to the other ladies as I didn't really want to talk about it; it was something that I wanted to try my hand at without the stress of people asking me how I was getting on.

It turned out to be an amazing experience. Paul, the director was patience personified with not only me but also the rest of the team. I sat back and watched everything. I absorbed how the other actors got themselves into the 'zone' as each scene was set up. The discipline of filming was the same as some TV work I had done before; I was used to the terminology, the standing around waiting for cameras and lighting to be set up; I was even used to learning lines. What was different was having to be someone else. I had spent so long being myself in front of the camera that I was nervous about how to portray my character, Audrey. Danny Midwinter, who played my on-screen brother and the main 'bad guy' in the film, was generous and helpful, and I learned a lot from him in a very short space of time. He took himself off quietly to learn his lines and slowly transformed from the smiling cheeky man he really is to the moody, snappy and dangerous character he played. Christina Baily, who played Suzy my dippy secretary, was the same; she could be chatting about wedding venues one minute, earnestly and

315

sensibly, and then the next she was almost cross-eyed with dumbness as she became Suzy. Being surrounded by everyone else in character changed everything, and from my dry read-throughs at night in bed with Steve playing every other part, suddenly the film came to life and my character made sense. On the first day I had to film a scene where I was being a caring and supportive psychiatrist one minute, then behind closed doors I was a snarling, heavy-breathing maniac struggling to hold it together. Now this I could relate to!

The part called for a real departure from my normal 'good girl' on-screen personality, and the new me relished it. I may not have been brave enough to behave badly in real life, but as Audrey Grey I was able to do all the things I would never have the nerve to do! I dressed provocatively in tight diva dresses, with push-up bras and a slash of red lipstick. I snarled as I led my innocent secretary to a secret underground club where anything can happen, and delighted in shocking her by leaning in for an unexpected and passionate kiss. I held hands with another woman while chatting up a man at the bar, and then allowed myself to be thoroughly snogged by my brother in full view of other club-goers. I got drunk and I went home with a stranger, waking up dishevelled and confused the next morning. In all, I did everything that I have never done and would never do in real life, and it was brilliant! No wonder people become actors!

I was so lucky that my first foray onto the big screen involved working with such lovely people while playing such a fantastic part. It would have been easy to cast me as the nice wife or sweet daughter, but I'm so glad they didn't. The timing was perfect as well, as it allowed me to dip my toe into a world where I didn't have to be good, or nice, or compliant; I could be mean and hard and devious — even if it was only on screen.

I hope I will get another chance to act as I thoroughly enjoyed it. And when people said to me after I came back to work following the summer break on *Loose Women*, 'You seem different somehow ... More confident, less scared,' I smiled and said, 'Thank you,' because I knew they were right. It's amazing what a near-death experience and playing a psychopath can do to a woman!

# 19

## Keepin' it Real

Looking at my nine-year-old son's twisted smile as he realized the children weren't laughing at his funny little joke but were laughing at *him* sent a bolt of pain shooting through my body. We were on holiday in Spain, and he had asked me quietly if he could help the children's entertainer make balloon animals, as he knew how to make one into a dog. I had watched him stand shyly back, waiting to catch the brightly dressed man's eye and offer his services. I saw him speak to an older boy and a girl next to him; it looked like he was telling them that he could make a dog. They looked him up and down, and with a sneer turned to each other and made 'L' for 'loser' signs and sniggered.

My eyes flew to Finlay's face and I saw his smile falter; then he flushed with embarrassment and edged away from the now laughing pair. Rage surged through me, and I fought the desire to leap over the railing separating us to grab the two of them and smash their heads together. Finlay regained his composure and ignored them as he tapped the entertainer and asked for a balloon to make something for himself. The Spanish man didn't fully understand, and handed him an inflated twisted balloon already shaped into a poodle. Finlay thanked him and

318

walked away, then quietly untwisted it and put it back together again himself. I watched, quietly sipping my drink while the other parents chatted, as the boy and girl sidled up to him again, asking what he had done. Finlay held out his balloon dog and the two of them glanced at each other again and collapsed into sneaky giggles. This time they were close enough for me to get involved, and I couldn't hold myself back. Shaking with rage, I beckoned them over.

'What are you laughing at?' I asked, a smile on my face, but keeping my voice low.

The girl had the grace to look embarrassed. 'Nothing,' she mumbled.

'I don't think you were,' I said firmly. I gestured for her brother to come closer. 'What were you laughing at?' I asked him. He looked at the floor. The girl piped up, 'My brother made a funny noise!' she said, pleased with the lie she had thought up on the spot.

Slowly I brought my gaze over to her. I smiled again, knowing it wasn't reaching my eyes. 'Is that right?' I said. She looked me straight in the eye and said 'Yes.' Little cow. I leaned down so my face was close enough to speak quietly, still smiling so that anyone watching would think I was just having a friendly chat with this little huddle of children. 'Well, you take your little joke, and your little hand gestures and your laughing behind people's backs, and you go and do it somewhere else, all right?'

I stared quietly at her and her sniggering brother, then stood up, towering over the two of them. I looked across the room at their mother, who was watching us. Her eyes met mine, and I saw them widen with recognition. Her children ran to her, and I could see them telling her that a lady had told them off.

I folded my arms and watched, unblinking, as she listened to their version of events, took in Finlay twisting his balloon, and saw things as they really were. She smiled at them and then shooed them away, still looking at me. I kept staring at her and her eyes remained glued to mine, a silent warfare of mothers, unnoticed by the rest of the noisy room. I heard Amy call for me, and I decided to look away first, but not before I gave her a slow, lingering up-and-down look of disgust. When I looked over next, as I did many times for the rest of the hour the kids were there, she was on her phone, talking animatedly and looking over in my direction. Brave enough to bitch about me, but not brave enough to say anything to my face. Just like her kids.

Bullying doesn't get any easier, however old you are, and having dealt with my fair share of bullies in my time I'm going to do everything in my power to prevent my children from going through the same thing. Finlay and Amy both need to learn to stand on their own two feet and fight their own battles, but I plan always to be there if they need a little helping hand.

Just as I've learned to deal with bullies over the years, I've also learned to deal with the many ways in which I've changed as a person, and have learned to appreciate the new Andrea I've become. Physically I am getting stronger by the day, and, although my tummy will never win any accolades when it comes to appearance, the fact that it works and I am no longer in constant pain is a wonderful compromise. Internally my stomach is still the nightmare it has always been; following on from my illness in India and Thailand in my twenties I am still intolerant to dairy, and am now sensitive to wheat, raw vegetables and soya. Luckily I can still eat chocolate, otherwise my life wouldn't be worth living! Only the darker stuff, as the milk content is so low, but I see that as a good thing . . . And I try not to dwell on the things I can't do, as there are so many other ways in which my life is rewarding.

Sometimes, being on the telly gives you the opportunity to do something so outrageously exciting that you cannot say no. I make most of my decisions based on the question, 'Will I regret not doing it when I am eighty?' If the answer is yes, then I do it. One of those things was performing the Girls Aloud song 'The Promise' on *Children in Need* with Carol, Denise, Zoe Tyler and Sherrie Hewson. We were all completely terrified; we actually saw Carol's knees knocking together. We got on stage, shaking and convinced we'd forgotten everything, then the lights went up and the music started and we were off! I can't remember anything except trying not to fall over, and grinning inanely. As we made our way off stage, I was overwhelmed that we had actually done it! Not only had we sung a song and moved our arms vaguely at the same time live in front of millions of viewers, but we'd had a little giggle on a stage at the infamous BBC Television Centre with the legendary TERRY WOGAN!

Later that evening, after much wine and back-patting, I swayed back to our dressing room to collect my things. 'I'll just lie down for a minute,' I thought to myself, and woke up hours later to find everyone gone. The room had been tidied round me by the cleaners, and it was 4 a.m. I wandered the empty corridors of the BBC, convinced I would set off alarms and end up surrounded by security guards and police, only to miraculously find my way to the reception, where exhausted-looking people were sitting behind the desk, waiting for the last stragglers (i.e. me) to bugger off home. By the time I'd got a taxi home, it was 5 a.m. and I had started to feel that half-drunk, half-hungover feeling creeping in. As I fumbled around in my handbag I realized I'd left my keys at home in my work bag so I had to call Steve to let me in. He was NOT happy!

This is definitely the exception rather than the norm, though, as my day-to-day life is nowhere near as exciting. But even when I get to do lots of wonderful things like this, I never have to tell myself to be careful not to get caught up by all the excitement, not to let it go to my head. Life does that for me, on an almost daily basis. With two children, the younger of whom is adverse to sleep, and being disorganized to the point of ridiculousness in real life, things just kind of 'happen' to keep my feet on the ground.

The most recent was at a lunch with Owain, a long-lost friend. It all started when I turned up at the Ritz for high tea to meet him. We hadn't seen each other since we were teenagers, and our families had moved apart. We had grown up together for a few years in Trinidad and then again in the Midlands when his family moved to just outside Birmingham, but now he is a banker living the high life in New York, and I am the host of an award-winning daytime talk show for women . . . so what a triumphant meeting this would be! How we would pat ourselves on the back and laugh at how well two gawky, never-that-popular-at-school kids had done, and weren't we just great? I arrived wearing jeans and my favourite cowboy boots, a black jumper and leather jacket, feeling more Kate Moss than Jeremy Clarkson, despite what it sounds like. I was stopped at the door by a very grumpy security guard, who told me in a gruff voice that I wasn't allowed in. 'Why on earth not?' I asked, taken aback.

'You are wearing jeans. You are not allowed in in jeans.'

I looked helplessly at him, as he fingered his earpiece, keeping his eyes fixed on me the whole time. What did he think I was going to do? Make a run for it into the tea room, so he'd have to call for back-up?

'Well, can I just go in and tell my friend what has happened, please? He is waiting for me inside.'

The security man looked at me through narrowed eyes, just as the mirrored, gold-framed door opened, and out walked a large, sandy-haired man. 'Sorry,' I said, as I stepped aside to let him pass, wondering if I should in fact make a bolt for it and slip through the door shouting, 'Owain! I'm here but they won't let me in!' before being rugby-tackled to the floor. But it turned out that I didn't have to, as the large, sandy-haired man was my friend, who was now laughing at the fact that I wasn't allowed in.

'I'm staying here, and she's my guest,' he said nicely to the security man (told you he'd done well!), but the guard wouldn't budge. The only way he would let me in was if I borrowed a skirt from their cloakroom. So that was what I had to do, and ten minutes later I was walking across the marble floor of the Ritz wearing a black jumper, my brown cowboy boots and a black pencil skirt roughly twenty-seven times too big for me. I hadn't even shaved my legs, never mind put on moisturizer. I just put my head down and walked over to our table as quickly as I could. Coiffed heads turned, and delicately plucked eyebrows were raised in my direction, as Owain roared with laughter and said, 'You've not changed a bit!' He was right. Bugger.

My family are the main reason I stay level-headed. My dad is now retired and always watches me on *Loose Women*, texting me after each appearance to give me his views either on my outfit, the guest, or the questions I should or shouldn't have asked. It's fine; I really don't mind, even though my heart does skip a little when the phone pings on my way home from work. But the main leveller is my daughter, Amy Jane. She is five. She rules our house. She is *very* scary.

The days when I'm not working can be challenging to say the least. I remember one Saturday in particular, which is, rather worryingly, quite a typical day at home for me. It wasn't quite 5 a.m. when Amy started tugging on my shoulder to tell me she was very pleased and proud of herself that she had been a 'big girl' and had stayed in bed all night. Even though 'all night' meant rising before the birds had even begun to tweet outside the window, technically she was right, and she insisted I got up and moved her higher on her reward chart. So, by 7 a.m., when we had finished playing dominoes, snap and matching pairs, I let her play on the Playhouse Disney website on my laptop while I had a shower, and stood dozing upright while pretending to wash my hair.

As I was getting dressed I heard a sing-song 'Oh, no . . . ' and then quiet. The kind of quiet that only mums can hear; the calm before the storm quiet when you know something terrible has happened. I made my way downstairs, calling, 'Aim-meee . . . Whatcha do-ing?' She ran out of my office and into the kitchen, shouting, 'Nothing!' I walked into my office and towards my brand-new shiny laptop . . . She had removed EVERY SINGLE KEY from the keyboard. I didn't even know you could do that. Now *I* was quiet, the way you are when you want to scream but nothing comes out . . .

Spurred on by the need to cook something for the children's breakfast to prove I wasn't a bad mother, as I wasn't *actually* going to act out the dark fantasies that whirled round my head when

I thought of Amy, my laptop and a lifetime on the naughty step, I waited until Finlay got up, and then made them a lovely pile of pancakes. Amy drowned hers in maple syrup, and then tried to drink it off the plate by tipping it into her mouth. She missed, badly, and dribbled most of it over herself, the table and her chair. Finlay inhaled his and muttered, 'Thanks, Mum,' before rushing back into the living room to watch *iCarly*, quickly followed by a very sticky Amy. The kitchen looked like it had been overrun by a child-and-pancake tsunami.

While bending down to wipe the floor, my hair got stuck to the sticky table; I looked like Cameron Diaz in *There's Something About Mary*, without being a blonde Hollywood bombshell, just with the sticky fringe. Coffee was the answer.

I noticed a tiny crack in the cafetière as I poured in the ground coffee and added boiling hot water. I thought to myself that we must get a new one, as it is the most used piece of equipment in our kitchen, after the bottle opener. I wondered quietly whether it was safe as I pushed the plunger down, and BAM! The glass cracked and I was showered in boiling brown grainy water, all down my front. I leapt back and it bubbled out onto the kitchen surface, the cupboard door and onto the floor. Thank God I need help in the boob department and was wearing a padded bra, because it could have been really nasty, not to mention time-consuming, having to take two children to A&E to explain third-degree burns and a Lavazza smell to a doctor. I ripped off my clothes and threw kitchen roll at the mess.

At the same time, Amy came roaring into the kitchen, having fallen off the sofa and bumped her head. I cuddled her in my damp Italian coffee-smelling bra and pants, and tried to stop the flow of brown molten water dripping onto the floor, while she wailed and clung on. Eventually she got it out of her system and padded back into the playroom, leaving me sitting on the floor in my pants surrounded by pancake mix, maple syrup, soggy kitchen roll and a steady drip of leaky coffee.

Later, after the carpet on the naughty step had been worn very thin, I decided to take the kids out for the afternoon as we were all getting cabin fever. The local garden centre beckoned, as they have huge tanks of fish and Amy thinks it's a zoo. I filled the trolley up with plants to kill, and the kids tried to smuggle on board SpongeBob SquarePants figures for our fish tank. I smuggled them back onto the shelves when they weren't looking. After cake and drinks in the café, and struggling back to the car with things that will never grow in my garden, we headed home. Amy insisted on having the satnav on for the entire journey and setting it herself, and then yelled all the way back that I was going the wrong way. She was apparently very cross that we weren't heading towards Blackpool. Finlay ignored the shouting, as he always does, by sitting quietly in the back seat and staring out the window; perhaps wondering what it would take to get adopted by a normal family?

The evening was just as difficult . . . Then the next morning — Sunday morning, when people all across the country were getting a chance to have a much-needed lie-in — it all began again: at 5.12 a.m., to be precise. After visiting me twice in the night to tell me her bed was funny, Amy thundered in shouting that it was her birthday and she wanted fireworks and her face painted with the England flag. She did not take kindly to being refused, and so began another day.

And that's why I never feel guilty about being a working mum. I adore my family — my world wouldn't exist without them. But I also love having something for myself, and that's where *Loose Women* comes in. It gives me a chance to escape from all the madness and a way to keep in touch with who I am. It's also a damn sight easier than being a stay-at-home mum, and doesn't involve children, maple syrup or kitchen roll . . .

However normal or exciting each day is, and whether the children are behaving like angels or driving me round the bend, my life is my life and I love everything about it. Mine and Steve's relationship has continued on its roller-coaster too, and we have faced the normal ups and downs that any married couple does. While my career has gone from strength to strength, work has been difficult over the past few years in the building industry, and Steve's company went through a rough patch as the world fell into recession. It has been a difficult time for us, as it has for many families, and we have tried to deal with things in our own way, muddling along as people do. I would never claim that our marriage or even that our relationship is perfect; I am experienced enough now to know that there is no such thing. I craved that idea of perfection in my first marriage, and I am not going to make the same mistake in my second. We are what we are and we have what we have, and long may it last. Will it last forever? I certainly hope so.

I'd like to believe that marriage is forever, and the good girl in me wishes that it could be so for everyone who falls in love and decides to spend the rest of their lives together. But I have realized, perhaps later than most, that life is often not like that. Hopefully we will be one of the lucky couples and we will see out our days into our dotage, with me grumbling about his messiness and him moaning about my lateness. I'm sure there will still be days in the future, as there are now, when we argue over the most trivial things and I don't even want to talk to him. As there will also be days when I can't bear to be apart from him, and I smile and feel my heart lift with love when I see his name flash up on my phone. That's life. That's my life. Most people say that life begins at forty. Not so for me — my life most definitely began at forty-one. And I can't wait to find out what exciting things it has in store for me.

# Acknowledgements

I wrote this book myself — no ghost writer; every single word, comma and full stop has come from me. Probably because of that it took longer than I thought it would, and I know I've left some bits out because I remembered them too late, but if you like this book, then maybe I'll be able to write another one and I can include all the stuff I forgot — it might take me a while though, as now I need to have a long lie down and a big glass of wine!

Without the following people, this book would never have come about, and I want to say a massive thank you to them. You may not know who they are, but they are very important to me and they deserve a mention. Actually, they deserve more than that, but for now, this will have to do.

First of all, thank you to my husband Steve, my knight in shining armour who manfully held the fort while I tapped away on my computer, and made sure that the family was fed and watered, that homework was done and the house carried on as normal. Thank you for understanding that I needed to shut myself away and write, that I wasn't just reading the *Mail* online or looking at nice pictures of shoes (even though it might have looked like I was doing that sometimes, honestly, I was actually working). I love you, and you have your wife back again! Thank you to my children, Finlay and Amy, for understanding when I had to chuck you off the computer, even when you were in the middle of playing a Nick Jr game or watching a *Doctor Who* clip. I love you both so much I could burst.

Thank you to my mum and dad for letting me write about our family, for keeping all those hideous photos of me and for reading this book chapter by chapter before anyone else got a look in. Thank you for being the best parents in the world, for loving and supporting me even when I got things wrong. I am so lucky to have you both, and I love you. To my sister Linda, thank you for being there when things were tough, when I probably didn't make much sense and was very annoying to live with. You're brilliant, and I love you. To Jane, you are much more than a best friend, you're my soul sister and I could not have got through the past ten years without you. We have laughed, cried and been ridiculous together and long may that continue. I love you.

★ ★ ★

To Andrea's Angels; you know who you are and I am blessed to have you as my friends. To Lin, our honorary family member who keeps us all going, thank you. To Ingrid and Lorraine, thank you for editing my book with friendly compassion, so that it is still mine,

331

only better! And to my agent Neil, thank you for seeing something in me that nobody else did and for believing in me. Thank you for supporting me and making so many of my dreams come true. I was already a good girl when I met you, but you have made me great!

Love Andrea x

# Picture Acknowledgements

The author and publisher would like to thank the following for permission to reproduce the images used in this book:

Rex features — page 6, bottom; page 8, all; page 10, bottom; page 13, top; page 16. Ray Burmiston (www.rayburmiston.com) — page 14

All other images provided courtesy of the author.